COUNTERING ONLINE PROPAGANDA AND EXTREMISM

Exploring the 'dark side' of digital diplomacy, this volume highlights some of the major problems facing democratic institutions in the West and provides concrete examples of best practice in reversing the tide of digital propaganda.

Digital diplomacy is now part of the regular conduct of International Relations, but Information Warfare is characterised by the exploitation or weaponisation of media systems to undermine confidence in institutions: the resilience of open, democratic discourse is tested by techniques such as propaganda, disinformation, fake news, trolling and conspiracy theories. This book introduces a thematic framework by which to better understand the nature and scope of the threats that the weaponisation of digital technologies increasingly pose to Western societies. The editors instigate interdisciplinary discussion and collaboration between scholars and practitioners on the purpose, methods and impact of strategic communication in the Digital Age and its diplomatic implications. What opportunities and challenges does strategic communication face in the digital context? What diplomatic implications need to be considered when governments employ strategies for countering disinformation and propaganda? Exploring such issues, the contributors demonstrate that responses to the weaponisation of digital technologies must be tailored to the political context that make it possible for digital propaganda to reach and influence vulnerable publics and audiences.

This book will be of much interest to students of diplomacy studies, counter-radicalisation, media and communication studies, and International Relations in general.

Corneliu Bjola is Associate Professor in Diplomatic Studies at the University of Oxford and Chair of the Oxford Digital Diplomacy Research Group.

James Pamment is Associate Professor and Head of the Department of Strategic Communication at Lund University, Sweden, and an external faculty member at the University of Southern California (USC) Center on Public Diplomacy.

Routledge New Diplomacy Studies

Corneliu Bjola, University of Oxford, and Markus Kornprobst,
Diplomatic Academy of Vienna

This series publishes theoretically challenging and empirically authoritative studies of the traditions, functions, paradigms and institutions of modern diplomacy. Taking a comparative approach, the New Diplomacy Studies series aims to advance research on international diplomacy, publishing innovative accounts of how 'old' and 'new' diplomats help steer international conduct between anarchy and hegemony, handle demands for international stability vs international justice, facilitate transitions between international orders, and address global governance challenges. Dedicated to the exchange of different scholarly perspectives, the series aims to be a forum for inter-paradigm and inter-disciplinary debates, and an opportunity for dialogue between scholars and practitioners.

Gender and Diplomacy
Edited by Jennifer A. Cassidy

Secret Diplomacy
Concepts, contexts and cases
Edited by Corneliu Bjola and Stuart Murray

Diplomatic Cultures and International Politics
Translations, spaces and alternatives
Edited by Jason Dittmer and Fiona McConnell

Sports Diplomacy
Origins, theory and practice
Stuart Murray

Countering Online Propaganda and Extremism
The dark side of digital diplomacy
Edited by Corneliu Bjola and James Pamment

For more information about this series, please visit: https://www.routledge.com/
Routledge-New-Diplomacy-Studies/book-series/RNDS

COUNTERING ONLINE PROPAGANDA AND EXTREMISM

The Dark Side of Digital Diplomacy

Edited by Corneliu Bjola and James Pamment

Routledge
Taylor & Francis Group

LONDON AND NEW YORK

First published 2019
by Routledge
2 Park Square, Milton Park, Abingdon, Oxon OX14 4RN

and by Routledge
52 Vanderbilt Avenue, New York, NY 10017

Routledge is an imprint of the Taylor & Francis Group, an informa business

© 2019 selection and editorial matter, Corneliu Bjola and James
Pamment; individual chapters, the contributors.

British Library Cataloguing-in-Publication Data
A catalogue record for this book is available from the British Library

Library of Congress Cataloging-in-Publication Data
Names: Bjola, Corneliu, editor. | Pamment, James, editor.
Title: Countering online propaganda and extremism: the dark side of
digital diplomacy / edited by Corneliu Bjola and James Pamment.
Description: Abingdon, Oxon; New York, NY: Routledge, 2019. |
Series: Routledge new diplomacy studies |
Includes bibliographical references and index.
Identifiers: LCCN 2018039421 | ISBN 9781138578623 (hardback) |
ISBN 9781138578630 (pbk.) | ISBN 9781351264082 (e-book)
Subjects: LCSH: Mass media and propaganda. |
Mass media and international relations. |
Internet and international relations. | Propaganda, International. |
Information warfare. | Extremist Web sites. |
Social media—Political aspects. | Internet—Political aspects.
Classification: LCC P96.P72 C68 2019 | DDC 303.3/75—dc23
LC record available at https://lccn.loc.gov/2018039421

ISBN: 978-1-138-57862-3 (hbk)
ISBN: 978-1-138-57863-0 (pbk)
ISBN: 978-1-351-26408-2 (ebk)

Typeset in Bembo
by codeMantra

CONTENTS

List of figures   *vii*
List of tables   *viii*
List of contributors   *ix*
Acknowledgements   *xv*

Introduction: the 'dark side' of digital diplomacy   1
Corneliu Bjola and James Pamment

PART I
Strategic communication   **11**

1 Propaganda as reflexive control: the digital dimension   13
   Corneliu Bjola

2 Information influence in Western democracies: a model
   of systemic vulnerabilities   28
   *Howard Nothhaft, James Pamment, Henrik Agardh-Twetman
   and Alicia Fjällhed*

3 A digital ménage à trois: strategic leaks, propaganda and
   journalism   44
   Emma L. Briant and Alicia Wanless

4   The use of political communication by international
    organizations: the case of EU and NATO   66
    Eva-Karin Olsson, Charlotte Wagnsson and Kajsa Hammargård

5   The unbearable thinness of strategic communication   81
    Cristina Archetti

PART II
Countering violent extremism   **97**

6   The democratisation of hybrid warfare and practical
    approaches to defeat violent extremism in the Digital Age   99
    Alicia Kearns

7   The aesthetics of violent extremist and counter-violent
    extremist communication   121
    Ilan Manor and Rhys Crilley

8   Virtual violence: understanding the potential
    power of ISIS' violent videos to buttress strategic
    narratives and persuade foreign recruits   140
    Sean Aday

9   The battle for the battle of the narratives: sidestepping the
    double fetish of digital and CVE   156
    Akil N. Awan, Alister Miskimmon and Ben O'Loughlin

    Conclusion: rethinking strategic communication in
    the Digital Age   172
    James Pamment and Corneliu Bjola

Works cited   *181*
Index   *211*

FIGURES

1.1	Tactical Model of Reflexive Control	18
1.2	Strategic Model of Reflexive Control	19
1.3	The 4E Funnel of Digital Reflexive Control	24
2.1	Four Principles of Human Cognition	31
2.2	The Epistemic Chain and Vulnerabilities of Opinion Formation	35
2.3	The Epistemic Chain and Techniques of Information Influence	39
7.1	'A Better Alternative Future' @Coalition Tweets	131
7.2	'Exposing Daesh Lies' @Coalition Tweets	132
7.3	'Debunking the Myth of Daesh Military Success' @Coalition Tweets	132
7.4	'A War for Islam' @Coalition Tweets	133
7.5	Visualizing Liberation	134
7.6	Visualizing Rehabilitation and Reconciliation	135
7.7	Average Levels of Engagement with @Coalition Tweets	136
7.8	Images with Low Audience Engagement	137
7.9	Average Levels of Engagement with @Coalition Tweets	138
8.1	Still from Nicholas Berg Execution Video	143
8.2	Cover of ISIS Video Mimicking Call of Duty Video Game Cover	145
8.3	Still from ISIS Execution Video Mimicking First-Person Shooter Video Game "Call of Duty"	145
9.1	The Strategic Narrative Cycle	162
9.2	Core Components of Strategic Narrative	162

TABLES

1.1   Processes and Outcomes of Reflexive Control   16
1.2   Cognitive Filter Mapping   21

CONTRIBUTORS

Sean Aday is an Associate Professor of Media and Public Affairs and International Affairs at George Washington (GW) University. His work focusses on the intersection of the press, politics and public opinion, especially in relation to war and foreign policy, public diplomacy and the role of digital media in democracy movements and countering violent extremism. He has published widely on subjects ranging from the effects of watching local television news to coverage of American politics and media coverage of the wars in Iraq and Afghanistan. He has been involved in global media and government capacity training projects, including work in Iraq and Afghanistan, and participated in International Security Assistance Force (ISAF)'s Counterinsurgency Leadership course at Camp Julien outside Kabul in 2010. For seven years, Dr Aday directed GW's Institute for Public Diplomacy and Global Communication and its Global Communications MA program. He received his PhD from the Annenberg School for Communication at the University of Pennsylvania.

Henrik Agardh-Twetman is a researcher at the Department of Strategic Communication at Lund University and an analyst at the Swedish Civil Contingencies Agency's counter influence branch. In the lead-up to the Swedish parliamentary election in 2018, he conducted seminars and trainings on countering information influence for national, regional and local civil servants and decision makers, military and academic experts, media and members of the foreign service. Henrik holds an MSc in Global Governance and Diplomacy from University of Oxford, a specialist officer's degree from the Military Academy of Halmstad and a BA in Politics and Development Studies from SOAS, University of London.

Cristina Archetti is Professor in Political Communication and Journalism at the University of Oslo, Norway. Her research interests cover the intersection of security, politics and strategic communication. She is author of three books: *Explaining News: National Politics and Journalistic Cultures in Global Context* (Palgrave, 2010), *Understanding Terrorism in the Age of Global Media: A Communication Approach* (Palgrave, 2012) and *Politicians, Personal Image and the Construction of Political Identity: A Comparative Study of the UK and Italy* (Palgrave, 2014). She won, among other international prizes, the 2008 Denis McQuail Award for Innovating Communication Theory. Beyond academia, she taught about the role of communication in Countering Violent Extremism (CVE) on courses provided to officials and community stakeholders by the US Institute of Peace (USIP) and the Hedayah Center (Abu Dhabi); she has lectured for the NATO Centre of Excellence-Defense Against Terrorism in Ankara (Turkey) and the NATO StratCom Centre of Excellence in Riga (Latvia).

Akil N. Awan is Associate Professor in Modern History, Political Violence and Terrorism at Royal Holloway, University of London, and Senior Fellow with the Center for Global Policy. His research interests are focussed around the history of terrorism, radicalisation, social movements, protest and new media. He has written widely in these areas, both academically and in the popular press, and is regularly consulted by government bodies, think tanks, media and other organisations in his fields of expertise. He has served in an advisory capacity to the United Nations (UN), United Nations Development Programme (UNDP), UK Home Office, the Foreign Office, the US State Department, the US Defense Department, the US Military, Council of Europe, NATO and the Organisation for Security and Co-operation in Europe (OSCE), amongst others. Most recently, he served as special advisor on Radicalization to the UK Parliament, as academic expert on Genocide to the UK House of Lords delegation to Srebrenica and as expert advisor on Youth Radicalisation to the UN. He has held major research projects with Research Councils UK, the Economic and Social Research Council, the Leverhulme Trust, the British Council and the US Department of Defense Minerva Programme. He is Founder and Chair of the Political Science Association's Specialist Group on Political Violence & Terrorism. His books include *Radicalisation and Media: Terrorism and Connectivity in the New Media Ecology* (2011, Routledge) and *Jihadism Transformed: al-Qaeda and Islamic State's Global Battle of Ideas* (2016, Hurst/Oxford University Press).

Corneliu Bjola is Associate Professor in Diplomatic Studies at the University of Oxford and Chair of the Oxford Digital Diplomacy Research Group. He also serves as a Faculty Fellow at the Center on Public Diplomacy at the University of Southern California and as a Professorial Lecturer at Diplomatic Academy of Vienna. His current research interests relate to the impact of digital technology on the conduct of diplomacy with a focus on strategic communication and digital influence as well as on theories and methods for countering disinformation and propaganda. He has authored or edited six books, including the recent co-edited volume on *Secret Diplomacy: Concepts, Contexts and Cases* (Routledge, 2015, with S. Murray) and *Digital Diplomacy: Theory and Practice* (Routledge, 2015, with M. Holmes). His work has been published in the *European Journal of International Relations, Review of International Studies, Ethics and International Affairs, International Negotiation, Cambridge Review of International Affairs, Global Policy, Journal of Global Ethics* and the *Hague Journal of Diplomacy.*

Dr Emma L. Briant is a Senior Lecturer (equivalent to Associate Professor) in Journalism at University of Essex, UK. She specialises in researching and publishing on the topics of propaganda and international security, and media debates of politics, inequality and human rights. She analysed the coordination and increasing impacts of the digitalisation of defence propaganda for her book *Propaganda and Counter-Terrorism: Strategies for Global Change* (Manchester University Press, 2015); as part of this, she became an expert on Strategic Communication Laboratories (SCL) Group, the parent company of the controversial contractor Cambridge Analytica. She is currently a visiting scholar at Stanford University as she writes a forthcoming co-authored book with George Washington University Professor Robert M. Entman, *What's Wrong with the Democrats? Media Bias, Inequality and the rise of Donald Trump.* This and her US election, Brexit campaign and defence propaganda research has formed the basis for important evidence submitted to the UK Digital, Culture, Media and Sport Committee inquiry into Fake News in April 2018, among other public investigations. Dr Briant's first book was *Bad News for Refugees* (Pluto Press, 2013, co-authored with Greg Philo and Pauline Donald), which examined UK political and media discourse on migration prior to 'Brexit'. For her forthcoming publications on propaganda in the European Union (EU) Referendum and US election she gained unparalleled access to interviews with senior executives at Cambridge Analytica and Leave.EU.

Rhys Crilley is a Post-Doctoral Research Associate in Global Media and Communication in the Department of Sociology at The Open University. His research explores how political actors use visual media to claim legitimacy for the use of force, and in 2016 he was awarded the International Studies Association International Communication Section's Best Paper Award. He has published in *International Affairs, Middle East Journal of Culture and Communication, Critical Studies on Terrorism, Critical Studies on Security* and *Critical Military Studies* and has a book chapter published in a Routledge edited collection, *Understanding Popular Culture and World Politics in the Digital Age.* He is currently working on his first monograph.

Alicia Fjällhed is a PhD candidate at the Department of Strategic Communication, Lund University. She has an MA in Communication in the Public Sector from University of Gothenburg and has worked with communication in public, private and non-profit organisations.

Kajsa Hammargård is a PhD candidate in International Relations at Stockholm University. Kajsa's research focusses on how the practices of the European Commission and EU agencies are affected when international crises hit their political sphere. Kajsa has a BA in Sociology from Stockholm University and an MA in Political Science, with a focus on crisis management and international coordination from the Swedish Defence University. Moreover, Kajsa is a consultant in the field of societal security at Secana AB in Stockholm and has previously worked as an analyst at Crismart, a centre for crisis management studies at the Swedish Defence University.

Alicia Kearns is an expert in countering violent extremism and countering disinformation and hybrid warfare interventions. During her career, Alicia has worked for the UK's Foreign and Commonwealth Office, where she led UK government interventions in Syria and Iraq, and advised over 70 governments on how to defeat the terrorist group Daesh (ISIS), insurgent groups and counter malign state disinformation efforts. Alicia also worked at the UK Ministry of Defence and Ministry of Justice. An expert in managing major incidents, Alicia now delivers counter violent extremism and counter disinformation interventions as an independent consultant to support vulnerable communities in fragile and hostile environments. Alicia is regularly interviewed in the media as an expert on national threats, including by BBC Radio 4, the Daily Telegraph, The Times, Sunday Times, the Guardian, Financial Times and the Huffington Post.

Ilan Manor is a digital diplomacy scholar and a DPhil candidate at the University of Oxford. Manor's research focusses on diplomats' use of digital technologies during times of geopolitical crises. His monograph *Are we there yet? Have MFAs realized the potential of digital diplomacy* (2016) was recently published as part of Brill's Research Perspectives in Diplomacy and Foreign Policy. His analysis of *America's Selfie Diplomacy* was published in *Digital Diplomacy: Theory and Practice* (2015). Manor has also contributed to the *Cambridge Review of International Affairs, The Hague Journal of Diplomacy, Global Affairs, Global Policy, International Affairs, Media, War & Conflict* and *Place Branding and Public Diplomacy*. His book *The Digitalization of Public Diplomacy* will be published by Palgrave Macmillan in 2018.

Alister Miskimmon is Professor of International Relations and Head of the School of History, Anthropology, Philosophy and Politics at Queen's University, Belfast. In addition to research interests in German and European security policy, he has authored two books on strategic narrative with Ben O'Loughlin and Laura Roselle: *Strategic Narratives: Communication Power and the New World Order* (New York: Routledge) and *Forging the World: Strategic Narratives in International Relations* (University of Michigan Press, 2017).

Howard Nothhaft is Associate Professor (docent) at the Institute for Strategic Communication (ISK) of Lund University in Sweden. He studied communication and media science, Anglistics and philosophy at Leipzig University in

Germany. Howard's PhD thesis was a shadowing study of communication managers in eight German companies. His main research interest lies in communication strategy.

Ben O'Loughlin is Professor of International Relations and Director of the New Political Communication Unit at Royal Holloway, University of London. He is co-editor of the Sage journal *Media, War & Conflict*. His latest book is *Forging the World: Strategic Narratives and International Relations* (2017, University of Michigan Press). He was Specialist Advisor to the UK Parliament's Select Committee on Soft Power, producing the report Power and Persuasion in the Modern World. In 2016 he won the Walter Lippmann Award for Political Communication at the American Political Science Association (APSA) for his work on digital engagement. His book *Strategic Narratives* (2013, Routledge) won the best book prize for International Communication at the International Studies Association (ISA) in 2016. He is completing a book on narrative diplomacy and the 2015 Iran nuclear deal. He has recently completed three projects exploring different dimensions of influence in Ukraine, funded by Jean Monnet, Marie Skłodowska-Curie and the British Council/Goethe Institute.

Eva-Karin Olsson is Professor of Political Science at the Swedish Defence University. Her research interests include crisis management, political communication and international organisations. She has published her work in journals such as *Journalism, International Journal of Press/Politics, Public Administration* and *Media, War & Conflict*.

James Pamment is Associate Professor and Head of the Department of Strategic Communication at Lund University, Sweden, and an external faculty member at the USC Center on Public Diplomacy. Pamment researches state influence across borders, including diplomacy, public diplomacy, information operations and foreign aid. He is author of *British Public Diplomacy & Soft Power: Diplomatic Influence & Digital Disruption* and *New Public Diplomacy in the 21st Century* and editor of *Communicating National Image through Development and Diplomacy: The Politics of Foreign Aid* (w/ K. Wilkins), among other publications. He is currently leading a project for the Swedish Civil Contingencies Agency entitled *Countering Information Influence Activities* in preparation for the upcoming general election.

Charlotte Wagnsson is Professor of Political Science at the Swedish Defense University. Her research interests include European and global security, NATO and political and strategic communication in crisis and war. She is author of *Security in a Greater Europe: The Possibility of a Pan-European Approach* (Manchester University Press), is co-author of *The NATO Intervention in Libya: Lessons Learned from the Campaign* (Routledge) and *European Security Governance* (Routledge) and has published in journals such as *International Political Sociology, Journal of European Public Policy, New Media and Society* and *Journal of Common Market Studies*.

Alicia Wanless is an internationally recognised researcher of information warfare and strategic communications in a Digital Age. With more than a decade of experience in researching and analysing the information environment, focussing on propaganda and disinformation, Alicia conducts content and network analysis and has developed original models for identifying and analysing digital propaganda campaigns. Alicia applies this learning to integrating information activities in support of government and military training exercises. Since 2017, she shared her work and insights with senior government, military and academic experts at Wilton Park and Oxford and Ryerson Universities; the Hedayah Centre; NATO Allied Rapid Reaction Corps (ARRC) and the Multi National Information Operations Experiment; the NATO-United States Special Operations Command (USSOCOM) Joint Senior Psychological operations Conference; the UK Joint Information Activities Group (JIAG); and the Lawrence Livermore National Laboratory. Alicia's work has been featured in the *CBC*, *Forbes* and *The Strategy Bridge*.

ACKNOWLEDGEMENTS

This project was born out of initial conversations that took place at the workshop on "Managing societal threats in the digital age: The case of propaganda and violent extremism", convened by the two co-editors and hosted by the Department of Strategic Communication, Lund University, in October 2016. We would like to thank Riksbankens Jubeliumsfond for funding the workshop as well as fellow panellists and participants in those discussions, including Benjamin Heap, Alicia Kearns, Paul King, Katherine Brown, Ben O'Loughlin, Alastair Miskimmon and Akil N. Awan, Ilan Manor, Ali Fisher, Sean Aday, Lotta Wagnsson, Saara Jantunen, Katja Valaskivi, Jesper Falkheimer, Cristina Archetti, Emma L. Briant, Shawn Powers and Greg Simons. Corneliu Bjola is particularly grateful to Jennifer Cassidy and Ilan Manor as members of the Oxford Digital Diplomacy Research Group (#DigDiploRox) for the inspiring conversations and intellectual exchanges on the topic of the 'bright' and 'dark' side of digital diplomacy that they have had in the past few years. James Pamment is particularly grateful to Howard Nothaft, Henrik Agardh-Twetman and Alicia Fjällhed at Lund University, and to colleagues at the Swedish Civil Contingencies Agency, Center for Asymmetric Threats Studies, Swedish Foreign Ministry and Swedish Institute for their collegiality and contributions to developing this research field in Sweden. In addition, we would like to thank the three anonymous reviewers whose useful criticisms and constructive suggestions helped strengthen the volume. Lastly, special thanks to the editorial team at Routledge, including Bethany Lund-Yates and Andrew Humphrys, who provided excellent support and guidance throughout the publication process.

INTRODUCTION

The 'dark side' of digital diplomacy

Corneliu Bjola and James Pamment

When Alec Ross, the former Senior Advisor for Innovation to Secretary of State Hillary Clinton, tweeted that "the 21st century is a terrible time to be a control freak" (Ross 2013b), many found that his observation captured something important about the series of societal transformations that the Digital Age had set in motion: the use of digital technologies to generate far-reaching change; to 'empower the powerless'; and to engineer a more pluralistic, responsible and democratic global society. To a certain extent, this vision still remains feasible, but the optimism of the early days of the digital revolution has been replaced by growing public cynicism, social distrust and even technophobia as the rise of echo chambers, fake news, disinformation and the deliberate weaponisation of information by state and non-state actors has fuelled fears of digital technologies having unintended consequences that may actually undermine rather than strengthen the social fabric of Western societies.

Initially dismissed as an inherent, albeit undesirable side effect of the digital revolution, digital propaganda has now reached a point whereby diplomats and foreign policymakers have no recourse but to take it very seriously and to seek credible solutions to containing and/or countering it. If basic understandings of the social reality are systematically falsified and reshaped to serve the foreign policy interests of the day, then the epistemological foundation that allows diplomats to bridge some of their differences simply collapses. The digital construction of 'alternative realities', that is, of public frames of social interpretation loosely linked or utterly unconnected to verifiable facts and evidence-based reasoning, becomes a form of undermining confidence in societal institutions and, by extension, in the diplomatic sphere, an ominous prelude rather than an alternative to war.

Certainly, digital diplomacy is now part of the regular conduct of international relations. Foreign ministries use social media to promote their countries, policies and values, contributing to a transparent and mostly cordial exchange of promotional materials and political views with anybody interested in global issues. However, some international actors, both state and non-state actors, make use of digital diplomacy techniques for nefarious purposes. In the case of state-sponsored information warfare, the resilience of open, democratic discourse has been severely tested by a 'firehose of falsehoods' of disinformation, fake news, trolling and conspiracy theories, many attributed to institutions affiliated with or promoting the geopolitical interests of the Kremlin. In the case of Daesh, stemming the flow of recruitment propaganda has proven to be a highly complex task, exacerbated by the decentralised profile of digital media technologies. It may be thus argued that by disrupting the way in which information is generated, circulated, interpreted and used, the digital revolution has not only created opportunities for progressive change but also ensured that digital propaganda, that is, the deliberate attempt to disseminate information on digital platforms with the purpose to deceive and mislead, is here to stay.

Like many other technologies, social media platforms come with a dual-use challenge, that is, they can be used for peace or war, for good or evil, for offence or defence (Evans and Commins 2017). The same tools that allow ministries of foreign affairs (MFA) and embassies to reach out to millions of people and build 'digital' bridges with online publics with the purpose of enhancing international collaboration, improving diaspora engagement, stimulating trade relations or positively managing international crises can be also used to "pierce, penetrate or perforate the political and information environments in the targeted countries" (Walker and Ludwig 2017), and in so doing undermine the political and social fabric of these countries. In fact, the 'dark side' of digital diplomacy, by which we refer to the use of digital technologies as disinformation and propaganda tools by governments and non-state actors in the pursuit of strategic interests, has expanded to the point that it has started to have serious implications for the global order.

More than 150 million Americans were exposed, for instance, to the Russian disinformation campaign prior to the 2016 presidential election, which was almost eight times more than the number of people who watched the evening news broadcasts of the ABC, CBS, NBC and Fox stations in 2016 (Lang 2017). Even more far-reaching, some two hundred unique targets – including politicians, diplomats, United Nations (UN) officials, military personnel from 39 countries and members of 28 governments – were found by a research centre affiliated with the University of Toronto to have been part of an extensive Russia-linked phishing and disinformation campaign (Hulcoop et al. 2017). The numbers are staggering, but probably even more disturbing are the findings of a recent study, which has discovered that fake news and false rumours travel six times more on average than accurate stories (Vosoughi et al. 2018). Simply put, disinformation reaches more people, diffuses much faster and replicates itself much deeper into the social network than fact-based statements. For resource-strapped governmental institutions, this is clearly a major problem as, with a few exceptions, many simply do not have the necessary capabilities to react to, let alone anticipate and pre-emptively contain, a disinformation campaign before it reaches them.

We consider these issues highly salient for many reasons. First, these topics represent major political challenges that undermine social cohesion, media ecologies and ultimately our security. They are major social problems with a shared emphasis on the online circulation of information and knowledge, and its manipulation for destructive purposes. Second, these are current challenges faced by the international community as a whole. Sharing knowledge and best practice is beneficial to all. There is a clear social utility in scholars and practitioners exchanging knowledge about the 'dark side' of digital diplomacy in order to contribute to societal resilience and collective responses. With these factors in mind, this edited volume brings together some of the world's leading experts on strategic communication, digital diplomacy and counter-propaganda, including academics and practitioners from the US and Europe. It highlights some of the major problems facing democratic institutions and provides concrete examples of best practice in reversing the tide of digital propaganda.

The volume is the result of a workshop held at Lund University in October 2016, which was funded by Riksbankens Jubeliumsfond. The workshop was innovative with respect to the fact that it established a strategic communication and digital diplomacy framework upon questions that are normally approached from technical, legal, ethical, doctrinal or social-psychology perspectives. By bringing the issues of strategic communication and countering violent extremism (CVE) together under this framework, participants were encouraged to unravel the communicative dimensions of these problems in ways that generated new insights. This volume seeks to collect the most important of those insights and to establish an agenda for future research on the 'dark side' of digital diplomacy in a way that takes into account the most pressing issues of our time.

The volume, the first of its kind to explore the 'dark side' of digital diplomacy, sets out to examine how governments make sense, manage and respond to two forms of digital propaganda that have proved particularly corrosive for Western countries in recent years: state-sponsored disinformation and violent extremism. The book is therefore divided into two broad themes that complement and inform each other: (1) strategic communication as a coherent set of governmental activities seeking to map, understand and respond to information threats of relevance for national security and (2) strategies for CVE, which include programmes, initiatives and measures focussed on preventing and dismantling networks that promote and sustain ideological radicalisation, violent extremism and terrorist recruitment. This simple yet effective topography helps frame the overarching question of the book – *how do democratic countries address the challenge of digital propaganda?* – as well as the response to this question by focussing on the ways in which strategic communication tools are used to counter false-hoods, incitements to violence and deceptions designed to undermine trust in expertise and institutions.

By instigating collaboration between scholars and practitioners on the pur-pose, methods and impact of strategic communication in the Digital Age, the book aims to make three important contributions to the existing literature. From a descriptive perspective, the volume provides a comprehensive overview of the challenges and opportunities that the 'dark side' of digital diplomacy poses for governments, in the context both of state-sponsored propaganda operations and of the radicalisation agendas pursued by extremist groups online. From an an-alytical perspective, it offers a pragmatic matrix of concepts and approaches for studying issues of digital disinformation as problems of strategic communication, drawing upon both the very latest practitioner insights and scholarship. From a prescriptive perspective, the book delivers a coherent set of analytical contribu-tions and best practices to contemporary challenges of information warfare and violent extremism, which can be reliably used by researchers and practitioners. The book thus demonstrates that while the weaponisation of information that the Digital Age now enables requires carefully designed response mechanisms, these responses must be tailored to the broader contexts that make it possible for digital propaganda to reach and occasionally influence vulnerable publics and audiences.

Strategic communication

Borrowed from the field of business and corporate management, the term stra-tegic communication (SC) has entered the lexicon of diplomatic scholars and practitioners relatively recently, initially as an add-on to instil coherence in the burgeoning literature on public diplomacy (Taylor 2009; Hayden 2013; Pam-ment 2015) and later as a valuable concept in itself to help make sense of and manage crisis situations (Cassidy and Manor 2016) or inform solutions to prob-lems generated by digital disinformation and propaganda (Bjola and Pamment 2016). By shifting the discussion away from the tactical use of communication by embassies and MFA to a more structured and goal-oriented form of pub-lic response and engagement, strategic communication has promised to create a more conducive environment for reaching out and engaging target audiences in a more coordinated, consistent and effective manner. At the same time, questions persist about the use of strategic communication as a (counter-)propaganda tool in support of foreign policy objectives; the processes and mechanisms by which strategic communication is supposed to deliver results; its broader relevance be-yond state-centred institutions; and, more critically, its theoretical added value and coherence.

Is there a strategy behind the digital disinformation campaigns attributed to the Russian government, and, if so, what conceptual tools can make better sense of the objectives of the strategy, and how can one build resilience against it? Drawing on the literature on Russian information warfare, Bjola argues that the theory of reflexive control offers a good framework for understanding how a state can be strategically influenced to pursue a predetermined course of action in international affairs. More precisely, reflexive control creates the conditions by which one party can 'hack' the diplomatic game so that it can shape the preferences of the other actors towards a desired outcome. By mapping the cognitive filters of the target audience, the party engaged in reflexive control seeks to offer tailored information to the opponent so that he/she will voluntarily make a decision to pursue a course of action in a predetermined direction. Most problematically, digital platforms now offer the opportunity to take the reflexive control theory to the next level by making filter mapping and micro-targeting of the relevant audiences more accurate and potentially more impactful. To counter reflexive control, Bjola suggests that a 4E funnel (entice, engage, elevate and exploit) can prove useful for developing guidelines about how a party can defend itself against reflexive control and how to build resilience against it. The response strategy should include, for instance, media literacy programmes for strengthening the informational environment against the risk of disinformation, a close monitoring of the potential for the viral dissemination of 'hot button' issues, a rapid response procedure for neutralising amplification effects and careful political analysis of the potential implications of the actions that parties are urged to pursue in reaction to disinformation campaigns.

In an effort to clarify what makes strategic communication valuable as an instrument for addressing disinformation, Nothhaft, Pamment, Agardh-Twetman and Fjällhed turn the question on its head and ask themselves what makes information influence illegitimate to the point that it must be considered a hostile act. In other words, what turns persuasion, entertainment, news, the very expressions of free communication and democratic deliberation into political warfare? Drawing on studies of cognitive science and evolutionary psychology, their chapter introduces a model of opinion formation that helps locate the systemic vulnerabilities of democratic societies to disinformation and propaganda. More specfically, the authors argue that Western liberal democracies have developed a system of public opinion formation that is self-stabilising as long as actors watch each other and insist on adherence to a few simple rules. However, the ultimate reason why illegitimate influence thrives, and what makes Western systems less resilient, is as simple as it is circular. It lies in genuine insecurity, on the part of Western liberal democracies, *about what is legitimate*. Simply put, a system that relies on the sound judgement of its citizens, relies by necessity on a certain convergence of judgements, which, under certain conditions, can be easily hacked. To prevent this, strategic communication must address this preexisting gap that foreign influence operators have discovered as the key societal vulnerability of democratic countries.

Building on this insight, Briant and Wanless focus on an interesting technique of influence, journalist leaks, which are strategically used by state and non-state actors to shape public opinion, decision-making and the distribution of power between competing elites. Their chapter introduces readers to scholarly debates regarding strategic leaking, propaganda and journalistic reporting, and examines how key actors attempted to manage and exploit leaks during the 2016 US presidential election and the 'Panama Papers'. The authors demonstrate that leaking must be increasingly seen within wider surveillance capabilities, coercive and propagandistic security strategies, and that research on its relationship to governance and changing methods of propaganda is much needed. Furthermore, as leaks are increasingly incorporated into advanced systems of propaganda to sway the public, deepen mistrust in institutions and impair citizens' capacity to make informed decisions about polices and candidates during elections, serious consideration must be given to how governments oversee and regulate the use of data in political campaigning to protect democracies in this Digital Age. A key role for strategic communication is therefore to reveal and counter the narratives that are being shaped by the emphasis or obfuscation of the leaked content, the leaker and their supportive audiences.

In the next chapter, Olsson and Wagnsson criticise the academic focus on states' use of political communication and call attention to the need for systematic research on how international organisations (IOs) also engage with the global public to shape perceptions on critical issues, especially in the security area. Drawing on examples on how the North Atlantic Treaty Organization (NATO) and the European Union (EU) use both public diplomacy and information warfare in the security arena, the authors identify four types by which the two IOs use strategic communication in support of their objectives: mustering internal cohesion in order to keep the organisations together, promoting the organisations in the international arena, expanding the organisations through new members and partnerships, and managing threats and adversaries. The authors note that the fourth type, engaging with adversaries, poses a particular type of challenge for the two IOs, especially the EU, because of a growing tension between civilian and military practice. The more they engage in information warfare, the more they may hamper public diplomacy activities in other areas. Similarly, NATO's communication strategy risks being seen as less credible and consistent since, on the one hand, it seeks to project itself as a forceful military alliance, thus building upon the logic of 'othering' and exclusion while, on the other hand, portraying itself as a non-threatening cosmopolitan force for good. The authors conclude that both the EU and NATO face difficulties in conveying a coherent image of their organisation. The problem may further aggravate in the age of social media as the trend of personification may affect the overall prospect for success of communication by IOs.

Cristina Archetti concludes this section with a provocative chapter in which she challenges the very premises that theoretically inform the concept of strategic communication. The worst problems with strategic communication, she argues, are not the practical ones related to its implementation, be they connected to political leadership or organisation, or the wording of the concept. These only arise because strategic communication is fundamentally flawed theoretically. More specifically, strategic communication as a complete coordination of words and deeds across large organisations is unrealistic; it cannot be approached in isolation from the political and social context, and although strategic communication can be a useful tool, its 'power' should not be exaggerated, especially in the context of increasing political polarisation. She illustrates these points through empirical examples, ranging from governmental efforts aimed at CVE to public diplomacy, and measures to counter propaganda from foreign countries, especially when it comes to dealing with election interference and 'fake news'. Her conclusion is sobering and worth reflecting upon: digital propaganda works because of the deep fractures that exist within Western societies, so the best defence against further disinformation should be a more serious commitment of governments and political leaders to improving the economic and social conditions of their citizens.

Countering violent extremism

Terrorism is hardly, of course, a recent challenge for governments, but the context in which it operates and the tactics it uses never stop evolving. As former US President Barack Obama remarked when introducing the US comprehensive counterterrorism strategy back in 2013,

> in an age when ideas and images can travel the globe in an instant, our response to terrorism can't depend on military or law enforcement alone. [...] We cannot use force everywhere that a radical ideology takes root. And in the absence of a strategy that reduces the wellspring of extremism, a perpetual war through drones or special forces or troop deployments will prove self-defeating and alter our country in troubling ways.
>
> *(Obama 2013)*

CVE strategies are supposed to do exactly that, to use non-coercive measures to counter underlying drivers of ideological recruitment and provide 'off-ramps' for individuals who may have already taken steps towards embracing ideologically motivated violence (Selim 2016: 95). However, lessons from CVE programmes implemented in the UK, Australia, and Denmark have revealed a critical tension between how to better reach those who require assistance, on the one hand, and how to avoid the securitisation of social cohesion efforts and the stigmatisation of communities which are essential for the success of the programmes, on the other hand (Harris-Hogan et al. 2016: 19).

Alicia Kearns locates the source of this tension in the way in which the Digital Age has transformed the ability of violent extremists to radicalise, recruit and carry out acts of terror. Specifically, she argues that the democratisation of narrative control has aided the spread of violent extremism and created a new generation of agents of influence: no longer solely states, the media or well-financed terror or organised crime groups but also regular individuals. Because whilst the battle over 'truth' remains the same, it is the Digital Age which has given individuals the ability to become arbiters of truths, above and beyond traditional power and information transference structures. This gives violent extremists more opportunity than ever before, but it also creates an entirely new brigade of counter-extremism 'soldiers': *we*, the citizens. As individuals, across the world, have embraced, to lesser and greater extents, their new position as arbiters of truth and information, they need better conceptual tools for understanding how to protect their communities against violent extremism. Kearns responds to this concern by proposing nine practical approaches to tackle the new battle rhythm and the democratisation of agency. These recommendations are not exhaustive nor applicable in countering all cases of violent extremism but offer some feasible and practical solutions for governments, organisations and individuals seeking to counter violent extremism.

Manor and Crilley take Kearns's argument a step further and point out that CVE activities conducted on social media are still premised on the assumption that extremist recruitment and support is facilitated through the dissemination of simple, clear narratives and that there is subsequently a need for counter-narratives to draw people away from extremism. The problem with this approach, they argue, is that narratives do not simply appeal to people because of their content but because of how they resonate with their emotions. If extremist groups are able to elicit sympathy or inspire followers with images, CVE must also offer compelling images that resonate emotionally with publics. In other words, scholars of violent extremism and CVE must pay attention not only to the narrative but also to the broader aesthetics of communication. Using the Coalition against Daesh's Twitter content as a case study, the authors find that the aesthetic content elicits the strongest audience engagement, and, interestingly, content with positive emotions receives the highest levels of follower engagement. The implication is clear: CVE counter-narratives should be communicated through aesthetic media in a way that resonates, symbolically, culturally and emotionally, with the audience that is being sought.

Sean Aday recognises the value of the idea of the aesthetics of communication in the case of violent extremism but for different, darker reasons. More specifically, he sets out to examine the extent to which the violent videos that terrorist organisations use to spread their strategic narratives are as effective as some policymakers and pundits claim them to be and if so, what to do about them. As an analytical strategy for addressing these questions, Aday compares Islamic State in Iraq and Syria (ISIS) execution videos to those produced earlier in the century by Al Qaeda (AQ) and concludes that ISIS videos' utilisation of pop culture formats is what allows them to cast a wider net than AQ's violent videos. This technique helps create more emotional distance between the audience and the violence, and it may have stronger, more enduring effects because the videos prime preexisting efficacy-reinforcing mental models and induce cognitive elaboration. The implications of Aday's argument are that while we should not exaggerate, much less panic about, the kind of violent videos that shock us, we should take some of them more seriously than others. That means, for instance, focussing on who is producing those videos, who is watching them and how they travel across online networks. Most importantly, Aday argues, it means adopting community and culturally based approaches to counter-messaging, including working with local and regional messengers and media that are credible with the target audience.

Finally, Akil Awan, Alister Miskimmon and Ben O'Loughlin take a critical view of the 'dual fetishisation' of CVE activities, that is, the framing of newer media and newer terrorist groups as being something special, even exceptional, thus ignoring the 'banal reality' of their evolution and transformation. This is a serious problem, they argue, because it creates an unrealistic account of communication and persuasion that ignores decades of research on radicalisation and a century of research on media effects. The 'battle of the narratives' becomes thus conceptualised and practiced as the quantitative online dominance of 'our' content over 'theirs'. Rather than admitting how intractably difficult persuasion is, and rather than responding to the real-world concerns of those persuadable by radical narratives – political disenfranchisement, socio-economic marginalisation, personal identity crises and xenophobia – removal of social media accounts and content affiliated with terrorist groups is instead considered the key mark of CVE progress. As an alternative approach, the authors propose a model of narrative contestation through which governments can address real-world concerns. By charting possible narrative alignment about how the world works, how we fit into that world and how that bears on current problems, we can identify how and why some radicalising groups may offer a coherent and compelling narrative, and why counter-radicalisation offers a less coherent and compelling narrative for certain audiences. In short, the authors warn that unless real-world concerns are taken seriously and addressed holistically, these very same issues will no doubt be taken up and mobilised towards the messaging of whichever extremist group inevitably emerges next.

In the concluding chapter, Pamment and Bjola consider some of the broader questions and issues facing this research field. First is the question of how the various insights from different academic disciplines can be consolidated into a common interdisciplinary discussion. Second is the balance between approaches that focus on the threat, whether that be a specific actor or issue, and approaches that focus on social vulnerabilities and resilience. A third dimension is ensuring that the best practice collected from two decades of counterterrorism experience is drawn upon in this new context. Fourth is the challenge of moving beyond contemplating the problem and instead taking a consistent approach to counteracting the threat. Fifth is the question of how the new public diplomacy and digital diplomacy relate to information influence activities in terms of their techniques and purpose. Fifth, the chapter considers the difficulties of attributing disinformation activities to specific actors, particularly in relation to the demands of democratic discourse. Sixth, the question of the ethics of countering digital propaganda is discussed in the context of how states should react to acts of dis-information without losing the moral ground that they seek to protect. Finally, the authors advance a set of policy recommendations for democratic countries to deal with the context of information influence, including a sustained dialogue between governments, academia, civil society and citizens on the importance of truth and transparency in the public sphere.

PART I
Strategic communication

1

PROPAGANDA AS REFLEXIVE CONTROL

The digital dimension

Corneliu Bjola

Introduction

Reacting to the poisoning of the Russian double-agent Sergei Skripal and his daughter Yulia on British soil on March 4, 2018, the UK Prime Minister, Theresa May, called the incident, in her statement to the House of Commons, an "unlawful use of force" by the Russian state against the UK (Asthana et al. 2018). Two days later, the leaders of Great Britain, US, Germany and France released a joint statement strongly condemning the Salisbury nerve agent attack as "an assault on UK sovereignty" and saying it was highly likely Russia was behind it (Walker and Roth 2018). The Russian government tried to distance itself from the incident (Osborne and Carroll 2018), but its denials made little impression on the UK government and its allies. As the situation soon evolved into a full-scale information war (Barojan 2018), the public discussion turned to examining and understanding the potential strategic implications of the attack.

The act of engineering a confrontation with the UK a few days before the Russian presidential elections on March 18 could have generated a number of political benefits for the Russian President, Vladimir Putin, starting from boosting voter turnout and by extension, the legitimacy of the outcome in a campaign dominated by voter apathy. Furthermore, the attack could have served to drive a wedge between a Brexit-weary Britain and its allies or even to push the UK to retaliate against wealthy and prominent Russians in London, thus forcing them to seek closer relations with the regime back home (Harding and Roth 2018). In view of the track record of recent Russian interference in the domestic affairs of other countries for strategic gains, some of these explanations could sound reasonably plausible (Hille, Foy, and Seddon 2018), but short of a credible conceptual framework to validate them, these claims largely remain in the realm of informed speculation. With that in mind, would it be possible to reduce the degree of overdetermination of the effects of Russian actions by better understanding the patterns by which such actions are designed and implemented? In other words, is there a way by which we can make sense of whether a state can be strategically influenced to pursue a predetermined course of action in international affairs, especially against its own interests?

Enter the theory of reflexive control (RC), which, as discussed further below, represents one of the long-standing and influential doctrine of information warfare employed by the Russian intelligence services. In basic terms, RC can be defined "as a means of conveying to a partner or an opponent specially prepared information to incline him to voluntarily make the predetermined decision desired by the initiator of the action" (Thomas 2004, 237). Unlike the case of physical coercion ("sticks") or economic inducement ("carrots"), RC seeks to exert influence by infiltrating the decision-making process of the opponent, who is thus covertly encouraged to pursue a course of action that favours the strategic goals of the initiator. In foreign policy terms, this is very powerful, as it could make the difference between war and peace or perhaps less dramatically, between diplomatic success and failure. Basically, RC allows one party to "hack" the diplomatic game so that it can shape the preferences of the other actors towards a desired outcome.

The RC strategy can hardly be faulted for lacking ambition, but it creates a level of expectation that might be hard to deliver in practice. After all, the ambition of influencing "collective attitudes by the manipulation of significant symbols" or simply put, by propaganda (Lasswell 1927, 627), has informed the thinking of political leaders, military strategists and diplomats for centuries with very mixed results, to put it mildly. RC could suffer the same disappointment, largely because people learn quickly how to resist efforts that seek to control them against their will. In addition, the concept of RC rests on a set of Hobbesian assumptions about the international system that are likely to induce international actors to see each other in very dark colours, so that even positive forms of diplomatic engagement could be interpreted as signs of deception and strategic manipulation.

This is why it is important to carefully unpack the conceptual underpinnings of RC: so that we can acquire a better understanding of how RC works; what limitations it faces; to what extent its claims can be validated empirically; and, equally importantly, to what extent RC can be "reverse-engineered" so that effective means of protection against it can be designed. What probably lends extra credibility to RC today is the arrival and spread of digital platforms, and the opportunity they create for RC proponents to use social media data to build detailed cognitive profiles on the basis of which RC controllers could imitate the reasoning process of the target audience and then to use this information for micro-targeting specific audiences. This chapter starts by providing a brief background to the concept of RC, discussing its mechanism and mode of operation; continues by reviewing the analytical contributions and limitations of the concept to understanding patterns of disinformation, especially in a digital context; and concludes by suggesting a four-layered funnel of digital RC by which the scope, reach and effectiveness of the strategy could be assessed and influenced.

The theory of reflexive control

In a study commissioned by the US Naval Postgraduate School in Monterey, California, towards the end of the Cold War (Chotikul 1986), the scientific development of the theory of RC was traced back to the early 1960s and the work of Dr Vladimir A. Lefebvre, a military researcher in the former Soviet Union, who later emigrated to the US. As Lefebvre indicated in one of his first books on the topic,

> one gains an advantage in conflict if one has an accurate image of the opponent's image of the situation and of how the opponent applies a particular 'doctrine' in an attempt to solve the problem as 'he' sees it; above all, if one is able to influence the opponent's perception of the situation or his goals or his doctrine and at the same time conceal from him the fact that one 'is' influencing him.
>
> *(Lefebvre and Smolyan 1968 (1971), 45)*

In short, by understanding the thinking process of a particular individual, one should be able to steer him/her to taking actions in a desired direction. The key question is, of course, how to do this?

RC theory, as Lefebvre and his team conceptualised it, has a dual aspect that considers both the process and the outcome of the disinformation strategy. On the process side, RC can be conducted through the transformation of the opponent's information processing (the cognitive dimension) or through the careful selection of messages presented to the person subjected to RC (the informational dimension). For example, a tourist could be induced to travel to city X if appealing information about the destination is made available to him/her or if his cognitive mechanism of evaluating touristic destinations is altered to include criteria that favour attractions in city X. On the outcome side, RC can facilitate a "constructive" result, in which the opponent is influenced to voluntarily make a decision favourable to the controlling side, or a "destructive" result, in which means are employed to destroy, paralyse or neutralise the procedures and algorithms of the enemy's decision-making processes (Lefebvre and Lefebvre 1984, 144–145) (see Table 1.1). Using again our earlier example, the tourist could be "constructively" induced to travel to city X or "destructively" prevented from travelling to the competition, city Y, either by offering him/her negative information about city Y or by heightening the appeal of those criteria in his mechanism of assessing tourist destinations that do not favour the type of attractions offered by city Y.

Informational control for either "constructive or destructive" purposes is the most common form of propaganda, and it has been used for centuries in various

TABLE 1.1 Processes and Outcomes of Reflexive Control

	Constructive	Destructive
Cognitive	B is induced by A to alter his/her decision-making algorithm to facilitate outcomes beneficial to A	B is induced by A to revise his/her decision-making algorithm to avoid outcomes detrimental to A
Informational	B is induced by A to assess the situation in a manner that facilitates outcomes beneficial to A	B is prevented by A to assess the situation in a manner that may lead to outcomes detrimental to A

manifestations. Diplomacy in Byzantium was characterised, for instance, by an elaborate propaganda system intended to impress "barbarians" of the political and military superiority of the empire, its longevity, grandeur and the contrasting fates of its enemies (Hamilton and Langhorne 1995, 16). The strategic objective of the entire court ceremonial was to discourage vassals and rivals from challenging the authority of the emperor by controlling the informational context based on which visitors could assess the political or military situation of the empire. The idea introduced by the theory of RC of altering or corrupting the decision-making process of the opponent goes a step further by seeking to control not only what B perceives (e.g., the dazzling symbols of power of the imperial office) but also how he/she takes decisions on matters relevant to A (e.g., whether it attaches the same weights and benchmarks to assessing the geopolitical situation as the emperor). The RC theoretical ambition is clearly high, but does it work in practice? Lefebvre's suggestion that "in contrast to a scholarly debate, the most inventive liar wins in conflict" (Lefebvre and Smolyan 1968 (1971), 18) does little to alleviate doubts and leaves the question open to interpretation.

In a more recent overview of the theoretical developments in the field of RC, Timothy Thomas, a former director of Soviet Studies at the US Army Russian Institute, traced the evolution of the theory since 1960s and found that the concept did not fade with the collapse of the Soviet Union, but it actually remained high on the research agenda of the Russian military and intelligence community at the end of the Cold War. Furthermore,

> at the present time, there is a reflexive control movement underway in Russia that is influencing approaches to various branches of knowledge. This embraces philosophy, sociology, psychology, pedagogy, problems of artificial intelligence and computer science in general, computer 'control' influence, military affairs, intelligence, counterintelligence, and a number of other areas.
>
> *(Thomas 2004, 248)*

Thomas's observation is important because it demonstrates continuity in strategic thinking between the military and political elites of the Soviet Union and those of post-Cold War Russia.

Some of the RC tactics recommended by the new generation of Russian military analysts sound, for instance, eerily similar to the type of disinformation operations that the European and American public has faced in the recent years: offering information that discredits the government in the eyes of its population, frequently sending the enemy a large amount of conflicting information, convincing the enemy that he must operate in opposition to coalition interests (Thomas 2004, 248). In a separate article, focussed on the Russian intervention in Ukraine in 2014, Thomas examines the extent to which RC measures have moved from theory to practice. The use of false analogies (Crimea vs Kosovo), military provocations (unannounced flights over the Baltic countries) or blame projection (accusing the West of targeting Putin with an information war) are, for instance, some of the RC measures deployed by Russian authorities, prior and during the annexation of Crimea, as a way to control the informational context, shape favourable perceptions about Russia during the crisis and prevent Western countries from taking actions detrimental to Russia (Thomas 2015, 456–458).

While the first generation of RC studies largely focussed on conceptual development (what RC means as a process and outcome), current investigations conducted by Russian military researchers seek to understand how the concept works in practice from a tactical and strategic perspective. At the tactical level, the issue of concern is the "reflex" component of the theory, that is, the process of unpacking and imitating the mode of reasoning of the opponent. Gaining access to the cognitive "filter" of the opponent (knowledge, ideas, experience) would presumably help one understand and copy how the opponent makes sense of the situation he or she faces and how he or she takes decisions. Close knowledge of the opponent's "filter" (habits, socio-psychological profile, preferred modes of social interactions, etc.) is therefore critical for maximising the chances of success of RC, but this is a challenging task as such volume of information is not easy to collect or interpret and to render it into actionable recommendations.

The alternative to developing detailed maps of the cognitive "filter" is to locate its "weakest links", that is, those intellectual, moral or personal characteristics on which the opponent relies the most for making judgements about matters of interest to him (see Figure 1.1). For example, if one is prejudiced, then feeding the source of his prejudice becomes the "weak link" to be exploited against him. Alternatively, if one is prone to narcissism, then boosting his ego with flattery and compliments could make him react more positively to your ideas. Drawing on writings of Russian military strategists, Thomas calls the process of locating the "weakest link" the "chief task of reflexive control", and rightly so as the side with the highest degree of reflex (i.e., with the best capacity to imitate the opponent thoughts or predict its behaviour) has the best chances of winning the influence "game" (Thomas 2004, 241–242).

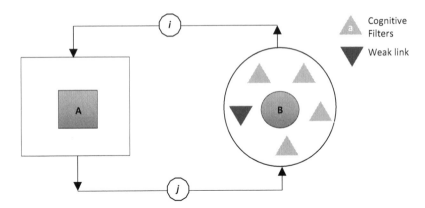

FIGURE 1.1 Tactical Model of Reflexive Control: A uses information *i* about B's cognitive filters and "weak links" to induce B via information *j* to take decisions in line with A's goals.

From a strategic perspective, the issue of concern is how the opponent reacts and adapts to RC. As one of the leading RC theorists, Colonel S. Leonenko, points out, RC is an interactive process, in which parties seek to influence each other to different degrees. For example, if side A acts independently of the behaviour of side B, then his degree of reflex relative to side B is equal to zero (0). If, on the other hand, side A makes assumptions about side B's behaviour based on the thesis that side B is not taking side A's behaviour into account, then side A's degree of reflex is one (1). If side B also has a first-degree reflex (takes A's behaviour into account), and side A takes this fact into account, then side A's reflex is two (2), and so on (Leonenko cited in Thomas 2004, 242). A higher degree of RC demonstrates strategic sophistication, but it also makes more difficult for the parties to stay in control of the strategic game.

As Lefebvre and his team note in a recent article, methods of RC work best under the condition that the party that is being controlled does not know about this fact (see Figure 1.2). Otherwise, RC can damage the controlling party, since after discovering the influencing attempt, the controlled party may be able to reconstruct the intentions of the opponent (Kramer et al. 2003, 99–100). In other words, once resilience against RC is developed, the controlling Party A may compromise its ability to "constructively" induce B to take decisions in line with A's strategic goals, but it may still retain the capacity to prevent B from taking decisions against A by "destructively" influencing his decision-making process through power pressure, deception or artificial time constraints (Ionov 1995).

To sum up, the theory of RC offers good analytical insight for understanding the conditions under which propaganda campaigns may work and why. By gaining access to the cognitive filter by which an opponent makes sense of the world, the controlling party might be able to induce him/her to voluntarily take decisions in favour or at least not against its interests. At the same time, the model comes with some important limitations. First, the theory carries reasonable

(I)   A uses info *i* to influence B (no resilience, R0) leading to 'constructive' reflexive control (RC_{++});

(II)   A uses info *i* to influence B (medium resilience, R1), prompting A to use revised information (Aii) leading to 'constructive' but reduced reflexive control (RC_+);

(III) A uses info *i* to influence B (strong resilience, R2), prompting A to use revised information (Aii) leading to 'destructive' reflexive control (RC_-);

(I) $Ai \longrightarrow B_{R0}$ $[RC_{++}]$

(II) $Ai \longrightarrow B_{R1} \longrightarrow Aii$ $[RC_+]$

(III) $Ai \longrightarrow B_{R1} \longrightarrow Aij$ $[RC_-]$

FIGURE 1.2   Strategic Model of Reflexive Control.

analytical currency at the individual level, but its applicability arguably narrows at the group or society level. It is not very clear, for instance, how "cognitive filters" could be mapped for large groups and with what degree of efficiency. Second, the model works well when the controlled party is unaware of RC efforts against itself, but once the parties develop resilience against such strategies, it becomes increasingly difficult to measure the impact of RC.

Reflexive control in the Digital Age

Within less than a decade since the launch of the first social media networks, 90% of all United Nations (UN) member states have established a Twitter presence, and 88% have opened a Facebook account, with a combined audience of 325 million and 255 million, respectively, of followers, likes and users (Twiplomacy 2016). The main reason why governments, ministries of foreign affairs (MFAs) and embassies have migrated online is influence as large and diverse audiences can now be directly reached and potentially convinced to adopt views and positions in line with the objectives of the source. To put the issue into the broader context, about 3.2 billion people have actively used social media in 2018, an increase of 13% from last year (Chaffey 2018) for the purpose of listening to, communicating and engaging with each other. In so doing, they have generated a vast amount of data about their social, economic or cultural preferences, but most of it comes in an unstructured format, as text and multimedia content, featuring an internal structure but lacking a pattern of self-organisation that can fit predefined data models or schema (Taylor 2018).

From an RC perspective, this is "good news" as the data generated online can be theoretically used to build detailed cognitive profiles of target individuals and groups with potentially strong implications for political behavioural prediction, thus filling an important empirical gap in the model. However, in order to be able to do this, one needs to find a way to convert unstructured social media data into a structured format so that its various attributes (number of likes, geolocation, type of connections, conversation topics, etc.) can be organised in a fashion that allows for easy identification of trends, patterns and relationships.

Depending on the method by which this conversion is done, four layers of cognitive filters could present relevance for RC, ranging from broader views of thematic or interactional preferences, at the group level, to a more granular insight of the demographic and psychographic data, at the individual level:

- Conversation filter: At the most basic level, social media platforms offer the possibility of monitoring trending topics of relevance for specific audiences in specific locations. Hashtag analysis is, for instance, a good tool for capturing events-triggering themes of online conversation (Lee, Abdar, and Yen 2018), examining the dissemination reach of controversial topics (Lycariāo and dos Santos 2017), or evaluating the reception spectrum of certain messages (Agarwal, Singh, and Toshniwal 2018). The filter is therefore useful for building a thematic profile of a particular audience (preferred or sensitive topics of conversation), thus allowing the message to be suitably tailored to group preferences. It also faces minimal technical obstacles, as the necessary data could be relatively easily collected with tools available online.

- Network filter: While the thematic profile is good for understanding how to make a message resonate with an online community, a networking profile can reveal how the members of a group interact with each other and with other groups. Social network analysis (SNA) has emerged, for this reason, as the key analytical instrument for mapping and exploring patterns of interaction between users, but it requires some extra knowledge from those who would like to make use of it. A network filter can, for instance, classify online conversations based on their patterns of information flow (Himelboim et al. 2017), identify and assess the "hidden" influence of potentially influential actors in the network (Dubois and Gaffney 2014; Jörgens, Kolleck, and Saerbeck 2016) or track the formation and evolution of online communities (Eugene 2015; Berntzen and Weisskircher 2016). From an RC perspective, the value of the network filter thus rests with its ability to create a profile of contacts and interactions of the potential subject: whom she interacts with more regularly, how influential these contacts are and what type of sub-networks and online communities the subject prefers to connect with and inhabit.

- Demographic filter: Socio-economic characteristics, such as age, gender, education level, income level, marital status, occupation, ethnicity and religion, can offer powerful indicators of people's political preferences and behaviour. In British politics, for instance, age is a key predictor of the voting intention, while the level of education and income largely inform party or ideological preferences (Curtis 2017). While substantially differing from the general population on many politically relevant dimensions (Mellon and Prosser 2017), social media demographics can nevertheless offer good insight for understanding patterns of political interaction online (Artime 2016), political value trade-offs (Swigger 2013) or the nature of impact of online political content (Anderson 2016). Using the relatively accessible advertising services provided by the tech companies, a demographic filter could be thus instrumental for segmenting the target audience using key demographic criteria and tailoring one's messages accordingly.

- Psychographic filter: By measuring psychological attributes (such as introversion-extroversion, openness to experience, conscientiousness, agreeableness and neuroticism), psychographics offer deep and actionable insight into users' personality profiles in a way that was nearly impossible before the arrival of Google, Facebook and Twitter (Samuel 2016). One important study has found, for instance, that computer models need 10, 70, 150 and 300 Facebook Likes, respectively, to outperform an average work of a colleague, cohabitant or friend, family member or spouse, respectively, in predicting someone's personality profile (Youyou, Kosinski, and Stillwell 2015, 2). This is arguably the most intimate type of filter from the list as it comes the closest to understanding the thinking process of the opponent, which is, of course, the main ambition of the RC theory. It is also the hardest filter to create, unless those developing it are able to gain access to the data collected by tech companies.

From an RC perspective, filter mapping may thus prove useful for gathering relevant data online about target groups (the B-*i*-A route in Figure 1.1), so that specific issues that motivate groups and individuals can be accurately identified and users can be then micro-targeted based on their distinct preferences. Social listening can be thus used to locate or by case engineer online communities that resonate with these topics and then feed them content, in an RC fashion, for maximum political impact. Cambridge Analytica allegedly used, for instance, a powerful combination of demographic and psychographic data in support of the Trump campaign,[1] but the results were rather inconclusive.[2] However, as Table 1.2 suggests, the more precise the filter, the harder to collect the data, and by extension, the more difficult to leverage the power of big data for RC (the A-*j*-B route in Figure 1.1). If the profiling data of online users is not easily accessible, then the capacity of Party A to use digital RC against Party B is arguably diminished. Furthermore, as online communities are generally volatile, issue oriented and prone to fragmentation, one may wonder whether filter mapping can provide sufficiently reliable data so that the right group is targeted at the right time and with the right message.

TABLE 1.2 Cognitive Filter Mapping

Filter Type	Profile Scope	Profile Depth	Profile Data Accessibility
Conversation	Group	Moderate	High
Network	Group	Moderate	Moderate
Demographic	Individual	Moderate	High
Psychographic	Individual	Strong	Weak

From an RC perspective, one solution to the problem of data scarcity and the limitations this can have for building an accurate cognitive profile of the opponent is to go "destructive" and use social listening for identifying "hot button" issues and relevant online communities that could be exploited to corrupt the opponent's decision-making algorithm. To be sure, each country has its own political vulnerabilities, ranging from racial tensions, socio-economic inequalities, secessionist aspirations, corruption scandals, to lingering effects of war traumas. The goal in this case is not to induce the opponent to pursue certain actions that can facilitate positive outcomes for Party A, but to distract or prevent Party B from taking decisions detrimental to the controlling party, either by paralysing his decision-making algorithm or by reshaping it in such a manner that some of the priorities to avoid of the party engaged in RC become the priorities of the opponent as well.

The Twitter user known as @TEN_GOP followed this pattern of digital activity prior and during the US presidential elections in 2016. For almost two years, it strongly commended the Republican candidate, Donald Trump, praised the American military, and interacted with dozens of leading conservatives, while attacking Trump's election rival Hillary Clinton, liberals, Muslims and the mainstream media. The account was suspended in July 2017, when Twitter confirmed that @TEN_GOP was a fake, run by a Russian operative connected to the notorious "troll factory" in St. Petersburg (Nimmo 2017). What this example suggests is that by seeking to exploit "weak links" with highly divisive messages, such accounts serve to sharpen ideological polarisation, maximise political disunity and weaken democratic institutions. In so doing, destructive tactics of RC can reset the decision-making algorithm of policymakers, by ensuring the country would stay focussed on issues that are less threatening to the interests of the opponent.

In sum, RC theory may help explain why digital propaganda has become such a dominant tool of Russian foreign policy influence, as digital platforms significantly reduce the cost of cognitive mapping (B-i-A) and especially microtargeting (A-j-B). It also provides a plausible explanation for the thematic and temporal tailoring of disinformation to the political context of Western countries (e.g., refugee policy in Germany, Catalonian separatism in Spain, race relations in the US) in line with the "weak link" argument. The intensity of Russian disinformation campaigns around elections is reasonably explained by the two-level logic of digital RC: influencing the views of the online public so that the subsequent elections results will drive decision makers to adapt their policies accordingly. The theory also predicts well the varying impact of disinformation as the more active the response to disinformation, the weaker the reflexive effect as suggested by the case of the UK and Baltic states. Last but not least, the theory explains the "destructive" escalation to follow from increased resilience as seen in the Skripal and MH17 cases, when the intention of the Russian authorities was to confuse and prevent Western audiences from developing a clear understanding about what had happened. On the critical side, the theory does not fully account for the independent contribution of RC relative to organic developments with impact on policy outcomes (e.g., whether certain policy outcomes would have happened regardless or because of RC). Most importantly, it fails to provide clear benchmarks for evaluating the success or failure of strategies of RC in a manner that is not subjectively connected to the authors' preferences.

The funnel of digital reflexive control

Developed at the height of the Cold War and refined conceptually in the 1990s, the theory of RC still remains an empirical "black box". In the absence of clear data about its use, it is hard to know the extent to which the theory successfully crossed the border from academic discussion to practical application during that period and if so, how well it supported the Soviet and later the Russian foreign policy agenda. Mindful of the explosion of online disinformation in recent years, one also feels compelled to ask a similar question not only about whether digital platforms have managed to inject new life into the theory, as discussed in the previous section, but most importantly about whether they have increased the policy impact of RC and, if so, whether countries subjected to such practices can develop effective responses in their defence. As the possibility of falsifying the success or failure of RC strategies remain rather weak in the absence of inside information, one way to address this question is by using counterfactual analysis and asking ourselves what kind of challenges Country B would likely face *if* B is subjected to digital RC by Country A.

Four considerations are particularly important to discuss if such situation arises. The first one relates to the *context* of the information environment of Country A and the extent to which a sudden influx of digital messages that are closely tailored to domestic political circumstances would start shaping online conversations, especially in pre-election periods. The second consideration concerns the *content* of these messages, whether they are fact-based and informative, and sustain political discussion, or they are emotionally charged and possibly misleading and serve to undermine a fair exchange of political views. The third consideration refers to the issue of amplification and the extent to which the *dissemination* of these messages, especially those with an inflammatory character, takes place organically, in a predictable fashion, or whether they are deliberately accelerated by the use of botnets or other media channels. The fourth consideration informs the potential *outcome*, that is, whether the online public is encouraged to take an offline political step and whether this call has a "constructive" (in favour of a particular objective) or "destructive" intention (against a particular objective).

The four considerations come together to form a 4E funnel of digital RC: entice, engage, elevate and exploit (see Figure 1.3), by which Party B could be induced to voluntarily take a decision that favours Party A's interests. The growing volume of politically tailored messages might not represent by itself a sign that Party B is exposed to RC as political discussions tend to multiply and become more intense in pre-election periods. The context layer simply calls attention to

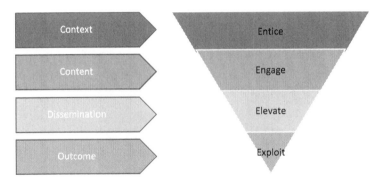

FIGURE 1.3 The 4E Funnel of Digital Reflexive Control.

the fact that the digital environment provides a conducive medium for conducting RC, and therefore Party B may want to check whether any unusual patterns of online political engagement can be detected and, if so, whether they are the result of an effort to entice the audience through the systematic use of tailored messages based on the four type of filters mentioned above. The next layer of the funnel represented by the content and profile of the message is critically important for understanding the extent to which online conversations cover a wider spectrum of positions, or they are artificially skewed towards political topics that seek to engage the audience in a manner resembling the "weak link" logic. The presence of botnets and of other instruments of media amplification could be a further sign of a deliberate attempt by Party A to tactically hack the information environment, if dissemination is pursued in an RC fashion by elevating the volume and intensity of the online conversation with the purpose to weaken or undermine Party B's decision-making algorithm. Finally, the call to action, either in favour or against a particular objective, completes the funnel by making explicit the political objectives that Party A seeks to exploit and accomplish through its RC strategy.

From an analytical perspective, the funnel offers a coherent framework for disentangling conventional forms of online political engagement from potentially strategic uses of digital platforms by foreign actors for RC purposes. The more the informational context of Party B is infiltrated by tailored messages, especially by "hot button" issues, the more the audience is prevented from making sense of what it is happening through algorithmically induced methods of information overload, and the more calls to action in favour or against certain political objectives, the more likely that Party B has become a target of digital RC.

The "Lisa case" provides a good illustration to this model as it touches upon all four components of the 4E funnel. Shortly after the incidents of sexual assault in the German city of Cologne on New Year's Eve 2016 (BBC 2016b), a 13-year-old Russian-German girl living in Berlin was reported by First Russian TV to have been kidnapped and raped by migrants. The story, which the German policy proved to be fake as the girl had been with a friend that night (Knight 2016), was subsequently amplified by Russian foreign media like RT, Sputnik and RT Deutsch, both offline and especially online via social media. Demonstrations were soon organised via Facebook involving representatives of the German-Russian minority as well as neo-Nazi groups. Most problematically, despite the story being debunked by the German authorities, the Russian Foreign Minister, Sergej Lavrov, took the unusual step to criticise German authorities for their inability to take such cases seriously because of "political correctness" (Meister 2016).

The case is important because it reveals the conditions under which the 4E funnel of RC may work. The story benefited from a conducive informational environment for dissemination as the public had been already sensitised by the sexual assault incidents in Cologne and thus enticed and primed to make intuitive connections between migrants and sexual improprieties. Aside from the emotionally charged content of the story and in line with the "weak link" argument, the immigration angle of the story aimed to engage the public on a "hot button" issue. Chancellor Merkel's refugee policy was highly controversial in Germany at the time and faced serious criticism both from the public and the policymakers, including members of her own government (The Guardian 2016). The amplification of the message done by the Russian media channels served to keep the issue in the attention of the public, but it was the intervention of Russian Foreign Minister, Sergej Lavrov, who misleadingly challenged the official account of the German authorities, which added confusion to the story. The fact that some people decided to protest on the streets could be seen as a partial success of the disinformation campaign, but the main target, Chancellor Merkel, refused to change course on issues of interest for the Kremlin, including Ukraine and the EU sanctions against Russia.

The "Lisa case" is instructive for understanding not only how the 4E funnel of RC may work but also how one can defend itself and build resilience against it. Interestingly, one year after the Lisa case, in February 2017, a similar campaign took place in Lithuania, claiming that German soldiers, who had just been deployed in the country as part of the North Atlantic Treaty Organization (NATO) "Enhanced Forward Presence" battle group, raped a teenager (Schultz 2017). However, this time, the campaign failed to gain traction with the public, and the reasons are telling. The general public had been made aware of the dangers of disinformation attacks, the angle of the story (e.g., the presence of the German troops) failed to ignite negative memories of the Second World War as intended and attempts to amplify the message online proved technically unsuccessful. As a result, the only political impact of story was to further raise awareness about the ongoing threat of Russian disinformation campaigns, exactly the opposite that a RC strategy would seek to accomplish.

Conclusion

Is there a strategy behind the digital disinformation campaigns attributed to the Russian government, and if so, what conceptual tools can make better sense of the objectives of the strategy and how can one build resilience against it? Drawing on the literature on Russian information warfare, this chapter has argued that the theory of RC offers a good framework for understanding how a state can be strategically influenced to pursue a predetermined course of action in international affairs. More precisely, RC creates the conditions by which one party can "hack" the diplomatic game so that it can shape the preferences of the other actors towards a desired outcome. By mapping the cognitive filters of the target audience, the party engaged in RC seeks to offer tailored information to the opponent so that he/she voluntarily makes a decision to pursue a course of action in a predetermined direction. RC can be used to facilitate either a "constructive" (in favour of a particular objective) or "destructive" result (against a particular objective), and it works best when the other side is unaware or unable to react to the strategy.

Digital platforms now offer the opportunity to take the RC theory to the next level, by making filter mapping and micro-targeting of the relevant audiences more accurate and potentially more impactful. These cognitive filters may provide insight about the audience's thematic or interactional preferences or even about specific individual reactions in line with their demographic and psychographic profile. By examining the informational context, content of the message, dissemination pattern and the potential impact of online conversations, especially in pre-election periods, one may develop a better understanding of whether these conversations are a reflection of an organic form of online political engagement or a strategic use of digital platforms by foreign actors for RC purposes. As full confirmation of the presence of an RC strategy is rather difficult to obtain without inside information, the 4E funnel of digital RC (entice, engage, elevate and exploit) provides a good model for making sense of the scope and intensity of the disinformation campaign. The more a party is exposed to "hot button" issues, prevented from making sense of what it is happening, and urged to take action in favour or against certain political objectives, the more likely that has become a target of digital RC.

The 4E funnel can also prove useful for developing guidelines about how a party can defend itself against RC and how to build resilience against it. The response strategy should include, for instance, media literacy programmes for strengthening the informational environment against the risk of disinformation, a close monitoring of the potential for viral dissemination of "hot button" issues, a rapid response procedure for neutralising amplification effects and careful political analysis of the potential implications of the actions that parties are urged to pursue in reaction to the disinformation campaigns. One should be also mindful of the fact that the RC strategy serves certain foreign policy goals, so by learning how to adapt and react to it, one can reduce its negative impact on oneself, but she/he might not be able to stop or prevent it unless the underlying foreign policy disagreements are resolved as well. On a similar critical note, one also needs to be careful about the long-term effects of using and reacting to reflective control in international politics. The concept evokes a Hobbesian world view of the international system, which is likely to induce international actors to see each other with severe mistrust, so that even positive forms of diplomatic interaction might be construed as "clear" signs of deception and strategic manipulation, thus reinforcing the RC cycle.

Notes

1 Voters in areas where people were likely to be Trump supporters were shown a triumphant-looking image of the nominee, and they were offered help to find the nearest polling station. Those whose geographical information suggested they were not fervent Trump supporters were shown photos of his high-profile supporters to induce them to vote for him (Lewis and Hilder 2018).
2 Theresa Hong, a member of the digital arm of Trump's presidential campaign, suggested in a BBC interview that "without Facebook, we wouldn't have won", but she failed to produce any "hard data" about how micro-targeting translated into votes in support of her claim (Glaser 2018).

2

INFORMATION INFLUENCE IN WESTERN DEMOCRACIES

A model of systemic vulnerabilities

Howard Nothhaft, James Pamment,
Henrik Agardh-Twetman and Alicia Fjällhed

The study of information influence activities has ballooned in the recent years. After concerns about the US presidential election and the Brexit referendum, faced with the expansionist ambitions of Russia and under threat from Islamic fundamentalist terrorism, Western governments have commissioned a plethora of investigations into the ways opinion formation in democratic systems is influenced by foreign actors in subtle and not so subtle fashions. Concerned by polarization, radicalization and other domestic dysfunctionalities, political parties and their associated think tanks have followed suit. So have intergovernmental agencies like the North Atlantic Treaty Organization (NATO), so have media and so have the social media giants like Facebook and Twitter, giving rise to a veritable ecosystem of experts, reports, projects, initiatives and centres.

Although the authors recently engaged with the ecosystem's output for a report commissioned by the Swedish Civil Contingencies Agency (Pamment, Nothhaft, Agardh-Twetman, Fjällhed 2018), the following contribution does not attempt to give an overview of current knowledge. Our aim here is to make a conceptual contribution. We offer a model that has shown itself capable of integrating most of the insights and results out there today, while at the same time addressing a key theoretical concern within the study of information influence activities. The key concern is the distinction between legitimate and illegitimate influence, and we argue that the distinction is unclear, amongst other reasons, because of a lack of theoretical integration.

The conceptualization of information influence: towards integration

From our point of view as communication researchers, with some years of experience in studying corporate and domestic disinformation at a more leisurely pace, the current state of information influence studies is characterized by two interesting tendencies. The first is that information influence studies in their present state appear to be by and large rooted in a pre-theoretical, somewhat tacit understanding of 'free' opinion formation. The second lies in the fact that information influence scholars increasingly drive a development that turns strategic communication research toward the mind sciences: toward psychology, cognitive science and neurobiology.

As for the first tendency, the tacit, pre-theoretical understanding, it must be presumed that the unwillingness to engage with fundamental questions of democracy theory is not due to incapability of the authors involved in the ecosystem. Very likely it is due to the nature of the reports, most of which were commissioned by and for decision makers under pressure – hasty readers, who do not appreciate being lectured on fundamentals. However, making the implicit explicit it is not only a matter of scholarly propriety. At present, scholarly pragmatism in the field manifests itself as a tendency to leave some of the big and tricky questions to the good sense of the reader. In many contributions it is taken for granted, for example, that Western democracies are 'free' (recently, e.g. Committee on Foreign Relations 2018). Despite the fact that disinformation operators are successfully attacking the very notion that Western media are 'free', e.g. suggesting that established media are controlled by globalists, that public broadcasters pursue corrupt leftist agendas, authors rarely ever outline what it is, exactly, that constitutes Western freedom. As influence is often conceptualized as hostile simply because it is assumed to be conducted, controlled or instigated by agents of a foreign power, it does not become clear in what ways hostile *intent* – again, often only assumed – transforms otherwise unremarkable communication into acts of political warfare. National tabloids regularly run factually false but highly emotional stories, some clearly harmful and disruptive. If RT does so, there is an elevated sense of alarm to the point that false emotional stories are classified as *disinformation techniques* in a recent report (Committee on Foreign Relations 2018). Without an exact conceptualization of freedom, its limits and reasons for its limitations, there is a risk that borders blur, leaving *speculation about intent*, a notoriously difficult endeavour, as the only criterion.

The second interesting tendency is the increasing utilization of insights from psychology, cognitive science and neurobiology in the study of information influence (e.g. Palmertz, n.d.). Although marketing and management studies are increasingly utilizing insights from cognitive science and neurobiology – neuromarketing and neuromanagement are the keywords here – the study of society is characterized by a tendency to resist the mind sciences, especially where they too openly concede the role of biology, such as in sociobiology (Wilson 2012) or evolutionary psychology (see, e.g. Tooby & Cosmides 1992, 2005; Barrett, Dunbar, & Lycett 2002; Kurzban 2010). In the humanities, resistance is so prevalent that cognitive linguist Steven Pinker addressed 'an impassioned plea' entitled 'Science is not your enemy' to 'neglected novelists, embattled professors, and tenure-less historians' (Pinker 2013). Political scientists, sociologists and scholars of public diplomacy or strategic communication tend to be slightly more open-minded, perhaps because they have more to win, but there is evidently anxiety about 'scientism' (e.g. Sandhu 2017; Christensen & Christensen 2017).

In our view, the community should worry not about a hostile takeover but rather about a botched merger. Impressive as experimental results and progress in brain scans are, it is doubtful that the mind sciences will ever come to a point where they supplant social science as the centre of gravity for influence studies. Although the juxtaposition of individual brain vs. complex society is a strawman – societies exist because our brains are social brains – experience in applying results shows that the strengths of the mind sciences are also a limitation. The mind sciences are concerned with relatively stable patterns and are geared towards the question of how does influence work in general? Influence studies do not stop at that question and therefore require the more flexible disposition cultivated in the social sciences. Here, a nexus of interrelated questions is addressed. Bent Flyvbjerg (2001) formulated these questions as the concerns of *phronetic science*: (1) Where are we going? (2) Who gains and who loses, and by which mechanisms of power? (3) Is this development desirable? (4) What, if anything, should we do about it?

To be clear, we regard the current situation as an opportunity, but the academic community needs to get it right. Thus, we offer a model of opinion formation in Western democracies that is grounded in both worlds: theories of the public sphere, liberalism and free opinion formation as well as (meta-)theories of human cognition. Once again it must be emphasized that the challenge lies in *integrating* the two worlds. Empirical researchers need to acknowledge that our political system, what we consider 'free opinion formation' in the West, what we deem appropriate and desirable behaviour in the public sphere, has evolved over at least two centuries of democratic practice, yet remains a variation on Enlightenment ideals. Kant's classic treatise 'Answer to the Question: What is Enlightenment?', written in 1784, still resonates with students today as the clearest answer to the question what the 'free' in free opinion formation realistically means. People on social media hotly debate the very same questions that Mill treats in 'On Liberty', written in 1859. Can there be a public interest in circulating statements that are factually wrong, for example?

Kant, Mill and other key theorists of the public sphere wrote in the 18th and 19th centuries, before neurobiology, genetic and epigenetic research, cognitive science and psychology made significant contributions to our understanding of human cognition. It must be acknowledged, however, that many contemporary theorists remain as untouched by modern mind science as Immanuel Kant was. Jürgen Habermas, John Rawls, Seyla Benhabib, Chantal Mouffe or Nancy Fraser, to name just a few, are key political thinkers of the 20th century, yet they stay firmly rooted in a tradition of theorizing that owes more to Plato and Marx than to the mosaic gradually assembled by the mind sciences.[1] This is problematic because a simple side-by-side of classical thinkers and cognitive science might not be enough. The proper way of integrating democratic theory and cognitive science is not side-by-side, we argue, but in a hierarchical relationship (albeit one where below simply means more fundamental, and above means more complex). Consilience, as the idea of a unified edifice of science has become known (Wilson 1998), suggests that the mind sciences should underpin the social sciences in the same way as physics underpins chemistry. Social scientists should build theory on conceptualizations of the human being that are in line, to the best of our knowledge, with empirical research in the mind sciences. Consilience also means, of course, that the physicist cannot answer the chemist's questions, because they are qualitatively different. Similarly, the four 'phronetic' questions addressed earlier cannot be answered by psychology or any other behavioural approach, because they are, metaphorically speaking, on a higher level.

The contribution of the mind sciences: subjective viability

How can insights from the mind sciences be integrated with the liberal-democratic heritage? Certainly not by layering in opportune empirical results: Habermas 2.0, sprinkled with brain scans, is not what we are looking for. Something that we might be looking for is a radical synthesis of the scientific view on human cognition.

Our radical synthesis of the scientific view of human cognition (Roth 1996, 2003), as opposed to humanist views and the views in the social sciences, suggests that human cognition is not one-dimensionally geared towards developing an accurate representation of reality, as some philosophical views propose. Nor is human cognition one-dimensionally geared towards protection of one's own identity and integration in society, as some views in the social sciences suggest. Human cognition, as far as we can see it, seems to be governed by the interplay of at least four principles: a reality-principle, an identity-principle, a pragmatic-principle and a modularity-principle (Figure 2.1).

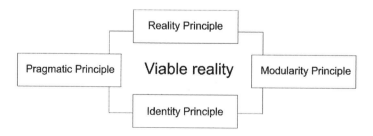

FIGURE 2.1 Four Principles of Human Cognition.

Reality-principle: hard facts of life

The reality-principle conceptualizes that the cognitive apparatus of *Homo sapiens* evolved to navigate the organism through life, with survival, not peace of mind, as key. As such, the apparatus is hardwired, to a considerable degree, to the biological facts of life. Healthy humans cannot and will not indefinitely ignore lack of nutrition, for example. The drop in blood sugar levels and other biochemical changes will *cause* the cognitive apparatus to increasingly shift attention to the acquisition of food. Admittedly, the executive system, which is strong in the human, can override attention shifting for a while, but eventually distracting thoughts of food become overpowering, i.e. command bottom-up attention (Baars & Gage 2010).[2]

Identity-principle: defensible position in the group

The identity-principle reflects that human cognition is not solely geared towards establishing the 'truth' of matters out there but constitutes a mechanism that protects the conscious experience of self, the identity of the person. The identity-principle also manifests the human being's social nature. This principle is specific to the species and our evolutionary history: for prehistoric hunter-gatherers, as for any behaviourally flexible social species, a socially viable identity, and consequently conformity with a group, was probably far more important than one-dimensional determination to see the world as it is. Peace of mind is by and large identical with the occupation of a defensible position in the group. Confirmation bias (e.g. Nickerson 1998), i.e. our inclination to discount information if it is at odds with what we already believe, fits into the picture. Confirmation bias constitutes a protection mechanism against continuous identity-perturbance.[3]

Pragmatic-principle: mental shortcuts, heuristics, cognitive misers

The pragmatic-principle once again captures that human cognition evolved to serve the organism, as opposed to an abstract epistemic ideal, but in a way different from the reality-principle. While the reality-principle hardwires cognition to the needs of the organism (or other organisms' needs since the cries of a baby are almost impossible to ignore) the pragmatic-principle reflects the limitations of the cognitive system itself, its limited capacity and considerable organic cost, i.e. energy expenditure (Roth & Dicke 2005). Kahneman's distinction between System 1 and System 2 (2011) acknowledges that humans are certainly capable of deliberate reasoning, but that deliberate reasoning is slow and costly. Insofar as 'thinking things through' is time-consuming and energy-intensive, there is a pragmatic logic in taking shortcuts. In everyday, routine life, and sometimes even when it comes to objectively important decisions, we often rely on 'mental shortcuts' or 'heuristics' to decide what to believe. Humans are 'cognitive misers'

(Source). When an individual does not understand the intricate political argument, she might decide to 'believe' the politician with the pleasant voice and the open face – Kennedy, not Nixon.

Modularity-principle: framing, triggering, cues

The modularity-principle is a concept drawn from evolutionary psychology, where the degree of the human brain's modularity is a contentious issue (Fodor 1983; Pinker 1997; Sperber & Hirschfeld 2004; Kurzban 2010). The basic idea is very simple: despite our introspective experience to the contrary, the human brain is best conceptualized not as a universal thinking organ, but as modular in architecture. Since it is hard to see how a universal thinking organ would have evolved, evolutionary psychologists assume instead that our mind constitutes as a collection of programmes (modules, adaptations) designed to solve typical problems, such as face recognition, kinship detection, mate selection and so on (Sperber & Hirschfeld 2004; Seiffert-Brockmann 2018). The Swiss Army knife is a popular comparison, and there is empirical research that suggests a similarity. Experiments with the Wason Selection-task conducted by Cosmides (1989), for example, have shown that humans solve a logical problem easily if it is framed as a social problem yet find a *logically identical task* incomparably harder when it is framed in abstract, purely mathematical terms. As the environment of a modern human bears very little resemblance to the environment in which humans originally evolved, contemporary humans necessarily utilize old modules to tackle new problems. Not every person approaches the same problem with the same module or set, it seems, and the pathway appears to depend on which module is triggered – which, in turn, explains the powerful effects of framing (Scheufele 1999). Moreover, psychological research conducted by, for example, Jonathan Haidt and colleagues, suggests that when it comes to moral reasoning not every human actuates or even possesses the same cognitive modules: research found striking differences between Democrat and Republican voters in the US, for example (see, e.g. Graham, Haidt, & Nosek 2009).

The variety of opinion formation

The interplay of reality-, identity-, pragmatic- and modularity-principles, we theorize, produces the variety of opinion formation: sometimes sober and analytical, sometimes passionate and emotional, sometimes logical and coherent, sometimes illogical and paradox. It also explains the typical effects communication practitioners, especially in political communication, are familiar with.

- People can be brought to ignore facts and realities if 'inconvenient truths' threaten their identity or way of life. Here, the reality- and identity-principle are in opposition.

- It seems impossible for people at different ends of the political spectrum to understand each other's arguments, no reconciliation seems possible. As psychological research shows, liberals and conservatives make substantially different ethical judgements because of cognitive differences. Here, the modularity-principle is at play. As their respective identifiers illustrate, proponents of pro-choice and pro-life see the same issue from a fundamentally different viewpoint, i.e. as a matter of personal freedom vs. a matter of murder.

- Quantity, i.e. the swamping of a debate with misinformation, by and large works because humans tend to be lazy in checking facts, 'cognitive misers' (Fiske & Taylor 1991). Here, the pragmatic-principle trumps the reality-principle.

- Some people cannot be influenced by arguments. Aristotle already noted that some people are susceptible to rhetoric, but impervious to dialectic argumentation, because dialectic necessitates instruction, and some people cannot be instructed (Aristotle, n.d., Rhetoric Book 1, Part 1). Psychological research suggests that it is not possible to influence certain people with particular types of arguments because the argumentation relies on modules that they do not possess (or, more likely, that are suppressed). Haidt's research (for a comprehensive overview see Haidt 2012) has shown that liberals score weakly on the perception of sacrality, for example. A thoroughbred liberal genuinely does not understand, in other words, why burning the flag should be as morally depraved as hurting an innocent animal.

The Western system of free opinion formation: a simple model

It is time to integrate our earlier thoughts into a model of opinion formation. Although we are well aware of the complexities of social dynamics, the model attempts to be very simple. Theoretical physicists sometimes make progress by radically simplifying a problem, e.g. by assuming that there is only one atom in the universe. Our model simplifies the problem of opinion formation by reducing it to opinion formation in one focal individual with regard to one focal issue, be that Brexit or the US presidential election or the dangers of overeating sugar. What we try to capture, exclusively, is opinion formation in liberal democracies of the Western type. The core argument is the following: opinion formation in a Western-type society is characterized by features which other types of society do not fully possess (although they might possess other useful features), e.g. a system of 'free' opinion formation. The features are a great strength, yet they also create vulnerabilities. A close look at recent information influence campaigns suggests that these vulnerabilities are becoming increasingly well understood by influence-operators.

What are the features? The first feature is that liberal democracies possess a reflective system for genuine public deliberation, i.e. a system of fora that is capable of sustaining a reasonably complex debate of societal issues while 'mirroring' society as a whole – a public sphere. The qualifier 'genuine' denotes, here, that this system must not only allow debate but that the debates must impact policymaking. The second feature is that Western democracies maintain, often at considerable expense, a system of institutions that operate by *evidence*, as opposed to ideology and political expediency. Independent courts and the scientific system come to mind here, although the de facto independence of these systems is always contested, of course. The third feature is that independent actors enjoy more or less unfiltered access to the public sphere. We hear and see not only elites and officials on a matter, in other words, but also experts and sources (i.e. eyewitnesses, the directly affected). At least as an ideal, evidence and scientific results are made visible in the public sphere even if they do not conform to the demands of the powerful. In the 20th century, this feature was seen as safeguarded by government-independent media and cultural forms; in the 21st century, digital media are valued for granting the public direct access to information and influence tools.

The constituents of the epistemic chain

Integrating our earlier thoughts, our model suggests that opinion formation in the individual can be understood as an *epistemic chain* that brings seven different instances of systems into dynamic interplay. Figure 2.2 illustrates the seven systems and the general principle.

With regard to *the individual*, the model is as much a depiction of the individual's outside world as a representation of its mental space. The seven systems are as much societal institutions as they are ways of thinking. Although it sounds prima facie strange, it is a very common duality: for an ordinary citizen, the police are as much an organization with physically existing people, cars, and buildings as it is a societal institution. In a functioning state, the police derive their effectiveness

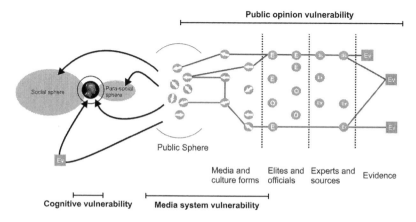

FIGURE 2.2 The Epistemic Chain and Vulnerabilities of Opinion Formation.

mainly from the fact that its symbols reside in the minds of the law-abiding citizen; its physical presence on the streets serves as a reminder.

- *Social and parasocial sphere.* The social sphere comprises the people with which the focal individual maintains an established social or parasocial relationship: 'people one kind of knows', in other words. Decades of research consistently show that opinion formation is predominantly social, not epistemic (early Horton & Wohl 1956).
- *Public sphere.* From the perspective of the focal individual, the public sphere is not only a space where ideas, arguments and evidence are discussed but also a generalized sphere of experienced public opinion. As Noelle-Neumann (1993) has argued, humans possess a 'social skin' and sense or at least believe they sense whether their beliefs, attitudes and opinions are in tune or at odds with society at large.
- *Media and culture forms.* Media and culture in this model are defined as forms the focal individual turns to more or less regularly: the newspaper you read daily, the TV show you watch weekly, the computer game you play with your kids, the museum you go to on rainy Sundays. Pewdiepie, with a followership on YouTube in the double-digit millions, serves as a good example for a media and culture form 2.0. The model thus acknowledges that people's ideas are formed not only by what they see in the news or information they seek out in order to deal with life's challenges but also by values conveyed in other forms of entertainment, art and culture, be it popular or highbrow. Another aspect is that media and cultural forms are in a way fragile containers: they can be used to expose individuals to content they would otherwise not be exposed to, but such a manoeuvre always carries the risk of destroying them, if the content is not palatable.
- *Elite personas and officials.* Elite personas are visible persons whom the focal individual perceives as prestigious and articulate. Elite personas are not necessarily experts in the area under consideration. Their prestige might derive from genuine expertise, as is the case with, for example, celebrity scientists (e.g. Richard Dawkins in the area of biology), in which case they are elite personas as well as experts. Most often, however, some more or less credible 'transfer' of expertise is involved, e.g. when Arnold Schwarzenegger – a highly successful but also a highly unusual immigrant to the US – comments on matters of work ethics amongst immigrants in the US. The formula seems to be that one should listen to this person because he is successful and visible. *Officials*, in contrast, derive their expertise from the authority invested in them by society: they probably know because it is their job to know.
- *Experts and sources.* In contrast to elite personas, who carry prestige in the area under consideration due to some transfer, genuine *experts* derive their prestige predominantly from true expertise, always as perceived by the focal individual, in the area under consideration: one should listen to this

person, because she obviously knows what she is talking about. It must be noted, however, that in the case of experts the currency is not necessarily knowledge of scientific evidence, but authority. A bishop is an expert in matters of faith, although he (or she, in rare cases) will have very little to offer in terms of evidence for their convictions. In some cases, expertise simply derives from authority, as only the institution in question can answer a certain question authoritatively. *Sources*, in contrast, derive their authority from 'being there'. An ordinary citizen with a smartphone at the scene of a terror attack becomes an indisputable source simply by virtue of presence.

- The defining characteristic of *evidence*, finally, is that it goes beyond opinion and authority. Although independent courts are supposed to base their verdicts on evidence, and so should rational policymaking, the source of evidence in modern society is ultimately science. (Note that evidence is only accepted in court if its validity is assured by science.) Science is a system that is unique to modern society, and indeed modernity could be described as the advance of science and the retreat of tradition and religion (and Max Weber does so, of course). Earlier and differently developed societies certainly boasted and boast expert systems, sometimes elaborate, but they did not possess a genuine scientific system. What does this scientific system do, at least in principle, that no other system in human history ever did? In very simple terms, it subjects opinions to scrutiny in accordance with the scientific method. The scientific method, in turn, replaces the distinction *opinion vs. other opinion* or *divinely sanctioned vs. unsanctioned* opinion with the tripolar distinction *tentatively proven vs. disproven vs. unknown*. The scientific system, in our conceptualization, is by no means congruent with the academic system. Modern academia, even in the West, remains largely an *expert system* with prestige and expertise, not evidence, as its primary currency. Frequently, expertise derives from knowledge of many opinions, not from the consideration of pro- and contra-evidence. The true impact of the scientific system lies in the fact that there is a general belief in a certain kind of fact, especially when established by means of technology. Note, for example, that during the emissions-scandal, once the programming of the car's computers was revealed, neither Volkswagen or other car manufacturers made efforts to substantially dispute the emissions-measurements taken by independent research institutes, as they knew that this would have been a losing game.

Consonance in the epistemic chain

The epistemic chain is normative insofar as it conveys that an argument is only valid if its epistemic chain is unbroken. This does not mean that there is only right or wrong, of course. But what elites and officials voice and what is consequently covered and represented in media and popular culture should not be, as far as factual claims are concerned, unsupported by experts and sources. What sources say should be scrutinized and should hold up to scrutiny. What experts voice should be supported by evidence, preferably scientific evidence, at least in areas that can be investigated scientifically. If that can be ensured, debate and discussion will, by and large, gravitate towards sound and reasonable ideas. In the long run, that will affect the content circulating on social media and in lunch-rooms, pubs, literary salons and coffee houses.

Free opinion formation

This ideal that debate and decision in society should be conducted in a rational, evidence-based fashion and that the public sphere is a forum where opinions, arguments and evidence are discussed openly and scrutinized vigorously for every citizen to see and to follow has served liberal democracies well. Few would claim that the ideal has ever been achieved, but by and large its acknowledgement seems to have given Western liberal democracies adaptability and responsiveness.

What may not be immediately clear is the relationship between the epistemic chain and free opinion formation. We contend that the epistemic chain and free opinion formation are two sides of the same coin. A society allows free opinion formation, we theorize, as long as public life is grounded in the belief that the epistemic chain is unbroken, that rational discussion and evidence-based debate will expose dubious arguments as dubious. As a consequence, there is no need to protect citizens from demagogues by silencing or censoring; society relies on the sound judgement of its citizens. The liar will reveal himself. This powerful idea, to emphasize again, is not new. It goes back to Kant's conception of Enlightenment as much as it echoes John Stuart Mill's conception of liberty. Over the centuries, it has been expressed in different ways by different authors. Its most sophisticated contemporary proponent is perhaps Jürgen Habermas, who has devoted large parts of his work to analyzing the exact conditions under which rational deliberation wins out. What we unpack here, are the constituents of the chain, the mechanism by which the liar is revealed. Moreover, the reason to do so, is that the epistemic chain in its current form, although it has worked well, might currently be unravelling under contemporary societal conditions. Hostile influence-operators have found ways and are continuously finding more ways, to gain unfair advantages in debate, undercut thorough scrutiny and shake public trust. All too often the liar is not revealed anymore, or revealed too late, or we find that the revelation of the lie does not matter anymore because the lie is believed anyway. Why is that so?

Systemic vulnerabilities of free opinion formation

The model developed by the authors for the Swedish Civil Contingencies Agency currently identifies systemic vulnerabilities on a general level as well as along the epistemic chain. Figure 2.3 gives an overview.

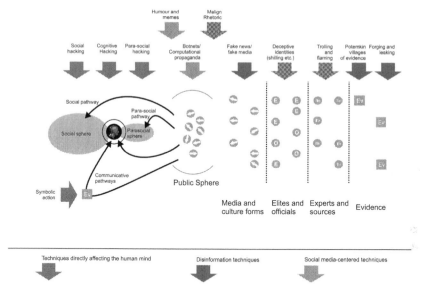

FIGURE 2.3 The Epistemic Chain and Techniques of Information Influence.

Vulnerabilities on a general level

On the general systemic level, three complexes of vulnerability are identified: namely cognitive vulnerabilities, media system vulnerabilities and vulnerabilities in public opinion formation.

Cognitive vulnerabilities. Some of the pathways of opinion formation resulting from the interplay of reality-, identity-, pragmatic- and modularity-principle have been discussed earlier. One of the key vulnerabilities of the current system lies in the fact, as has been mentioned, that the normative ideal of free opinion formation is built on an idealistic understanding of the human being which was by and large formed in Enlightenment era, and one that is not fully in line with empirical research. Kant's *sapere aude* – 'dare to know', commonly interpreted as 'dare to think for yourself' – is a noble ideal, but ordinary folks dealing with everyday life seldom aspire to it beyond mortgage, smartphone and diet. Observers of society, maybe most eloquently Walter Lippmann, have always pointed to the gap between ideal and reality, but only in recent years have the psychological processes and cognitive mechanisms come in to focus. Influence-operators still appear to be ahead of the curve, but at least the social sciences are catching up. To give an example, one of the many ways in which 'proper' academic form can be at odds with human cognition are the so-called 'backfire effects' encountered in debunking. Cook and Lewandowsky (2012, 2) remark that attempts to debunk myths about climate science often begin with a prominent exposition of the actual myth, sometimes even repeating the key falsehood in the headline. Experimental evidence suggests that there is a 'familiarity backfire-effect': merely mentioning the myth might lead to more people believing it, because familiarity, not intricate arguments, is what counts in the long run. Cook and Lewandowsky (2012, 2) elaborate:

> Immediately after reading the flyer, people remembered the details that debunked the myth and successfully identified the myths. As time passed, however, the memory of the details faded and all people remembered was the myth without the 'tag' that identified it as false.

Media system vulnerabilities. The current media system vulnerability stems mainly from rapid change that is inadequately understood. Western media systems are continuously evolving in terms of technologies, patterns of media consumption, audience fragmentation and economic models. The result is a hybrid media system, to use a phrase coined by Chadwick (2013), that is comprised of 'old' (newspapers, television, radio) and 'new' (social) media as well as an ambiguous, i.e. hybrid zone in between. Moreover, it takes time for ordinary citizens to internalize that their once-quality subscription-based newspaper still looks the same, but is produced under considerably different economic conditions. Thus, the new quality in information influence operations is not only that they exploit technological, regulatory and economic vulnerabilities in Western media systems but that they systematically exploit the lag between what becomes technologically possible and what is grasped by society.

Public opinion-vulnerability. Public opinion has always been targeted with intentions beyond the public interest. The 20th century has seen the emergence of a whole industry that offers the management of public opinion as a commercial service. Public relations, public affairs, public diplomacy and lobbying are examples of the legitimate efforts of organizations to influence public opinion in support of their interests, partly by genuinely engaging in public debate, partly by mimicking such engagement. The new dimension of hostile influence lies in the resources available to state or non-state actors. While Western societies have dealt with commercial actors powerful enough to fabricate scientific results in support of their interests (i.e. the tobacco and the fossil fuel industry), foreign hostile influence-operators can draw on a whole ecosystem of resources, and contrary to big tobacco and big oil they can also shield their ecosystems against legal scrutiny.

Influence techniques along the epistemic chain

On a more concrete level, the model currently inventories *techniques* that attack the epistemic chain at various points. As there are currently 12 techniques, each with several sub-techniques, we lack the space to discuss every technique. However, selected examples illustrate the general idea (see Pamment, Nothhaft, Agardh-Twetman, & Fjällhed 2018 for further details).

- *Forging and leaking* attacks the epistemic chain at the level of evidence. Forgery is, in essence, the production of false evidence. Leaks insert evidence into the system that was not supposed to be there, for good or for bad. Tainted leaks, as in the case of Emmanuel Macron, constitute a combination of leaks that contain partly forged elements.

- *Malign rhetoric* are techniques such as the Gish-gallop, named after creationist debater Duane Gish, who used to overwhelm his opponents with a veritable flood of arguments, many spurious and unconnected to the issue (sometimes called 'proof by verbosity'). Malign rhetoric manifests itself in the public sphere. Although it can and is employed to win arguments illegitimately (in that way, it is sophistry's evil sister), its effect goes beyond that: by toxifying the atmosphere in forums of discussion, it drives reasonable and civilized people away.

- *Social bots and botnets*, a final example, can be used to create fake social capital and create the impression of a social media-movement where no or very little popular support exists. By 'riding the wave of algorithmic curation', as *The Guardian* (Hern 2017) puts it, mutually reinforcing botnets can make content go viral, although very few real humans are overawed by it.

Conclusion: legitimate, illegitimate and hostile influence

In conclusion, we return to the question of what makes information influence illegitimate to the point that it must be considered a hostile act. What turns persuasion, entertainment, news into political warfare? Can our model illuminate the distinction between *legitimate* and *illegitimate* influence? What, exactly, makes information influence illegitimate?

We argue that Western liberal democracies have developed, evolved or stumbled upon, a system of public opinion formation that is self-stabilizing as long as actors watch each other and insist on adherence to a few simple rules. When hand in hand with free markets, this system apparently not only led to acceptable degrees of social harmony, it also supported, perhaps by allowing a freer exchange of ideas, the economic prosperity of liberal democracies (unmatched by other societal systems until only recently). The central institution is the public sphere – the communal fiction of a forum – where affairs of public importance, res publica, are debated genuinely, openly and freely. Genuinely means that public debate not only is for show, as Crouch (2004), for example, argues in his account of post-democracy, but really drives policymaking and truly holds governments and other organizations accountable. Freely means that no-one is excluded from participating and contributing *beforehand*. In Habermas's well-known words, '[a] public sphere from which specific groups would be *eo ipso* excluded was less than merely incomplete; it was not a public sphere at all' (Habermas 1962, 85). Openly means that public actors and their track records will be identifiable, and arguments made in public are held to certain epistemic standards. Very briefly, these standards require that serious suggestions, in order to make it into serious forms of media and cultural exchange, must be endorsed by persons of prestige; backed up by experts; supported by authority; covered by sources; and ultimately rooted in accessible, verifiable evidence. Everyone can try to have a say, in other words, but it will not be easy to be taken seriously.

The generosity of the system, once again, relied on the sound judgement of its citizens. It was predicated on the simple idea that the liar will sooner or later reveal himself. Dubious arguments will be exposed because they must fulfil the requirements or else are discarded. If they fulfil the requirements, they will become subject to scrutiny, and the scrutiny will quickly reveal that they are dubious. The system always had flaws, of course, two of which have been pointed out: first, the assumption of an ideal rational human that never existed; second, the assumption of highly engaged, politically well-informed citizens which might have existed at some point, in Habermas's bourgeois public sphere maybe or in the Athenian *polis* but cannot be taken for granted in mass welfare democracies.

By and large, flaws notwithstanding, the system has served liberal democracies well. However, presently, there are indications that this well-working institution is being turned against the very societies it supports. And it is here, we argue, that the root of illegitimacy lies. The illegitimacy of information influence derives not only from actual or potential harm, in other words, but from the violations of a fundamental *ethical precept*: i.e. the imperative that the 'other' should not only be treated as a *means* but also as an *end*. The issue with information influence is not legal, therefore, but multidimensional, contextual and ultimately *moral*[4]:

- Information influence *breaks the rules*. Liberal democracies are generous, but it is well understood by theorists – John Rawls, in particular, comes to mind here – that participation in open and free debate is granted in fictional exchange for a commitment to the rules of the game. One of the rules is that one should not knowingly tell the untruth.
- Information influence *exploits vulnerabilities*. By leveraging the system under false pretenses, information influence exploits the well-functioning system of opinion formation while at the same time hacking its weaknesses. One of the weaknesses that derives from the centrality of social media, for example, is the anonymity or quasi-anonymity of contributors that make it impossible to judge whether political comments represent a real majority of citizens or foreign influence.
- Information influence *deceives* people. Information influence mimics legitimate forms of public debate and copies established forms of media and engagement to leverage the existing system, and the trust people bestow upon it.

The moral nature of information influence, illegitimate but not illegal, should give pause to proponents of legal solutions and other government crackdowns. Social media, the digital revolution and other forms of innovation have stressed the system of public opinion formation, exposing fundamental flaws. Undoubtedly, there is also a foreign-driven influence; maybe at unprecedented levels, as is sometimes claimed. However, the ultimate reason that illegitimate influence thrives, and Western systems are less resilient is as simple as it is circular. It lies in genuine insecurity, on the part of Western liberal democracies, *about what is legitimate*. A system that relies on the sound judgement of its citizens relies on a certain convergence of judgements. It is this preexisting gap that influence-operators have discovered as the key vulnerability.

Notes

1　System theorist Niklas Luhmann, although reluctant to engage with empirical re-search, is perhaps the exception. Luhmann's later works borrow heavily from neu-robiologists Maturana and Varela. Moreover, and in contrast to many other social theorists, Luhmann insists that the social sciences, instead of continuously suggest-ing that humanity grow up by actualizing a normatively driven sense of deficiency ('Bewusstsein des Ungenügens'), should quite simply look at what is (1998, 21).

2　Psychological warfare operators, by the way, have long realized that the appeal to re-alities is universal and the most powerful. As Linebarger (2015, KL2506) puts it: 'The appeal of credible fact is universal; propaganda does not consist of doctoring the fact with moralistic blather, but of selecting that fact which is correct, interesting, and bad for the enemy to know'.

3　Beyond the individual, on the level of communities, the identity-principle explains the appeal of narratives, as they connect the identity now with a (continuously re-constructed) past and a (continuously re-projected) future (see, e.g. Schacter 2001). Ideological movements, first and foremost the great religions but also extremist ide-ologies, invariably offer a narrative that humankind is moving towards a brighter future, towards elevated identity, here or in the afterlife.

4　Rule-breaking, exploitation and deception point to the ethical grounds why infor-mation influence operations are in many cases illegitimate. For the practical purpose of identifying illegitimate influence the authors have developed the criteria further into a diagnostic tool, which is encapsulated in the acronym DIDI. DIDI stands for Disruption, Intention, Deception and Interference (for the following see Pamment, Nothhaft, Agardh-Twetman, Fjällhed 2018).

3

A DIGITAL MÉNAGE À TROIS

Strategic leaks, propaganda and journalism

Emma L. Briant and Alicia Wanless

While leaking isn't new, the scale of recent data releases and new methods deployed by political actors to influence public opinion transform the process. State and non-state actors controlling the flow of information (from politicians and governments to those seeking to undermine them, such as whistle-blowers) have long used leaks strategically to shape public opinion, decision-making and the distribution of power itself. Increasingly leaks are used within a networked propaganda strategy to offer pressures and opportunities unique to our globalised Digital Age. Powerful, competing elites, and those seeking to disrupt or question their power, combine leaking with emerging advanced methodologies in hacking, (counter-)surveillance and propaganda, meaning these cannot be understood in isolation in today's information environment. This chapter introduces readers to scholarly and popular debates regarding strategic leaking, propaganda and journalistic reporting. We focus on political, governmental and whistle-blowing disclosures affecting the US, analysing how key actors attempt to manage and exploit leaks in the case studies of the 2016 US presidential election and the 'Panama Papers'. We aim to generate discussion about the role of leaks in shaping public perceptions within democracies, ultimately questioning how such disclosures are used by whom and why.

Strategic leaks

A news cycle seldom passes without sensitive, scandalous disclosures.[1] Since 2006, data leaks internationally increased by nearly 500%. Most leakers are an employee inside the organisation, or an "external violator"/hacker (InfoWatch, 2017). Leaking is disclosure of covert information – but not all leaks are equal. Every relationship or power structure is shaped by degrees or types of secrecy engulfing it (Simmel, 1908: 331).[2] Given the nature and pervasiveness of secrecy, leaks are a common yet risky way in which those with little power wield asymmetric influence against the powerful. Unauthorised leaks are often made at great risk by leakers who may "lack easy access to journalists … they lack social capital … [and] are not skilled in handling the media" (Flynn, 2017: 257), while others emerge from political elites manipulating the media with few repercussions (Tiffen, 1989: 97). 'Strategic leaks' have a particular political objective: motives might include 'whistle-blowing'[3] or myriad other, possibly nefarious or self-interested motivations. Often media and political rhetoric reduce leaks to simplistic dichotomies, hindering understanding of competing interests and ethics involved. Leaks can be described as strategic, where they are a deliberate act by a powerful or asymmetric actor motivated towards achieving a specific political or security objective. This may include disrupting an opponent's existing political strategy, particularly "when others might frustrate one's plans because they have different and possibly opposing interests and concerns" (Freedman, 2015, xi). Strategic leaks achieve their aims by using the leaked material to influence public opinion and/or policymakers through the release of accurate, or misleadingly partial information. For these reasons, where they aid an adversary or domestic groups seeking to undermine the authorities, leakers may be accused of espionage (US Department of Defence, 2018). Depending on the sophistication of the leaker, to ensure the desired impact, strategic leaks will be mobilised within a wider propaganda strategy aimed at public audiences or political influencers. We break the concept down and illustrate the complex dynamics of strategic leaking in the digital domain, first, by analysing the important roles played by the following during a strategic leak: (a) leakers, competing interests and their relative power, (b) propaganda, leak dissemination and journalism; then in illustrating this through case studies, we further highlight (c) the role of target audiences.

Leakers, competing interests and power relations

Leaks emerge in diverse ways and may involve bureaucrats, politicians and journalists. Technologies enable those inside and outside of organisations to gain and share unauthorised access to information.[4] While hacking is different from leaking, hacks are sometimes obfuscated as leaks, and leakers may be hiding behind hacking collectives adding further complexity to analysing disclosures. We have seen in the recent case of Cambridge Analytica (CA) how firms can broker such hacks to smear a political opponent within a wider disinformation campaign are available for hire (Cadwalladr, 2018b). Indeed, Business Development Director Brittany Kaiser is accused of having facilitated CA's introduction to hackers for Nigerian then-presidential candidate Goodluck Jonathan's campaign. Kaiser said these were individuals who had joined their opponent Buhari's campaign, denying this was hacking:

> These people weren't hackers. [...] They brought information into the office that they obtained from what I understand, from the other campaign. [...]

And the campaign was fully aware that they were giving information to these people. There's a video of them participating in meetings with Buhari and the campaign manager [...] I mean obviously, that's like… might be sneaky… but it's not hacking. If you can hire people that are able to convince another campaign they are part of the campaign and trusted, that's pretty good… it's pretty good. But it's not hacking. They say 'they hacked the president's emails!' Number one, he was not president, Number two, his emails were not hacked and these people were not hackers. They were other campaign consultants to the same clients.

(Interview, 3 April 2018)

She said,

There were other consultants employed by the same client as SCL Group was employed by. No they are not "hackers" but they did give us the information about David Axelrod's engagements with the campaign and the foreign hospital visits of Buhari.

(Correspondence: Kaiser, 2 April 2018)

This takes a narrow 'popular' definition of hacking, as online attack, but access to computer systems is gained by hackers in various ways, including in-person deception or infiltration (Okenyi & Owens, 2007).

In an age when information travels quickly, passed between proxies and self-interested parties into media, a leak or hack can become confusing or misleadingly represented. Angry judgements flow rapidly making analysis of complex interrelationships between leaks, leakers, disseminators and beneficiaries tricky. Some actors have greater power and influence within society, others less. Critical are the relative power of the leaker and target of the leak. Low-power leakers do not leak lightly. Other leakers might be somehow implicated in activities they anticipate being revealed so 'blow the whistle', and may release important information publicly not only to right a wrong but also to protect themselves. In the CA case, Brittany Kaiser came forward only when the end was nigh for the company (MSNBC, 30 March 2018), and both whistle-blowers were implicated in the revelations. Whistle-blowing leaks challenging problematic systems and abuses of power emerge with other activities related to 'hierarchical sousveillance' (see Bakir, 2016; Mann, 2004) aimed at using technologies to strengthen the public's 'power to watch' authority figures and state institutions, often arising in reaction to expansion of government surveillance.[5] Pozen asserts that "The executive branch's 'leakiness' is actually an adaptive response to external liabilities (such as the mistrust generated by presidential secret keeping and media manipulation) and internal pathologies (such as over classification and bureaucratic fragmentation) of the modern administrative state" (2013). Leaks can be used by the powerful to "make the journalist somewhat obligated to the leaker," (Grattan, 1998: 42) – dependent on access and amenable to cooperation. Anti-leaking laws have rarely been enforced as it is hard to punish violators but also "because key institutional actors share overlapping interests in maintaining a permissive culture of classified information disclosures" (Pozen, 2013). This permissiveness is actually "a nuanced system of informal social controls" that "has come to supplement, and all but supplant, the formal disciplinary scheme" (Pozen, 2013).[6] A digital arms race has just begun; advancing technologies to target whistle-blower vulnerabilities, monitor, prevent further leaks or suppress and smear. Media activists focus "on the creation of alternative infrastructure that bypasses regulatory obstacles instead of lobbying against those obstacles" (Hintz, 2014: 352). But encryption does not guarantee security if a device is compromised. Systems also aim to stop whistle-blowing, watch, intimidate or channel dissent. Efforts to 'predict' whistle-blowing have a flawed methodology that should raise concern. Nigel Oakes, CEO of defence contractor SCL, described in an interview how the US Government is concerned with 'insider threat' preventing leaks like Snowden, and creating predictive systems to identify "before you employ people, the type of person who's going to do this? So they've started collecting more data on people when they go in. And can big data, algorithms, start identify- yeh, the leakers..." using

> any kind of behavior or data predictors, triggers that you could pick up flags in the dataset that could- you know, the sort of people who take more holidays... or sick days... are they likely to turn out to be - now of course, it's a very flawed model because there only are five leakers so you can't ever regress the data but that's the sort of thing *they're* doing.
>
> *(Interview, 24 November 2017)*

Surveillance is not passive watching; it has many purposes and outcomes, including intimidation and psychological impact, mapping of networks, targeting for propaganda, policing and securing evidence for eventual prosecution.[7] While unusual for all these reasons,[8] state secret leaks remain important. 'Whistle-blowing' has deep roots: the framers of the constitution "vested the authority to keep secrets in the executive because they saw it as best suited to exercise this power" yet "identified three means of countering its abuse: elections, the separation of powers, and unauthorized disclosures" (Sagar, 2016: 10). Despite lacking clarity over how these fail-safes work in practice, leaks remain important to US democracy ensuring governmental accountability.[9]

Other types of leaks are more self-serving, aiming to reinforce dominant elite interests. Relative power of the leaker relates to their ability to manipulate the context of the leak. Tech companies profit from and help to spread leaks. Non-governmental organisations (NGOs), activists, think tanks, lobbyists, public relations (PR) firms and ideological media also amplify and frame leakers and content following the initial disclosure. For governments and political actors, complicit actors and intermediaries are a strong feature and aligned interests may or may not imply that actors deliberately conspired. Governmental information release is necessarily selective: This can be overt and aid transparency or be covert and strategic, misdirectional to distract the public – it can even be offensively targeted. Governments and political actors deliberately leak information to garner popular support for ideological foreign policy initiatives.[10] The Bush Administration leaked information to punish Iraq War dissenters, exposing US Central Intelligence Agency (CIA) operative Valerie Plame-Wilson, whose husband, Joseph Wilson, a former ambassador, argued that the "administration had manipulated intelligence on Iraq to back its case for war" (BBC, 2007). Plame-Wilson said,

> Right before my husband's op ed piece came out there were quite a bit in the press, anonymous -quote- 'analysts' who were talking about the pressure that they had felt in the run-up to the war. And when they outed me, both Joe and I feel strongly that it was in fact a very clear signal. [To] Those that would speak out, that – look what we can *do* to you. We'll not only take you down we'll take your family.
>
> *(Interview: 11 August 2009, original emphasis)*

Leaks are also used for distraction; a political operator might release bad news during a greater event hoping to bury it.[11]

One leaker described

> a proactive approach to the strategic press leak is seeking out a sympathetic media outlet...to break the bad news to the public. While my stories may say, "sources close to the situation," those sources are sometimes the very people who go on the record with a "no comment".
>
> *(Silverman, Unknown Date)*

This leaker continues:

> The strategic press leak, if used properly, can be an excellent proactive crisis management tool. By effectively beating the media to a negative story, a company can limit the media's ability to delve deeper into a story, saving the company from a potential public relations disaster.
>
> *(Silverman, Unknown Date)*

Political actors might seek to use leaks to create 'power scandals' (such as Watergate) (Thompson, 2013), their success in doing so resting on their communicative ability to organise a campaign to raise the topic's salience in the media (Entman, 2012). We therefore turn to dissemination and propaganda's role in the leaking process.

Propaganda and dissemination

Before a leak has occurred, its anticipated impact will be considered in preparing an accompanying propaganda strategy. Legal advice may be sought by a whistle-blower. The selective preparation of leaked or revealed material might be the first stage in crafting its desired effect. The ability to leak 'strategically' with effect depends on the communicative environment that will carry the leak. The whistle-blower Chris Wylie was able to draw on immense skill from his communication background working on many political campaigns, including from his time as Research Director of CA itself, in planning his public interest release. This plus outstanding and determined investigative journalism by Carole Cadwalladr of the Guardian helped expose that company's unethical activities in an impactful way (Cadwalladr, 2018a). The communicative environment for any leak includes not only journalism, new propaganda technologies and an enabling media infrastructure, but also hosting sites, networks of powerful influencers and PR infrastructure and lobbyists – through which an actor may obscure or positively frame their own role and ensure their leak and framing of its contents are amplified. Actors have differing abilities to wield such communicative power, and other intervening actors may also exploit the leak, attempting to alter media framing.

Briant has defined propaganda as

> the deliberate manipulation of representations (including text, pictures, video, speech etc.) with the intention of producing any effect in the audience (e.g. action or inaction; reinforcement or transformation of feelings, ideas, attitudes or behaviours) that is desired by the propagandist.
>
> *(2015: 9)*

Propaganda is a controversial term. For Corner it "is too crude to catch at the more stealthy, partial ways in which discourses of power are at work in culture" (2007: 676). Viewed by early 20th century advocates as a tool for deliberately shaping public opinion (e.g. Bernays, 1928; Lippmann, 1922), propaganda challenges voters' ability to express real choice, threatening liberal democracy (Dryzek, 2000). In democratic societies, propaganda has gained a pejorative tone, and euphemistic terms such as PR have become popular (Garrison, 1999; Moloney, 2006). Briant argues for a move beyond focussing primarily on the intent of the propagandist and textual analysis, to deeper consideration of systems employed to manage information and processes as well as their outcomes. This is crucial given the role digital technologies play in shaping the information environment, including the use (and abuse) of algorithms, incentives to share our data, artificial intelligence (AI) and mass surveillance. King argues for resolving an infrastructure problem that makes it easier to profit from disseminating falsehoods (2017). Given that the internet enabled audiences to not only consume propagandistic messages but also engage in the creation, adaptation and sharing of persuasive content, Wanless and Berk argue that the role of audiences participating in the dissemination of persuasive messaging must also be analysed (2017). Within this changing nature of propaganda, strategic leaks fed through various types of media become one tool in an increasingly complex network of actors aiming to persuade target audiences.

Leaks are both drivers of positive transparency, and a powerful mechanism by which governments covertly shape or create media discourse on a range of subjects concerning themselves and others. Governments have ready infrastructure, fostering collaborative relationships with journalists (Boyd-Barrett, 2004; Johnson, 1986). Pozen argues that "focusing enforcement on employees [leakers], rather than journalists and publishers, reduces short-term backlash" for governments, and "the media may feel threatened", but this way the government avoids direct confrontation with them (2013: 606–607). For Pozen, the government has more to gain long term from maintaining a system that facilitates leaking and planting stories (by them when needed) than from destroying it. It declines "to clarify the law governing ad hoc declassification" (2013: 607). Intelligence agencies maintain channels for information that permit 'plausible deniability'. Leaked or planted information with propagandistic intent can follow interesting routes; former Weapons Inspector Scott Ritter claims "to have been recruited, in 1997, for MI6 propaganda campaign 'Operation Mass Appeal' to plant stories in the media regarding WMD in Iraq [that] would 'feed back' to Britain and America" (Rufford, 2003 in Briant, 2015: 45). With "playback", an information leak "appears to provide a distant, and deniable, route to leach propaganda into Western media" (Briant, 2015: 45).[12]

Real leaks exist alongside a powerful discourse of faked leaks, and *accusations* used to undermine credibility of real leaks – for example Trump branded reports that Jared Kushner, his son-in-law, tried to establish a communication channel to the Kremlin during the campaign, as 'fake news' (Newsweek, 2017). This relies on source ambiguity and difficulties of verification. As all leaks emerge with simultaneous impact on trust, amid competing attempts to frame disclosures in ways that legitimise and delegitimise them, and key actors, obscuring authenticity. Leaks are used for deception, particularly in an information environment where deception is common, and real leaking is frequently used. Fake leaks become easier to wield and harder to decry. Audiences become used to seeing leaks and media interpretations through an ideological frame. Leaks become by definition, cloaked by whoever aims to benefit from the romantic frame of underdog 'whistle-blower' enforcing accountability against the corrupt elite. Easily invoked and difficult to differentiate. Journalists working to get an exclusive 'scoop' from Brittany Kaiser facilitated her 'whistleblower' claim, allowing her to push forward a critique of Facebook designed to advance the interests of her cryptocurrency business (MSNBC, 30 March 2018).

Technological investments and developments in the communicative environment to embed monitoring and persuasion environments masquerading as innocuous tools for consumers (through Facebook, Google, etc.) are a deliberate part of the propaganda process. Indeed, a product of the complex relations between powerful competing actors, including elite investors, intelligence agencies and often complicit profit-making PR, technology and media organisations. Emergent journalism is "neither purely networked nor purely traditional, but is rather a mutualistic interaction between the two" (Benkler, 2011). Digital distribution of leaks, for example, through platforms like Facebook and Twitter, complicates leaking, obfuscating an original source's identity. New platforms enhance ability for 'big data' releases with mechanisms to sort, filter, consume and analyse. Advances transforming strategic leaking involve big data, algorithms, mass surveillance, AI and computational propaganda – even the use of encrypted apps like Telegram and Signal. Technologies made direct and individualised targeting possible within and between states, by dominant and asymmetric political actors. We must consider how the emergence of many communication technologies out of investment in warfare and politics might influence and aid their deployment for coercive power. The securitisation of the dual issues of leaking and digital propaganda is further likely to preclude cooperative and symmetric solutions.

Leaks are now deployed in a media environment where mass surveillance increasingly encroaches on citizens' privacy and whistle-blowers' and journalists' rights (Briant, 2017). 'Black boxed' commercial systems with no transparency cloak strategic processes by which algorithmically targeted and deployed strategies see bots, machine learning and AI engaged in sorting and distributing information on a massive scale, propagandistically tailored to maximise effect. Unauthorised leakers and whistle-blowers may be extremely vulnerable and attempt to mitigate a power imbalance. Yet being able to use a leak strategically depends on competence in the communicative environment, as well as ability to both obscure their own role, and ensure their framing is amplified. The leaker cannot control who else aims to manipulate the leak, which complicates accountability.

Media and journalism remain important for disseminating and framing leaked information, influencing 'national agendas' (King et al., 2017) and informing the public. They offer credibility and anonymity for whistle-blowers who fear repercussions (Sagar, 2016). The identity and motivations of sources, if protected by intermediaries such as journalists (or *Wikileaks*), might never be revealed.[13] As intermediaries, traditional journalists and newer outlets become gatekeepers and arbiters of what is disclosed, and in the process become the most visible actors with responsibility for the leak.

Wikileaks, struggling to publicise its 2008 release of US counter-insurgency manuals (Roberts, 2011), nurtured relations with journalists and sought credibility as a journalistic entity itself (Eldridge, 2017). It was criticised for contextualising footage it released of "US air crew shooting down Iraqi civilians" in a journalistic way (McGreal, 2010). Marlin notes,

> 'Collateral Murder' can certainly be seen as a kind of propaganda itself, particularly with the commentary added to it by *WikiLeaks*. The facts selected, and the interpretations placed on them, can all arguably be in need of supplementation by other facts and interpretations.
>
> *(2011: 5)*

To gain increased exposure and credibility, and avoid criticism for distorting the leak, *Wikileaks* used media partnerships in 2010–2011 for Afghanistan releases (Coddington, 2012). A celebritisation of leaking by Edward Snowden, *First Look Media* and the *Intercept*, hides the profit-driven nature of media outlets who publish disclosures.[14] For Natsios and Young of *Cryptome*,[15] "It's deeply cynical to sensationalize the trusted transaction, when someone come (sic) to you with a document and puts it forward to you" (Shorrock, 2016). The *Intercept* almost totally controlled the release of the Snowden documents, publishing only a fraction – 7,361 of 58,000 (Cryptome, 2013b). In shunning "high-profile activity because we think it disrupts the process" (Shorrock, 2016), Young refers to a transformation of leaking into an increasingly strategic and media-managed activity. The romanticism of past leakers as pure in motive raises an important point about mediated leaking into the future.

When the leaker may not be obvious, coverage of leaks tends to focus on the content of the leak, not leakers (Cockfield, 2016), making it easy for authorities to leak, particularly where leaked information supports a dominant discourse (as in the Iraq War). There may be little exploration of the source or its motivations unless it violates the wishes of powerful actors and/or could arguably be a security concern. In such cases, the disseminator may become a focus. As disseminators, media become gatekeepers of what will be disclosed, and in the process become, the most visible actor with responsibility for the leak. This leaves scope for competing propaganda campaigns to shape discourse. As Marlin explains,

> A favourable assessment of WikiLeaks' ethics supposes the leaker to be sincerely motivated by the public interest, exposing some vital deceptions perpetrated on an unsuspecting public. But other motivations are possible: retaliation by disaffected workers, enhancement of career prospects by ensuring the demise of a superior, political or financial opportunism, or perhaps just sheer mischief.
>
> *(2011: 1)*

The context in which leaking occurs is complicated. Covert sources play a legitimate, necessary and long-established role in investigative journalism, particularly in foreign policy and security. They are also powerful tools for covert influence, and this must also be considered by journalists. Scholars have long debated journalism's ability to act as a 'Fourth Estate', upholding democracy and ensuring accountability (Robinson, 2012). Leaks are often accompanied and inseparable from campaigns to control their presentation by competing actors, who exploit news values that favour simple dichotomies – black and white, good and evil (Gripsrud, 1992: 88f), or increasing transparency versus hindering national security (Zenor, 2015). Entman (2012) found that "it is generally easiest for media to produce a scandal when the accusations do not pose much danger to existing structures of power and distributions of resources".[16]

Whistle-blowers still see journalism as a crucial platform for public dissemination and strategic collaboration brings credibility. Yet, journalists apply journalistic norms, practises that define newsworthiness and professional ethics, and such curation imposes restrictions inherent in the press. Journalism comes with its own interests and filters. Strategic leaks are disseminated and amplified by the media which may also apply its own self-interested or profit-driven lens to coverage and indeed celebrity or career incentives can also incentivise this process.

Despite the complex interests and ambiguity surrounding leaks, the public discourse tends to be simplistic or dichotomous. Even if the leaker is known or more often when they are hidden, dissemination conduits become the focus and are discussed as either making the government more transparent or imperilling national security (Zenor, 2015). Examining the Snowden revelations, Russell and Waisbord describe a predominant domestic lens 'fogged by nationalism', revealing heavy focus on the US political elite narrative, despite important global actors in the story. Coverage was framed on risks and benefits to the US and issues of whether or not surveillance was constitutional rather than more universal principles such as morality (Russell & Waisbord, 2017). Continuing dominance of elite legacy newspapers led to reduced attention on significant international elements of the story (Russell & Waisbord, 2017). Crucially, they highlight the role of elites' efforts to shape the news – "Peaks coincided with declarations (e.g. presidential speeches) made by and actions (e.g. congressional hearings, judicial decisions) taken by high government officials and new revelations involving government and corporate actors" (Russell & Waisbord, 2017: 873). Debate frequently centres on the leaked content, neglecting to investigate leakers and motives unless interested parties seek to make the leaker central to their framing of the leak (Cockfield, 2016).

The role of audiences

Complicating matters further is the role of audiences in the spread of leaks for propagandistic purposes. Through forms of digital communications, social networks in particular, the audience becomes active in the dissemination of persuasive messaging, which can then be exploited for propagating leaks. Propaganda has moved

> beyond a traditional, unidirectional "one-to-many" form of communication to one where vertical and horizontal propaganda (Ellul, 1973: 79–84) are in combination; a "one-to-many-to-many more" form where each 'target' of influence (an individual or group which is the object of persuasion) can in theory become the new 'originator' (subject) of content production and distribution, spreading persuasive messaging to others in a 'snowball' effect.
>
> *(Wanless & Berk, 2017)*

Woolley and Guilbeault argue that recent methods might be "democratizing propaganda through enabling nearly anyone to amplify online interactions for partisan ends" (2017: 28). Yet much of the online push of persuasive communications still comes from strategically organised campaigns, bolstered by automated and deliberate manipulation of the information environment, with regular internet users then co-opted to participate.

Encouraging digital audience engagement proved particularly effective through email lists (Plouffe, 2010) and social media are now engineered to assess what sort of content and connections users might want to consume and forge, and to then put that targeted information in front of them (Van Dijck, 2013). In the whistle-blowing case of CA, a series of releases were staggered over time. For a large release to be impactful it must be planned, ensuring the salience of the most crucial evidence at a rate it can be absorbed and reinforced without overwhelming audiences. AI and behavioural advertising (Matthew, 2017) may be used to segment users and provide them with the leaked content in a way that conforms to their world view, using echo chambers (Rainie et al., 2017). Within these, audiences can be encouraged to actively participate in dissemination including by lending or using their online accounts to share messaging (Katalenas, 2016), and even create persuasive messaging itself. Audiences are more engaged in the propaganda process as more active participants than would have been possible without such tools. If the right circumstances are created, audience members might also be encouraged to engage in trolling (Buckels et al., 2014), stifling the opposition in debate surrounding a leak.

In a Digital Age it is possible to frame leaks to provoke emotional responses among a specified target audience echo chamber (Wanless & Berk, 2017), encouraging users to share content (Tanz, 2017). Slanted content is then published across multiple sites and platforms comprising a complex ecosystem of hyperlinked digital media, that at once helps to collect more information about users as they consume such material (Albright, 2016a), as well as boosting search returns for other unsuspecting internet users (Moz, 2017). Shares on Twitter, automated or otherwise, also manipulate real-time newsfeeds and search returns, further distorting the information that the audiences are delivered (Mustafaraj & Metaxas, 2010). Emerging mass data-driven campaigns augmented by algorithmic targeting are increasing in sophistication, drawing on expertise from neuroscience and AI, which unlocks opportunities for targeted dissemination in strategic leaking.

The interplay with audiences, alongside the practice of astroturfing (Howard, 2004), makes propaganda much more insidious as the distinction between fake and real users blurs. Where persuasive communications come from a familiar source, perhaps a friend, target audiences are more likely to trust the content (Garrett & Weeks, 2013; Turcotte et al., 2015). Twenty per cent of those surveyed by Pew Research Centre in 2016 said "they've modified their stance on a social or political issue because of material they saw on social media, and 17%

had perspectives changed this way about a political candidate" (Anderson, 2016). This is particularly troubling, given that 93% of American adults get their news online (Pew Research Center, 2017).

Case study: 2016 US election

The exploitation of leaks for propaganda advantage, such as the disclosure of Clinton's presidential campaign chairman John Podesta's emails, was significant within communication strategies aiming to influence voter decision-making in the 2016 US presidential election. We will use our framework to discuss this case study, beginning with the hackers and leakers, and other competing interests, then discussing dissemination strategy and the role of audiences. A tapestry of events combined hacking attributed by US intelligence agencies to Russia (US National Intelligence Council, 2017); *Wikileaks'* leaking of Democratic National Committee (DNC) emails; amplification by CA; counter-disclosures, including opposition research on Trump (Chmielewski, 15 June 2016); and the CA Files (The Guardian, 2018). The present author, Dr Briant, was named in the latter journalism, her evidence based on academic research for an upcoming book was compelled by the Digital, Culture, Media and Sport Committee Inquiry into Fake News (Briant, 2018); it was published as parliamentary evidence and *not* leaked. However, it was released amid other evidence revealed by insider whistle-blowers. Such releases, whatever their source, can be seized upon by parties looking to present them to their advantage and much nuance of the process and motivations, not to mention the process of their release and how they were obtained, can become obscured by deliberate propaganda and media spectacle by the various parties. The unauthorised posting of Podesta's emails by *Wikileaks* on 22 July 2016 was exploited by Trump and his supporters, as well as Julian Assange, to discredit Clinton. The election was accompanied by extensive 'fake news'; prolific lying (particularly by the Trump campaign); and 'computational propaganda' (Kollanyi et al., 2016). There were, of course, competing political interests in the leak, and we will deal with these separately. One must be wary of assuming that all outcomes happened in the way intended by the leaker, as these are shaped by competing interests. Motives may become clearer with time, but the exploitation of leaks for propaganda by actors competing to shape events invites closer examination.

Competing interests

Leakers: Wikileaks and Russian involvement

The Federal Bureau of Investigation (FBI) warned the DNC in September and November 2015 that their security had been compromised, and information had been transmitted to Russia. The Podesta hack occurred after this, in March 2016, and in June, the *Washington Post* reported that the DNC had been breached "by those thought to be Russian hackers, something supported by the CrowdStrike report" (Uchill, 2017). In June, Assange promised further Clinton leaks (ITV, 2016). The leaks occurred in July; the first documents via Guccifer 2.0 on 14th and then the DNC emails were released via *Wikileaks* on 22nd (Uchill, 2017). *Wikileaks* chose not to reveal the source of the Podesta emails and tweeted, "Note on sourcing #DNCLeaks. We have, as usual, not revealed our sources. Anyone who claims to know who our source is has no credibility" (2016a). *Wikileaks*' Tweets in the month before the 8 November 2016 election suggest that Assange was running a determined campaign to prevent Clinton from winning. Every day, the *Wikileaks* account mentioned the Podesta Email disclosure, often multiple times a day. On 14 October 2016, *Wikileaks* made 10 posts referencing the Podesta Emails. The *Wikileaks* account also shared GIFs belittling Clinton and attacked her supporters. When *The Economist* Twitter account declared support for Clinton, *Wikileaks* rebutted with a leaked email connecting Clinton and the magazine's publisher (2016f).

Assange's motives in publishing Podesta's emails, as well as his source, which is still under dispute, are important to consider, if difficult to discern. Beyond Assange's professed commitment to increased transparency, one motive for publishing the Podesta leak could be hostility towards Clinton. When asked by an interviewer if he prefers a Trump presidency, Assange states:

> From my personal perspective, well, you know the emails we published show that Hillary Clinton is receiving constant updates about my personal situation, she has pushed for the prosecution of Wikileaks which is still in [inaudible], so we do see her as a bit of a problem for freedom of the press more generally.
>
> *(ITV, 2016)*

This wasn't Assange's first disclosure about Clinton. The Podesta Emails followed the launch of a searchable database of an earlier leak, on 16 March 2016, of Clinton's correspondences sent via a private email server while Secretary of State (Wikileaks, 2016e). This database was introduced by Assange's framing to implicate Clinton in a bribery scandal and the 2010 partial sale of Canadian firm Uranium One to Russian interests (2016b), a myth that Trump as president has continued to perpetuate (Kwong, 2017).

Defensive interests: Clinton and the Democrats

The DNC were reported in the *New York Times* on 22 July as saying "that Russian hackers had penetrated its computer system" (Shear & Rosenberg, 2016). The Russian Government denied involvement but, viewing the hack through the lens of their own forced exposure, inevitably shaped DNC and Clinton Campaign responses. Concern that cooperation might have occurred between Russia and the

Trump campaign became increasingly central to the Clinton Campaign's framing of events and campaign strategy, particularly after Trump tweeted, "Russia,
if you're listening, I hope you're able to find the 30,000 emails that are missing. I
think you will probably be rewarded mightily by our press" on 29 July (Uchill,
2017). Democrats quickly concluded that the DNC had been hacked and "that
Russian hackers had penetrated its computer system" (Shear & Rosenberg, 2016).
Opposition research files on Trump were also leaked (Buzzfeed, 10 January 2017;
Chmielewski, 15 June 2016).

Exploiting interests: Trump versus 'Crooked Hillary'

At the time of publication, Trump's campaign team have been shown to have
some ties to Russia which were at first denied (Prokop, 2018), the extent of this
is still unclear. In one CA-driven campaign (Channel 4, 20 March 2018), Trump
used the released Podesta Emails to attack Clinton, referencing 'Wikileaks' in 12
Tweets between the July disclosure and the 8 November vote,[17] helping frame
the DNC and Clinton within a corrupt media and political elite conspiracy:
"Very little pick-up by the dishonest media of incredible information provided by
WikiLeaks. So dishonest! Rigged system!" (2016b). Such mentions of *WikiLeaks*
became inflammatory content, fuelling the Trump Campaign's participatory
propaganda model (Wanless & Berk, 2017).

Dissemination in a Digital Age

Clinton campaign: Trump and Russian collusion

This reactive narrative was repeated by liberal-leaning political blog *Talking
Points Memo*, which accused Trump of colluding with Russia (Marshall, 2016).
And two days after *Wikileaks* published the Podesta Emails, Clinton's Campaign
Manager, Robby Mook, told *CNN*: "experts are telling us that Russian state
actors broke into the DNC, stole these emails. And other experts are now saying
that the Russians are releasing these emails for the purpose of actually helping
Donald Trump" (2016).

Post-election the question of whether Trump or his team colluded with
Russia in hacking and disclosing the emails was advanced to a salient position by
the FBI investigation into the matter, and more successful Democratic framing
of the leak in mainstream media.

Wikileaks' counter-framing: Russia and deflection

Wikileaks countered these claims on 24 July. Assange tweeted that the Clinton
campaign was "pushing lame conspiracy smear that we are Russian agents. Last
time we were Mossad. Get it right" (2016b). A second tweet insinuated that the
Podesta Emails had been leaked by an insider: "the hack? DNC has been hacked

dozens of times by multiple hackers & we never stated whether our source was inside or outside" (Wikileaks, 2016c). Assange reinforced this narrative in an interview with *Democracy Now* on 25 July 2016, saying many "consultants… lots of programmers" had access to DNC servers (2016a).

Assange's insinuations that an insider leaked the Podesta Email disclosure fostered conspiracy theories that murdered DNC staffer Seth Rich was the source. Trump supporters propagated this; one posted to subreddit /r/the_donald, saying, "DNC Data Director Seth Rich was likely assassinated by the Clintons" on 27 July and including a timeline of events (MyKettleIsNot-Black, 2016). These claims gained more traction on 9 August when *Wikileaks* announced on Twitter a "$20k reward for information leading to conviction for the murder of DNC staffer Seth Rich" (2016d). This persisted into May 2017, when *Fox 5* repeated the story (Kiely, 2017). Emails from 20 September 2016 until at least July 2017 reveal Julian Assange attempting to solicit assistance from Donald Trump Jr to amplify the leak, some of which appears to have been acted on (Ioffe, 13 November 2017). Some of the Russian output was discussed by politicians, including Trump himself, and to some extent influenced the agenda (Nimmo, 2018). Russian sources further amplified the leaks via online media shared widely by US voters, especially in swing states (Howard et al., 2017).

CA was reported to have reached out to Assange through an agency in September 2016 (Ballhaus & Bykowicz, 10 November 2017); in his testimony to the Fake News Inquiry Nix insisted that he had "never spoken to them" (Patrick, 28 February 2018). Despite Assange's interests, he was apparently reluctant to work with CA directly in dissemination, engaging instead with the Trump campaign team via Donald Trump Jr.. Emma Briant interviewed the CEO of SCL, the parent company of CA, who said,

> Alexander [Nix], if he got the release… of the Hillary Clinton emails it would have pushed her down in the polls. But there's nothing wrong with that… that's perfectly legitimate, Julian Assange was releasing things every day and Alexander rang up and said 'Any chance we can help you release the Hillary Clinton things?'
>
> *(Interview, 24th November 2017 in Briant, 2018)*

Assange declined. When asked about the wisdom in attempting to help Assange, given the accusations that the leaks had come from Russian sources, Oakes said, "At the time, at the time, you didn't know there was an-…that anyone's ever going to mention the Russians." He defended the decision, citing low risk of exposure, saying, "In hindsight… remember, this is 18 months before… and it was a year before the election. No-one had *been* in the press" (Interview: Oakes, 24 November 2017 in Briant, 2018). Oakes's claim that this may have been 12–18 months before the November election is interesting, given Assange's tweet confirming "an approach by Cambridge Analytica [prior to November last year] and can confirm that it was rejected by WikiLeaks" – but not confirming how *long* they had been talking (2017). Nix publicly claimed they approached Assange in early June 2016 (Ballhaus & Bykowicz, 2017). Oakes's statement implies earlier contact.

Trump campaign: Cambridge Analytica and supporter memes

Revealed in an exposé, the then CEO of CA, Alexander Nix explained how messaging was propagated by CA and described how supposedly 'independent' but actually coordinated groups are used, potentially illegal in US (Channel 4, 20 March 2018). Along with the Podesta Emails, the FBI investigation into Clinton's use of a private email server was used by the Trump campaign to discredit Clinton through CA's 'Crooked Hillary' campaign, using populist rhetoric to position her within a corrupt establishment. Trump supporters' online participation was crucial to how the leaked emails were used to advance his candidacy. Trump utilised CA's digital campaign tool, which used illegitimately acquired personal data of Facebook users to hyper target them with provocative messaging (Cadwalladr, 2018b). Their invasive analysis of Americans and repeated experiments helped them craft messaging aimed at provoking emotional drivers and personality traits. The unethical behavioural advertising driven CA efforts operated with the spread of other content including fake news (Maheshwari, 2017), memes (Schreckender, 2017) and content from the leaks. This hyper-targeted model helped create and reinforce echo chambers, which were fed with this content (BBC, 2016a; Benkler et al., 2017; Dreyfus, 2017) and boosted by manipulation of online news feed and search algorithms through the hyperlinking and reposting of URLs and content (Albright, 2016b), and botnets (Kollanyi et al., 2016). Pro-Trump online accounts encouraged followers to take action, sharing content or trolling opposition (Katalenas, 2016; Marantz, 2016). Posts were picked up by other media and given salience, even though negatively in much mainstream reporting. Through initiation of their involvement, Trump's supporters fed the wider system of online propaganda support for top-down efforts, which together featured and framed email leaks. Participatory propaganda elements included an unidentified supporter who created a website outlining the most damaging leaks for Clinton, launching this via the /r/the_donald subreddit (LegendaryAmerican, 2016).[18] More disturbing is the blending of narratives and mediums by Trump supporters, producing a "His name was Seth Rich" meme. Posts used photos of the deceased super-inscribed with a version of "His name is Seth Rich, not Russia". These posts began appearing as early as 19 August 2016 in the aforementioned subreddit (Reddit, 2016).

The role of audiences

CA used their digital methodology to target and provoke emotions, including outrage and fear, encouraging audience participation in the spread of leaked material on Clinton. While Trump was characterised by some as a troll (Lapowsky & Marshall, 2017; Offman, 2016; Silver, 2015), he was not simply reactive, and his team led a campaign drawing from support of an army of other online trolls (Marantz, 2016), who helped spread fake news (Gallucci, 2016; Kang, 2016) and attacked Clinton supporters online (Chmielewski, 2016). One online community, the *United States Freedom Army*, provided its members with a monthly guideline of actions to take online to support Trump (Lotan, 2016), including lending influential social network accounts to the cause (Katalenas, 2016). In the lead up to the 2016 election, this group published 17 articles referencing *Wikileaks* on its website.

The *Wikileaks* disclosure was found to have impact on social networks. In a study of the most retweeted posts during the two months leading up to the election, "there were three times as many posts attacking Clinton than posts in her favour" (University of Edinburgh, 2017). The term 'Wikileaks' was found to be one of the most frequent attack terms used against Clinton on Twitter, with the *Wikileaks* website being the most shared, in particular the URL pointing to 'The Podesta Emails' (Darwish et al., 2017: 11). *Wikileaks* also accounted for 20% of the polarising content shared by American Twitter users during the 10 days leading up to the November election (Howard et al., 2017).

Monitoring and audience analytics have become central to propaganda targeting and content and "online monitoring tools enable the original propagandist to follow and assess the spread of their messaging, adapting strategies in a constant feedback loop and inserting additional content, as and if required" (Wanless & Berk, 2017: 6). Through CA's activation of participatory propaganda, Trump's Campaign was able to set the agenda on the leaks. Gallup surveyed American voters during the campaign and found 'email' the most salient Clinton association (Newport et al., 2016). Indeed, in the year leading up to the writing of this chapter in early 2018, 'The Podesta Emails' remains one of the most shared pages from the *Wikileaks* website (Buzzsumo, 2018). This case study shows how the propulsion and logic of strategic leaks was enhanced by a new online participatory media infrastructure. Although importantly it further illustrates that given a national security frame official investigations and traditional media still retain a key role in agenda setting in a Digital Age. The next case study examines the pressures facing journalism's role in a Digital Age.

Case study: Panama Papers

In this case study we focus on the relationship between leakers and disseminators – specifically, how this is shaping journalists practises in a Digital Age. As hacking and leaking increase, awareness of powerful interests use of leaks as tools of strategic transparency or covert propaganda raises concerns for both journalistic practise, integrity and real-world and online safety. We examine the 'Panama Papers' in April 2016 – this involved over 100 media organisations and 11.5M files from law firm Mossack Fonseca revealing financial information for more than 214,488 offshore entities. Push-back against disseminators post-Snowden has seen a considerable extension of public and private infrastructure available to governments for surveillance, with the stated intention of protecting liberties and security. Some argue this now threatens journalism. We consider the precautions taken and the adaptation of reporting by journalists working on the leak, which illuminate how leaks are transforming journalism amid surveillance and physical threats.

The leaker and competing interests

The journalist approached by the source of this leak, Bastian Obermayer, from *Süddeutsche Zeitung*, destroyed his phone and hard drive after their conversations (Greenberg, April 2016). Developments in leaking raise questions about sources' motives and interests. Regarding this, Obermayer stated, "you can't guarantee it's not a secret service. As you never can." But "Why would any given secret service offer this vast amount of data? Why not use it for itself?" He said, "We verified the documents and found we could trust them. *We* chose what we published", according to public interest (Interview: 3 May 2016). The security-conscious leaker insisted that data must be stored on "air-gapped" PCs, their security concerns shaping journalists' practises – "the whole way we communicate. No one in my team still communicates without encryption" (Obermayer, Interview: 3 May 2016).

Powerful interests were seen as likely to place them under pressure and attempt to surveil, censor and control the narrative with propaganda. Russia was seen as the key threat, although the leak released information on wealthy elites around the world, all of whom would seek to shape the narrative. British surveillance was seen as the most concerning in Northern Europe. Collaboration was important for support when working in a difficult and risky environment; Kristjansson said,

> I didn't know what the reaction would be and it's human to imagine... sometimes I ask myself why am I doing this? But the most important thing for me was to be able to communicate with all those great journalists abroad.
>
> *(Interview: 4 May 2016)*

Dissemination in a Digital Age

Journalistic collaboration is another development enabling journalists to navigate legal and constitutional differences between states, and ease financial pressures on small media organisations. It allows journalists from repressive states to work "in the US jurisdiction, where you feel protected constitutionally from the stuff being seized. And also there's no …libel risk" (Interview: Harding, 4 May 2016). ICIJ used encrypted forum 'iHub' to communicate and developed a two-factor-authentication-protected search engine for the documents ('black-light'). This forms a permanent infrastructure for future multi-organisation investigations. Other journalists were inspired to build similar tools; Johannes Kristjansson from *Reykjavik Media* said, "for the next project we are going to work on here in Iceland …we are going to build our own iHub – some kind of system that will be a platform for us to work on and share ideas" (Interview: 4 May 2016).

According to Pew 71% of journalists reporting on national security, foreign affairs or the federal government believe the US government has already collected data about their communications and this is transforming journalistic reporting practices (Williams, 28 April 2015). Default end-to-end encryption is increasingly expected on new apps. But "among those who work for news organizations … half say their employer is not doing enough to protect journalists and their sources from surveillance and hacking" (Holcomb et al., 5 February 2015). Johannes Kristjansson, whose work led to the Icelandic Prime Minister's resignation, thought, "I don't think any journalist thinks about this until he has to", despite the importance of being knowledgeable and prepared (Interview: 4 May 2016). Financial pressure means security may get less priority than it should (Holcomb et al., 5 February 2015). According to Pearce, "I know lots of journalists who say that they are willing to go to jail to protect the identity of a source, and yet they don't even take elementary precautions to safeguard the contacts in their smartphone" (Posetti, 30 June 2014). This doesn't just concern major media organisations; little protection exists for independent bloggers who are more vulnerable and exposed and perhaps unclear of their legal position. The National Union of Journalists stresses that "Freelance journalists, citizen journalists and bloggers would need to be sure that they have the technical know-how to safeguard their sources and understand the potential risks involved" (Williams, 28 April 2015). Media outlets and journalists are now hosting 'secure drop' facilities. With the rapid evolution of technology, journalism education is also lagging behind. Cyber-security and counter-surveillance should be taught but don't need to involve expensive software; Pearce says, "cyber-security is a mind-set", so creative responses might be more effective: "they can only see things if they know where to look. Mostly, we are dealing with computer logic. We have human logic. Our duty is to confound them all and operate in unexpected ways" (Posetti, 30 June 2014). Alan Rusbridger, James Ball (*The Guardian*) and Wolfgang Krach (*Suddeutsche Zeitung*) suggest 'low-tech' methods – not taking your phone to a meeting, to avoid geolocation, may help. Creative methods by security services might still mean a whistle-blower can be revealed by eliminating those whose location *is* possible to determine or *the absence* of a digital trail for a source (Pearson, 22 June 2015). *The Guardian*'s Luke Harding conceded that "it's an unequal battle because you're up against a state that may be bureaucratic but has a lot of resources and tech up its sleeves which most journalists… don't have…", but countermeasures still matter – "why make it easy for them?" (Interview: 4 May 2016). Harding remains positive: "we live in a golden age for investigative journalism, the leaks are getting bigger and the datasets are more and more amazing. There are more and more whistleblowers coming forward" (Interview: 4 May 2016). Whistle-blowing is not becoming any safer – for leakers or journalists. Panama Papers' journalist Daphne Caruana Galizia was recently murdered, her son said, because she "stood between rule of law and those who sought to violate it" (Henley, 2017). Journalistic protections remain vital in this context. It illustrates the resilience of the powerful. Iceland's dethroned Prime Minister Sigmundur Gunnlaugsson made a comeback, establishing a new 'Center Party' and securing joint third-party status, despite his forced resignation a year earlier due to conflicts of interest (Iceland Monitor, 2017).

Conclusion

While leaks play an important role in democracy, disclosures also raise complex questions. Beyond the leaker, a networked hierarchy of actors struggle over dissemination, manipulation and framing of the leak. Such competition aims to shape public understanding of actors and content. Narrative is shaped by the emphasis or obfuscation of leaked content, the leaker, disseminators and their motives. Audiences are involved more directly in content creation. Yet a picture emerges that resonates with Castells's discussions of networked power, and communication power, as asymmetric, coercive and necessarily dominative (2009). While technology enables the access to and spread of leaked information, it is also designed to support the interests of those creating such tools, helping them provoke target audiences in acting while obfuscating processes of engagement. Indeed, technology may have increased public participation giving more people a voice through social media platforms, but aren't necessarily "democraticizing" propaganda given the use of technology to distort that collective voice, as Woolley & Guilbeault assert (2017). Fuchs correctly reminds us, of an important corrective, that cooperation is the most fundamental process in society and that it *is* possible to create systems that *are* more symmetrical and protective – something we must work towards (2017). We raise important concern about the mediated leaking of the present, some of which is becoming more sensationalist and more subject to algorithmic sorting, filtering and communicated through propaganda. Dangers and pressures against journalists also remain. Leaking must increasingly be seen within wider surveillance capabilities, coercive and propagandistic security strategies and research on its relation to governance and changing methods of propaganda is needed. As media technologies and mass surveillance remain in continual flux, pressure must be placed on policymakers to act on existing resolutions on whistle-blower protection and constant vigilance is necessary to protect human rights and assess how corporate and state surveillance and monitoring activities are impacting on free debate. New research is needed on how leaking is evolving in the context of coercive and persuasive practises by politicians and states; and its effects on the exercise of democracy.

Leaking today presents new opportunities for propagandists and journalists alike, but as leaks are increasingly incorporated into advanced systems of propaganda to sway the public and distort their contents and meaning, their deliberate manipulation will ultimately deepen mistrust. This likely will increasingly confuse differentiation of whistle-blowing and other forms of leaking, potentially endangering whistle-blowers and undermining public interest transparency. In elections, this could impair voters' capacity to make informed decisions about candidates. Whistle-blowers are increasingly prosecuted, monitored and controlled, increasing risks involved. Far more consideration must be given to how we oversee and regulate the use of data in political campaigning to protect our democracies in this Digital Age. Currently, risks for powerful manipulators are few. This chapter sheds light on the complexity behind strategic leaks and propaganda, but ultimately, calls for further research on not only the content or motivations of leakers and how complex commercial systems allow leaks to be easily manipulated for political gain, but also how systems might be adapted to work better for citizens and stronger democracy.

Notes

1 While writing this chapter, a plan by the United Arab Emirates to "wage financial war against its Gulf Rival Qatar" was leaked to the media (Grim & Walsh, 2017) and two of the biggest data disclosures to date, the 'Panama Papers' and 'Paradise Papers' were also released (Garside, 2017).

2 Moreover, secrets hold special appeal, "those who know about the secret, but do not have it, desire it. They project their hopes and fears on it, and these passions are heightened by the unknown character of the secret" (Vermeir & Margocsy, 2012: 161). Simmel saw secrets as "one of the major achievements of humankind" as they enlarge our world and allow "the possibility of hiding reality and creating a second world alongside the manifest one" (Richardson 1988: 209).

3 Exposing wrongdoing with the aim of achieving political changes in the public interest.

4 Hackers affiliated with the group Anonymous, for example, "tended to seek materials themselves, rather than calling for whistle-blowers to pass data on to them" (Coleman, 2013: 210).

5 However, Bakir shows sousveillance may have limited agenda-setting ability compared to its powerful targets (2016).

6 The Obama Administration "prosecuted more leak cases than all previous administrations combined" (Risen, 2018), yet a former speechwriter for President George W. Bush, Marc Thiessen, used the DNC email leak to blame Democrats for having not done enough under the Obama Administration to crack down on leaking and whistle-blowing (2016).

7 In the US Food and Drug Administration, scientists were targeted with spyware after they wrote to Obama, anonymously asking him to restructure the agency (Brodkin, 2012). Citizen Lab researchers revealed a growing market in commercial spyware, such tools have been employed to chill whistle-blowing and target peaceful activists, journalists and "those …deemed political threats by government agencies" (McCune and Deibert, 2017).

8   4% of total leaks in the first half of 2017 (InfoWatch, 2017).

9   The 'Pentagon Papers' and 'Watergate' transformed the discourse around leaking and whistle-blowing. The former concerns Daniel Ellsberg's leaking of a top-secret Department of Defense study of US political and military involvement in Vietnam from 1945 to 1967. The latter, an FBI insider who leaked information to journalist Bob Woodward about the Watergate scandal which led to the president's downfall (Woodward, 2005). Two legal opinions on the Pentagon Papers case concurred that 'secrecy in government' was 'fundamentally anti-democratic, perpetuating bureaucratic errors' (*New York Times Co. v. United States*, 1971).

10 The Reagan Administration leaked falsified 'scare stories' about foreign adversaries to gain media attention (Solomon & Lee, 1990, 141). Selective leaking by President Clinton's press secretary Mike McCurry, included 'a symbiotic complicity of the media, reliant on highly crafted and planned out leaks which give them little more than a watered-down White House-approved portrait of event' (Kurtz, 1998).

11 See, for example, British political appointee Jo Moore, who suggested that 11 September 2001 was 'a good day to bury bad news' (a statement, ironically, leaked itself) (Sparrow, 2001).

12 A 1946 British Foreign Office guide details five ways to leak information to media: (1) "An inconspicuous leak to one newspaper", garnering little attention for the purpose of getting it on the public record for future reference; (2) Leaking to domestic and international media and acting as though the disclosure was done unwillingly; (3) Making "multiple leaks" to trusted journalists who publish stories based on the material with no connection back to the disclosure; (4) "Leaks to news agencies" who are trusted to pick up the disclosure in an acceptable manner without attribution; and (5) "Indiscriminate individual leaks" attributed to unnamed officials or inner circles (Jenks, 2006, 17–18). Other intelligence agencies around the globe aim to manage security interests online, placing pressure on journalism and creating deniable avenues for selective, strategic releases of information whether relating to government itself or other actors.

13 It took more than 30 years before the Watergate informer was identified (von Drehle, 2005).

14 A former *Wikileaks* volunteer, Daniel Domscheit-Berg, suggested that *Wikileaks* may have economic incentives for sensationalism: 'what will keep you in the news the most, your number of Twitter followers' (Ahmed, 2016). Indeed, two days before the US election on 6 November, following a month of posts about the Podesta Emails, *Wikileaks* posted a call for donations 'WikiLeaks.org was down briefly. That's rare. We're investigating. Increase our capacity' (2006g).

15 An online repository for leaked intelligence documents.

16 He observes how in traditional and online media alike the seriousness of a scandalous release is not what raises extensive publicity. However, the online media echo chambers of the online environment of 2016 perhaps somewhat challenges Entman's conclusion that 'online media cannot manufacture Presidential scandals or enforce accountability on their own' (2012).

17 The first was 'The Wikileaks e-mail release today was so bad to Sanders that it will make it impossible for him to support her, unless he is a fraud!' (2016a).

18 According to SharedCount the site was shared more than 242K times.

4

THE USE OF POLITICAL COMMUNICATION BY INTERNATIONAL ORGANIZATIONS

The case of EU and NATO

Eva-Karin Olsson, Charlotte Wagnsson and Kajsa Hammargård

In recent years, there has been growing interest in how nations and international organizations (IOs) communicate in order to be seen as attractive and competent in various areas ranging from sport and culture, to economy and security. Most of the research has focused on nation-states' use of various forms of political communication, whereas less attention has been paid to IOs. Yet, IOs play important roles in all policy fields at the global level. In recent decades, there has been a transformation in political communication from an 'us-versus-them' nation based worldview into a network mode of communication placing IOs, personal contacts and cultural competence at its forefront (Zaharna, 2007). IOs share certain characteristics, which make them interesting objects of study in understanding political communication in today's globalized world. IOs are the product of nation-states and, as such, exist in an environment where they need approval and support, not only from national politicians and citizens but also from other IOs, in order to get funding and legitimacy. Communication is crucial in IOs' quest for legitimacy and influence (Barnett and Finnemore, 1999). In this chapter, we examine IOs' political communication within the security field by way of a case study of North Atlantic Treaty Organization (NATO) and the European Union (EU).

NATO and the EU have been selected because they represent two of the most important IOs engaged in European security issues. They differ in origin and mandate: NATO was set up as a military alliance and defense organization, whereas the EU started out as an economic peace project. Given this, one could expect the EU's political communication to focus on sustaining legitimacy among its members and to function as a normative power toward its neighbors. On the other hand, one could expect NATO's communication to be dominated by deterrence and information warfare. However, the empirics show that NATO is also engaged in communication aimed at sustaining legitimacy among existing members, and attracting new members and allies, and that the EU is becoming engaged in information warfare. The empirics show that there are enough similarities for the two IOs to be analyzed jointly. Based on this, we propose that communication by IOs in the security arena can be divided into four types representing different drivers and purposes. We define political communication broadly, and based on our interest in security issues, we have a particular focus on public diplomacy and information warfare.

Political communication, public diplomacy and information warfare

IOs are created by nation-states for various purposes and founded by interstate treaties under international law. The treaty stipulates the structure of the organization, which in general consists of an assembly in which the member states are represented and a secretariat, which carries out the organization's decisions (Cassese, 1986; Archer, 2001). According to Barnett and Finnemore (1999), a great deal of an IO's authority is based on communication activities related to classification, labeling and the spreading of norms and values. Through their discursive power, IOs define what is legally, socially and culturally accepted at the global level. Due to the spread of new information technologies, IOs have better abilities to influence their surrounding world than ever before. According to Gilboa (2008), the post-9/11 era came to the fore based on two technological innovations, the Internet and the rise of global networks, such as CNN and Al Jazeera, which together transformed notions of time and space. Since then, the communicative tendencies in global politics have been further fueled by additional developments in communication technologies, such as social media. According to scholars in the field, the transnationalization of political communication requires new approaches to public diplomacy focused on how to engage with nongovernmental actors, understanding the emotional aspects of stakeholders' perceptions and reactions, and developing methods for two-way communication (Wang, 2006).

The literature in the field highlights the fact that the use of political communication and public diplomacy by IOs has expanded in recent decades. In this chapter, we aim to explore in more detail when and why IOs communicate, including opportunities for and obstacles to achieving the aims of their communication. We do so by proposing four types of communication practices based on different rationales. We use political communication as a broad term in describing IOs' communication activities. According to Hallahan (2004), political communication refers to efforts made by political actors in building consent "involving the exercise of political power and the allocation of resources in society". This can include efforts to influence elections or policies and, at the international level, "communications in support of public diplomacy and military stabilization" (6). Public diplomacy was originally defined in 1965 by Edmund Gullion, as "…the influence of public attitudes on the formation and execution of foreign policies" (Cull, 2009: 19). Modern public diplomacy methods often include two-way processes termed "new public diplomacy" that place an emphasis on listening and dialogue (Melissen, 2005b: 13). According to Rasmussen (2009), public diplomacy is defined as "... the efforts by which an actor seeks to transfer ideas and beliefs by influencing foreign political discourses through direct contact and participation in political debates" (266). Public diplomacy is a nonconfrontational communication practice that avoids dichotomization in terms of 'us-and-them' and aims to foster attraction. Information warfare differs from public diplomacy insofar as it is a more confrontational practice that is more prone to dichotomization. Moreover, in contrast to public diplomacy, it is characterized by military, technical and secretive aspects of communication, such as cyber-attacks and hackers (Denning, 1998; NATO, 1999; Bishop and Goldman, 2003). Modern information warfare is, however, more than a struggle over technology; it is also about influence by way of messaging, often through social media, in such forms as projection of narratives, propaganda, PsyOps and Cyber Attacks. It is, therefore, our assumption that IOs in the security arena in this day and age use both public diplomacy and information warfare.

Types of international organization communication

We propose that IOs engage in four types of political communication, one geared toward an internal audience and three toward external audiences. These four ideal types are characterized by different main goals:

- Mustering internal cohesion in order to keep the organization together
- Promoting the organization in the international arena
- Expanding the organization through new members and partnerships
- Managing threats and adversaries

Applying these models to the EU and NATO, we expect the EU to focus more on the first and third types as a result of its aims to uphold internal legitimacy and act as a normative power in relation to its neighbors; and NATO to focus more on the fourth one, given its fundamental goal of deterring adversaries and protecting from external attack.

Organizations have been struggling with these challenges for a long time, yet digitalization has transformed practices. We will display below how both organizations have taken advantage of opportunities created by new and social media and that this process has been facilitated by the personalization of politics and by progressive leaders with a belief in the potential of social media. Yet, there are also obstacles in the ongoing process of development and adjustment to new digital realities. In particular, lack of convergence within organizations hamper channeling cohesive messages on social media; both the EU and NATO partly rely on member states in their communication yet members diverge on the future direction of the organization (e.g. Wagnsson, 2011b; Hobolt, 2016; Keller, 2017).

A previous study also exposed that armed forces across Europe diverged in their views on social media (Olsson et al., 2016).

It should be noted that we make no claim to cover all activities involving political communication. In large organizations such as the EU or NATO, communication activities take place at various locations, which makes it almost impossible to get an overview of all venues, outlets and activities (Duke, 2013: 13; Missiroli et al., 2016: 46).

Keeping the organization together

IOs like NATO and the EU depend on their appeal to member states and their citizens. Communication is crucial in keeping the organization together and explaining the economic and security benefits to its members, as well as creating and nurturing a common identity. The ability to attract media attention plays an important role in communicating with citizens, and here IOs are at a disadvantage compared to nation-states. In national political systems, personalities, conflicts and divisions are the lifeblood of political reporting and the main way in which citizens make sense of politics. In the case of the EU particularly, the complex governance system does not fit well with media logic. There are impediments relating to the nature of the policy process, which is perceived as remote, technical and complex, and to the lack of clear political conflicts and charismatic personalities. Thus, within both the EU and NATO we can see a move toward clearly identified spokespersons as a way of increasing personification of communication.

Within NATO, the need to communicate with the public in member states dates back to the Cold War and the practices of NATO Information Service mentioned above. Former Secretary General Rasmussen (2009b) acknowledged the need to communicate NATO's purpose to the domestic public: "After all, people will only support what they understand and appreciate". The evolution of the role of the Secretary General has played its part in strengthening NATO communication. The Sec Gen became the spokesperson of the Alliance and in Risso's words "the personification of the alliance" (Risso, 2014: 261). Anders Fogh Rasmussen, who served from 2009 to 2014, was an enthusiastic and highly charismatic leader well versed in new media use. Running his own personal video blog, he in turn stimulated NATO's social media (Risso, 204: 261–262). The Strategic Concept process of 2009–2010 led by Rasmussen can be seen as the primary example of NATO's public diplomacy. The process was a way of engaging a wider audience – both internal and external – in view of the adoption of a new Strategic Concept at the NATO Lisbon Summit in November 2010. Openness was the catchword. NATO invited the public to engage, arranged open seminars and encouraged chat on its website. Twelve experts were appointed to arrange a series of conferences in different capitals. NATO representatives emphasized openness, transparency and the importance of public engagement (Appathurai, 2009; di Paola, 2009; Rasmussen, 2009c). The Secretary General declared that the process was to be the most inclusive in the history of IOs, i.e., a typical public diplomacy project:

> I intend to make this the most open, the most inclusive consultation process in NATO's history, and I dare say, in the history of any international organization. The experts will hold many consultations in many countries. I will do the same. And our web model is giving the world a window into the process and a way to provide input as well.
>
> *(Rasmussen, Albright, and van der Veer, 2009)*

NATO thus aimed to muster public support in member states for the Alliance and this required officials to use modern communication as a means of marketing. In the present era, there is a particularly urgent need to market NATO internally in order to get European members states to invest financially in order to strengthen the European contribution to NATO. The US Administration has indicated that the US will not maintain its commitment to the Alliance, if European allies do not fulfill their obligations (Sanger and Haberman, 2016; Lamothe and Birnbaum, 2017).

In order for the EU to increase support and legitimacy among its citizens, communication is vital. The turning point for the EU in understanding the importance of media came with the resignation of the Santer Commission in 1999. During the period leading up to the resignation, the Commission showed a lack of knowledge, will and institutional structures to cope with increased media scrutiny (Meyer, 1999). This was a period of significantly low trust in one of EU's key institutions and it highlighted the need for responsiveness and accountability toward the European public and journalists (Schmidt, 2013: 16). In order to reduce the gap between Brussels and European citizens, and increase the legitimacy of the EU project, over the years the Commission has tried to address problems associated with the lack of information and routes for feedback for the European general public within European governance (Karoliny, 2010; van Brussel, 2014). Insights into the importance of communication have, e.g., resulted in changes in communication policies emphasizing more two-way communication. Despite the ambition, not much has changed in practice, and communication is still focused on improving the public perception of the EU, rather than creating a genuine dialogue (van Brussels, 2014). In addition, Nulty et al. (2016) suggest that social media has not yet challenged the traditional political communicative landscape when it comes to EU elections (Nulty et al. 2016).

The EU narrative has centered on values related to democracy, diversity and human rights:

> *The EU is a pledge of greater liberty, prosperity and security for Europeans; the EU promotes a model of society inspired by solidarity and dynamism and respecting diversity; and the EU enables us to play a world role matching our values and commensurate with our weight.*
>
> *(European Commission, 2002; Michalski, 2005: 128)*

One key difficulty encountered by the EU in communicating with its citizens, and getting its message across, relates broadly to the lack of media adjusted institutional and personal conditions within the EU, which creates problems in matching established news values and norms. For example, in contrast to national political institutions, the multilevel governance of the EU lacks strong symbolic personalized leadership (Olsson and Hammargård, 2016). That said, like NATO, over the years the EU has worked on personification. One important such move came with the introduction of the Common Foreign and Security Policy (CFSP) in the Amsterdam Treaty, when Javier Solana was appointed spokesperson and High Representative. Interestingly, research on EU media coverage shows that CFSP coverage was more Europeanized than other types of EU coverage with news stories primarily featuring EU actors (Kandyla and De Vreese, 2011). The mandate of the High Representative was further strengthened in 2009 with the introduction of the Lisbon Treaty when the security and defense policy ceased to come under the rotating presidency of the Council (Duke, 2013).

In summary, both the EU and NATO have spent considerable time and resources on communication aimed at explaining and motivating their own organization by creating appealing narratives in order to engage members and strengthen support. Forward-looking individuals like NATO's Secretary Generals have helped introducing social media as a means to bolster the spread of narratives. At the same time, both organizations have been hampered by media structures that are nationally structured and focused.

Engaging with the international community to promote the organization

Nation-states engage in political communication in order to influence the world around them. IOs are no exception. Beyond engaging with their member states, IOs are also active in the international community and often have membership and contacts with other actors such as the UN, the World Bank, WTO and the OECD (Michalski, 2005: 139). IOs depended on their competences, capacities and soft power in order to influence policies, norms and decision-making in the international arena.

NATO communicates to promote its interests, including the deterrence of potential adversaries: "...NATO must have the full range of capabilities necessary to deter and defend against threats to the safety of its populations and the security of its territory, which is the Alliance's greatest responsibility" (NATO, 2012). Coherent political communication and signaling is central to achieve deterrence (Kulesa and Frear, 2017: 8). NATO's role as a military alliance with the purpose of defending its members against territorial attack is stipulated in Article 5 of the North Atlantic Treaty of 1949. The current Strategic Concept sets collective defense as the first of three core tasks (NATO, 2010b). However, spokespersons also portray NATO as a value-based force for good, in this sense similar to the EU (Wagnsson, 2011a: 593–596). The North Atlantic Treaty stipulates the

NATO's value base, beginning with an affirmation of the parties' adherence to the UN charter, to peace, and to safeguarding the "freedom, common heritage and civilization of their peoples", which in turn is based on the principles of democracy, individual liberty and the rule of law. According to Article 2, the parties to the Treaty will "contribute toward the further development of peaceful and friendly international relations by strengthening their free institutions, by bringing about a better understanding of the principles upon which these institutions are founded, and by promoting conditions of stability and well-being" (NATO, 1949). Recent practice confirms that the alliance cultivates its image as a value-based organization and its officials do see it as their mission to do what Barnett and Finnemore (1999: 713) argue characterizes such an organization: to preserve, spread and enforce global values and norms. Explaining NATO's Libyan intervention in 2011, Secretary General Anders Fogh Rasmussen stated

> NATO member states form a unique community of values, committed to individual liberty, democracy, human rights and the rule of law. We consider these universal principles that apply to all people of the world, including in North Africa and the Middle East. That's why NATO Allies support the legitimate aspirations of people throughout the region.
>
> *(Rasmussen, 2011)*

NATO's value-based public diplomacy was in part spurred by an acute need to keep in synch with modern political messaging in an era of new media and military interventions that unfolded rapidly. Risso (2014: 258–259) sees the intervention in the Balkans as a catalyst; suddenly NATO could not communicate by ways of output that had been agreed upon in advance and by ways of consensus; it had to professionalize its communication service in order to keep up with messaging on a daily basis in a new media climate. A Media Operation Centre was set up in 1999 in order to induce NATO military personnel to better keep up with modern broadcasting. In 2003, public diplomacy was further facilitated by the establishment of the NATO Public Diplomacy Division, which, in essence, is the successor of its Cold War equivalent, the NATO Information Service (Risso, 2014: 5, 260–261). The Alliance became very active on social media, using various sorts of media, such as YouTube, Twitter and the NATO video Channel. Secretary General Rasmussen utilized these new channels to promote NATO not only as an interest-driven but also as a value-driven, even cosmopolitan organization (Kuus, 2009).

The EU was designed to generate European integration. As a civilian power, it relies on economic and diplomatic means of influence. The EU has also an interest in spreading norms and values at the global level. The core idea is to achieve peace and prosperity through economic stability, respect for human rights, diplomatic solutions and regional cooperation, which will benefit not only the EU but also the world in general (Smith, 2000). In order to engage with the international community and pursue its foreign policy, the EU has capabilities similar to those of nation-states, in terms of a diplomatic structure, membership of key IOs, and the ability to undertake military missions. The EU engages in a variety of policy activities such as international negotiations regarding trade, climate change, development and finance (Manners and Whitman, 2013: 18–19). Communication plays an important role for the EU in pursuing its goals on the international scene. In the June 2016 EU Global Strategy, it is stated that the EU's foreign policy priorities should be directed toward defense, cyber, counterterrorism, energy and strategic communications.[1] Strategic communication should enhance the EU's public diplomacy efforts and "connect EU foreign policy with citizens and better communicate it to our partners". In addition, the EU will not only improve consistency and speed in communicating but also "offer rapid, factual rebuttals of disinformation" (23).

Over the years, various EU bodies have been engaged in communicating at the global level. The most important have been the Commission's delegations (Rasmussen, 2009: 273). Before 2010, the delegations came under the CFSP and were often described as "quasi-diplomatic services" that, on one hand, represented the Commission in third-party countries and served a supranational function and, on the other, played an intergovernmental role within the framework of the CFSP (Duke, 2002: 855). Beyond the delegations, external communication activities were also carried out by the so-called RELEX-family (The Directorate-General [DG] for the External Relations) (de Gouveia and Plumridge, 2005: 14–15). In order to coordinate public diplomacy and external communication activities, monthly meetings were held between DG RELEX, DG Development, DG Trade, AIDCO (Europe Aid), DG ECHO, DG ENLARGMENT, DG PRESS and ECFIN (Duke, 2013: 117). Other DGs, such as DG Trade, handled their own political communication activities without central guidance. Despite the EU's rather low-key ambitions when it comes to coordination, the coordination of voices, messages and positions has been a constant challenge. After the Lisbon Treaty went into force in 2010, DG RELEX was merged into the European External Action Service (EEAS), which moved a significant portion of the political communication out of the Commission. The establishment of the EEAS changed the role of the approximately 140 delegations around the world to one of "delegations of the Union", rather than "delegations of the Commission". Coordination of the EU's external communication is thus still problematic, and various actions have been taken to deal with the problem (Duke, 2013). Initially at least, the EEAS dependence on external resources caused problems, which it tried to solve by closer collaboration with the Commission and the Council (Bátora, 2013: 9).

In today's world, media diplomacy plays an increasingly important role. Yet, the EU is often vague and difficult to understand, with its slow decision-making processes and shared institutional leadership, which do not fit with media logic. For example, a representative of the Arab media network, Al Jazeera, states that

> the EU is a difficult topic 'to sell' since Arab viewers are used to dealing with strong individual political powers. They are not accustomed to 'softer

entities', where the decision-making process has to go through multiple rounds of negotiations and complex systems of collegial decisions.

(Donatella Della Ratta, 2009: 204)

There were high hopes that social media would facilitate EU's diplomatic communication, but there is a lack of research showing whether this is the case. For example, a study of how Japanese, EU and US delegations in China use Weibo shows that social media is primarily used for information dissemination, rather than to engage audiences in a two-way dialogue (Bioloa et al., 2015). In studying how the EU is perceived by various nations and IOs, Lucarelli and Fioramonti (2009) show that the EU is seen as weak and divided when it comes to foreign and security policy. In contrast to the US, the EU is often understood as a global promoter of democracy and peace, focusing its efforts on dialogue, incentives and soft power. On the other hand, when it comes to global economic matters, the EU is perceived as a key actor. In addition, when it comes to democracy and regional integration, perceptions are positive and the EU is often regarded as a role model. At the same time, the EU is criticized, primarily by countries belonging to the 'global south', for inconsistencies and double standards.

In sum, as can be seen, both the EU and NATO use political communication to engage with the international community and spread their values and norms globally, arguing that they are organizations set up to protect the common good (Barnett and Finnemore, 1999, 2004). Communication is used to export and promote universal values, sometimes for the general good, but also as a way of maximizing utility for the IO and its members, including enhancing the IO's reputation as a 'force for good'. Both organizations have adopted digitalization and social media in their work in the international arena, yet there is need for further research on how they have succeeded so far in this endeavor.

Expanding the organization

Beyond communicating with existing member states, both NATO and the EU use public diplomacy as a way of attracting and cultivating partners and potential new member states.

NATO has become heavily dependent upon partnership arrangements of different sorts. Some are allies who see NATO as a complement to the US; some are potential NATO members; some view NATO as a complement to the EU and some are potential NATO partners (Edström, 2011: 7). Public diplomacy is an important tool in cultivating such arrangements. By adopting the new Strategic Concept at the Lisbon Summit of 2010, NATO placed great emphasis on developing partnerships regionally and globally as part of fulfilling NATO's third task labeled 'cooperative security'. This move was interpreted as opening up a new role for NATO as a global security provider (e.g. Noetzel and Schreer, 2012: 28). The document mentioned partnerships with the EU, the UN, Russia, as well as the Euro-Atlantic Partnership Council, the Partnership for Peace, the Mediterranean dialogue and the Istanbul Cooperation Initiative. The aim was partnerships through 'flexible formats' and global dialogue and cooperation. Stuart (2004) reproduces a widely held view of NATO at the time; one of an expanding entity, both in terms of membership and of geographical reach. The globalization of NATO's tasks and relationships is contested, and some saw the Ukrainian crisis as strengthening the relevancy and raison d'être of the alliance (Daadler and Goldgeier, 2014; Traynor, 2014).However, although the globalization of NATO has been constrained, even halted, by the conflict with Russia, it may regain vigor and with it an increased need for global public diplomacy. Throughout the 2000s, NATO conducted public diplomacy directed at new partner countries to the east, e.g., through the Euro-Atlantic Partnership Council, launched in 1997 aiming to strengthen relations with European non-members. Risso (2014: 259) describes a new cultural diplomacy that included, e.g., cultural and scientific exchanges and joint research projects. Meanwhile, the enlargement process continued with Croatia and Albania joining in 2009, the same year France returned to full membership, and Montenegro joined this year. Digitalization is a key to these endeavors and NATO has displayed an awareness of this. The Public Diplomacy Division has, e.g., organized several expert fo-rums for IOs use of social media in 2015 and 2016, and NATO's spokesperson and the current Secretary General Jens Stoltenberg take advantage of twitter to promote the organization globally (Maronkova, 2016).

Enlargement lies at the very heart of the EU and over time the organiza-tion has received new members as they have turned into democratic market economies. EU integration has been framed as a natural progressive develop-ment, alongside those of economic and democratic prosperity (Michalski, 2005; Rasmussen, 2009; Nitoiu, 2013). In total, the EU has grown from founding initial member states to 28, with Croatia joining as the latest member in 2013. An important aspect of the enlargement process, and the prospect of member-ship, is fostering democratic norms in the EU's southern and eastern regions. For example, the Eastern Partnership was launched in 2009 with the ambition of promoting political and economic reforms in Armenia, Azerbaijan, Belarus, Georgia, Moldova and Ukraine (Dias, 2013).

Communication toward potential new member states has focused on values related to peace and democracy, advocated as an essential element of the EU as a model of good governance, embodied in policy areas such as the single European market (Michalski, 2005. Nitoiu (2013) identifies five types of narrative domi-nating EU external communication: the EU as a promoter of peace, the democ-ratization narrative, good neighborliness (this narrative is strongly connected to the European Neighborhood policy [ENP]), the security narrative and the "EU and the well-being of peoples around the world" narrative. EU narratives can be understood as 'identity driven', but also at times directed at and com-bined with concrete policy goals (Rasmussen, 2009: 285–287). DG Enlarge-ment has historically had an extensive communication budget, with a strategy aimed at satisfying the public's demand for information, to generate dialogue and to counter misperceptions about the enlargement process (De Gouveia and Plumridge, 2005: 17). DG Enlargement was also responsible for the ENP where communication aimed that

> ... portrays the Union as a good neighbor is based on the belief that the EU should build or is striving to build a partnership with its neighbors, through which it could spread a series of universal norms and values.
>
> *(Nitoiu, 2013: 246)*

In summary, we can see how public diplomacy to attract new members and strengthen partnerships is crucial. There is also an awareness within the organizations of the significance of social media as a tool in this process.

Dealing with adversaries

Finally, we would like to address the EU's and NATO's ability to deal with adversaries. Public diplomacy also plays a role in forging better relations with adversaries, although we now move into a gray zone in which both public diplomacy and information warfare are applied.

In both the cases of NATO and the EU, Russia has turned into the significant 'other'. NATO has a long-term engagement in Russia, involving public diplomacy activities. Throughout the 2000s, NATO tried to normalize relations with Russia. Mutual perceptions reflected a period of relative détente that made public diplomacy an option. An extensive interview study conducted in 2006 indicates that very few Russian and NATO diplomats regarded the use of force as a realistic scenario in mutual relations (Pouliot, 2010: 98–104). The Strategic Concept process of 2009–2010, led by Rasmussen, also became the peak of NATO's highly active and visible public diplomacy toward Russia. Relations had soured because of the war in Georgia in 2008, and NATO attempted to revitalize relations during the Strategic Concept process of 2009–2010. The narrative during the concept process did not focus solely on military defense; instead, NATO also characterized itself as a cosmopolitan military organization legitimized through '...outward-looking narratives of global security, stability, and peace' (Kuus, 2009: 558). The Secretary General explained that NATO needs Russia to solve major contemporary issues, stating that a strategic partnership with Russia would become one of the most important questions during the Concept process (Rasmussen, 2009a; Rasmussen, Albright, and van der Veer, 2009). The chair of the Group of Experts who headed the process, former US Secretary of State Madeleine Albright, held one of the seminars in Moscow. For the time being public diplomacy is difficult, due to the frozen relations with Russia, but in the future public diplomacy can once again become central to NATO's perennial attempts to normalize relations with its historically significant 'other'.

When it comes to information warfare, it is interesting to note that, throughout the 2000s, NATO retained and strengthened its intelligence capabilities and other traditional resources underpinning information warfare. For example, the 9/11 terrorist attacks spurred an increased focus on information sharing and intelligence sharing among member states (NATO, 2017d). NATO's focus has been on an environment characterized by states as adversaries. This has resulted in NATO finding it more difficult adjusting to the threat of terrorism based on its limited military capabilities and the nature of the new threat as such (De Nevers, 2007). After the Russian annexation of Crimea and incursion into the Ukraine, NATO became more focused on the defense of the territory of its member states (Gearan, 2014). With this came an increased focus on information warfare, as a reflection of the Russian Federation's so-called hybrid warfare and heavy reliance on information as a tool in the sphere of security (e.g. Russian government, 2000; Russian government, 2014 and Russian government, 2015). NATO took numerous concrete steps toward strengthening its information warfare capability. Several member states established a Strategic Communications Center of Excellence (Nato StratCom) in Riga, Latvia, in 2014.[2] It produces expertise and analyses on strategic communications. The Centre provides recommendations on how to produce effective information, as countermeasures to Russian information and propaganda, and how to disseminate it effectively to target audiences. Publications have covered the use of social media, hybrid warfare and Russian disinformation in Eastern Europe and the Ukraine, as well as Islamic State (IS) communication and influence in NATO member states. NATO's move toward information warfare is also visible in its support of a newly opened joint EU NATO project the European Centre for Countering Hybrid Threats. In connection with the opening, NATO issued a statement, saying "NATO's counter-hybrid strategy includes strengthened coordination with the European Union, and also involves our new Intelligence Division, more training and exercises, and our work to actively counter propaganda with facts" (NATO, 2017c). In December 2016, NATO created a new position central to information warfare, a first Assistant Secretary General for Intelligence and Security, who is to give intelligence support to the North Atlantic Council and the Military Committee as well as advising the Secretary General on intelligence and security matters. Thereby, NATO also merged its civilian and military intelligence strands (NATO, 2017b).

Thus, NATO currently communicates both through its military and civilian structures, conducting both information warfare and public diplomacy. Key agencies on the military side are the Public Affairs and Strategic Communications Advisor to the Chairman of the Military Committee, and NATO's two strategic commands (Operations and Transformation). The free-standing NATO Communications and Information Agency, which is also part of the NATO structure, deals with communication aspects that fall within the remit of information warfare, focusing on, e.g., communications and information systems and services, intelligence, surveillance and reconnaissance capabilities. The Committee on Public Diplomacy provides advice to the NAC on communication, media and public engagement (NATO, 2017a). The Public Diplomacy Division at NATO Headquarters, which is part of the civilian structure, coordinates the Alliance's public diplomacy and communication activities. The division's homepage states the over-all aim of the alliance's communication activities, which is in line with common definitions of public diplomacy: '...to promote dialogue and understanding, while contributing to the public's knowledge of security issues and promoting public involvement in a continuous process of debate on security' (NATO, 2017a). The Public Diplomacy Division includes several subunits and also promotes NATO by way of the presence on social media through its video channel, which broadcasts short videos on current affairs, feature stories on NATO operations and activities, NATO press conferences and speeches and so on. It provides a free e-mail service intended to supply timely information on NATO on various topics. NATO is also present on a wide range of social media sites, such as Facebook and Twitter.

The EU has had a long-standing dialogue with Russia, which over the years has occurred through various institutional arrangements and has experienced both ups and downs. According to Haukkala (2015), the relations between the EU and Russia can be divided into three phases. The first phase took place after the end of the Cold War, 1992–1994, and was characterized by optimism and cooperation. In the second phase, 1994–2000, the relationship became more strained and troubled, yet the cooperative ambition remained. The final phase started with a spirit of mutual understanding between Putin and the EU, em-bodied, e.g., by the launching of the four Common Spaces in May 2003, created within the framework of the Partnership and Co-operation Agreement. How-ever, Putin gradually began to refrain from the idea of shared interests, culmi-nating in the occupation of Crimea in 2014 (Haukkala, 2015). The Crimean incident, combined with the rise of the terror organization the IS created the impetus for the EU to start engaging in information warfare activities in a much more proactive manner than previously.

According to Mogherini, the EU has entered a new era called the "post-truth era", where EU public diplomacy also focuses on IS propaganda and Russian disinformation, and the EU is now targeting two seemingly new audiences, Arab and Russian speakers (Mogherini, 2016). The recent development indicates a new direction for EU public diplomacy, where EU policies are more directly geared toward threats of disinformation and propaganda from specific actors. In order to deal with these new challenges, two missions have been created: the East Stratcom Task Force and the Arab Stratcom Task Force, which to date are the most institutionalized issue-specific efforts in the history of EU public diplomacy. In the past year, the EEAS has increased the press and information budget for the delegations, and the task forces have worked on increasing social media presence and outreach projects to young people in the region (European Parliament, 2016). Thus, the EU has taken a step toward engaging in information warfare, if only to defend itself against it.

In summary, this section shows how adversaries play an important role in con-tributing to the development of new communication practices in an era of dig-italization, with recent developments concerning Islamic terror organizations, such as IS, serving as the best example.

The way ahead

Four types of political communication by IOs have been presented above and applied to NATO and EU communication. In this concluding section, we will discuss what we see as the main challenges ahead in each of the four types.

The way ahead in the first type, which is centered on the creation of a shared sense of belonging and identity, may well be to make identity into something that is not only talked about, but which becomes a reality for citizens. What happens when the demands of keeping the organizations together become more and more difficult, as in the case of the legitimacy crisis faced by the EU? Will the need to establish a stronger common identity have an impact on how the EU communicates in connecting existing and future members? Given the notion that identity is created around inclusion and exclusion, will we move toward more of an 'us-and-them' rhetoric, building on distinctions between citizens and non-citizens? According to Wodak and Boukala (2015), the developments in Europe, from the financial crisis in 2008 and onwards, have resulted in a European debate characterized by new distinctions between 'real Europeans' and 'them'. Will the EU follow the trend, and how does such rhetoric match the traditional messages of the EU as a union for solidarity and respect for diversity? NATO also faces a challenge in this regard, especially after the US Administration undermined the belief in Alliance cohesion and loyalty in 2016–2017. The Secretary General and political leaders of major NATO states may become even more important in communicating in favor of internal cohesion if this tendency is sustained.

In relation to the second and third types of communication – engaging with the international community and attracting new members – there is potential for two-way public diplomacy and engagement in spreading and creating dialogue in the global community, e.g., in concert with other IOs and nongovernmental organizations. However, the two organizations also face challenges. NATO's messaging risks being seen as less credible and consistent since, on one hand, it seeks to project itself as a forceful military alliance, thus building upon the logic of 'othering' and exclusion, while on the other hand portraying itself as a nonthreatening cosmopolitan force for good. The EU in turn is weakened by internal crisis and is likely to have become unattractive to the international community. Moreover, the two organizations face obstacles in merging their communicative efforts, since increased cooperation in this regard may damage the image of the EU. Critics, such as Thomas Diez and Ian Manners (2014), resist ideas of the EU becoming more of a self-interested, nation-state type entity, like NATO, since this might reduce its ability to spread universal values.

The fourth type, engaging with adversaries, poses a challenge because of a growing tension between civilian and military practice. When it comes to the EU, the organization has primarily been engaged in public diplomacy efforts and has, only recently, become more active in the field of information warfare, driven by a perceived change in threat level. One can assume that the suspicious and rather hostile view of Russia in the EU's conduct of information warfare may hamper public diplomacy activities in other areas. On a more abstract level, Rasmussen (2009) points to a latent conflict between, on one hand, the EU projecting its identity as an efficient political and economic actor, which is necessary to uphold internal legitimacy, and, on the other hand, the ambition to appear as a trustworthy, altruistic actor on the global stage (286). This conflict risks becoming even more severe, the more the EU needs to strengthen its internal image, which may then hamper its public diplomacy and norm spreading activities. We have demonstrated that two IOs, with different origins and purposes, are active in the same types of communicative activities in four domains and that they share common challenges and opportunities. Future research should examine how political communication in one domain impacts on communication in the other domains. For example, if an IO communicates with adversaries in a way that appears overtly hostile or incorrect, this may complicate their communication with the international community at large, and, if an IO increasingly engages in information warfare, this may serve to damage its capacity for public diplomacy, which is built upon attraction and the image of being a 'good' power. Another issue for future research is how IOs in the security arena, with many members, manage to form communicative strategies that promote a coherent narrative, linking the promise of success for their policies to preexisting ideas about the IO's role in security, all of which is likely to muster popular support (Jakobsen and Ringsmose, 2015: 216–217). This article indicates that both the EU and NATO face difficulties in conveying a coherent image of their organization. Furthermore, in the age of social media, the trend of personification is likely to continue and needs to be further investigated. How do the personal styles and communicative strategies applied by an IO's most prominent spokespersons affect the overall prospect for success of communication by IOs?

Notes

1 http://europa.eu/globalstrategy/sites/globalstrategy/files/regions/files/eugs_review_web_0.pdf

2 NATO Centers of Excellence are not part of the Alliance's command structure but formally recognized by the alliance for their expertise. The Center is financed by Latvia, Estonia, Lithuania, Germany, Poland, Italy, the Netherlands and the UK. France also forms part of the Centre as well as two partnership countries (Finland and Sweden). NATO also recognizes a Cooperative Cyber Defence Centre of Excellence in Tallin, Estonia, founded in 2008, which focuses more on the technical side of information warfare.

5

THE UNBEARABLE THINNESS OF STRATEGIC COMMUNICATION

Cristina Archetti

Introduction: a contested concept

"Strategic communication" is where it's at. No matter whether we are talking about managing counterinsurgencies in Afghanistan or Iraq, countering the radical messages promoted by terrorist groups like ISIS or extremist right-wing organizations, promoting a country's interests among foreign audiences through public diplomacy activities, or addressing hostile propaganda and "fake news" from foreign countries. "Strategic communication" figures in military doctrine (Department of Defense 2009; NATO 2009, 2010; Ministry of Defence 2011), in policy documents (White House 2010, for instance), think tank reports (Lord 2008, for one example), practitioners' papers (Murphy 2009, 2010; Zwiebel 2006), as well as research (see the *International Journal of Strategic Communication* and *Defense Strategic Communication*) on both sides of the Atlantic.

Although multiple definitions exist,[1] they all tend to converge on four main aspects. As Christopher Paul (2011, 4) outlines them, in a book that specifically examines this concept, strategic communication is based on the premises that '[i]nforming, influencing, and persuading is important; effectively informing, influencing and persuading requires clear objectives; coordination and decon-fliction are necessary to avoid information fratricide; actions communicate.' Although his analysis is mostly about strategic communication in the US debate, where the concept has undergone most development, this definition is well suited to capture approaches from a range of organizations operating in different countries and domains of activity.

When it comes to defense and security, strategic communication is regarded as crucial in an information environment that is increasingly transparent. The Department of Defense Strategic Communication Science and Technology Plan (2009, 2) states, for instance, that 'a compelling argument can be made today that the public perceptions and implications of military operations might increasingly outweigh the tangible benefits actually achieved from real combat on the battle-field.' The UK Ministry of Defence (2011, iv) adds,

> Everything we say and do is exposed to instantaneous global scrutiny, not just by conventional media with its own biases and agendas, but also by individuals able (and inclined) to transmit information and news via the world-wide-web; "What is heard in Helmand [Afghanistan] is heard in Huddersfield [West Yorkshire, UK]" and vice versa.

Beyond the battlefield, a Chatham House report by Paul Cornish, Julian Lindley-French and Claire Yorke (2011, 3) underlines how strategic communi-cation is in fact a constitutional obligation that belongs to the very mandate of a democratic government—'in the age of near-instant mass communication [...] how could government *not* communicate?' (11). The ability to convey clearly and consistently a set of defined objectives (strategic communication implies the development of an overall strategy in the first place) both domestically and ex-ternally, as they continue, further contributes to the government's competence, credibility and efficacy—not just to their perception by third actors, but their ac-tual realization (12–16). In this respect, the US National Framework for Strategic Communication (2010, 1, my emphasis) similarly states, with reference to public diplomacy, that '[a]cross all of our efforts, effective strategic communications are *essential* to sustaining global legitimacy and supporting our policy aims.'

Communication is additionally key to countering extremism (Archetti 2012; Casebeer and Russell 2005; Crelinsten, 2002; Council of the European Union 2014; National Coordinator for Counterterrorism 2010). As again the Chatham House report (2011, 34) suggests,

> Although strategic communications play a vital role across counter-terrorism policy, they can have particular potency in addressing [the] early phases [of radicalization], enabling preemptive, non-violent intervention and messaging for those most susceptible to radicalization.

It is thus of paramount importance, the mantra goes, to get strategic communica-tion "right." Failure to do so—this is the underlying argument—effectively spells government's inability to carry out its basic functions and face the most pressing threats of our time. To the point that Paul (2011, 183) concludes his analysis with an open plea: 'If strategic communication as a term is too vague, too contested, or comes politically untenable, abandon it. Just do not allow the underlying effort to coordinate government impact on the information environment to be lost.'

Yet, despite having become part of the policymaking vocabulary for at least the past 15 years—the term "strategic communication" has been used for longer in other contexts (see Hallahan et al. 2007)—the implementation of strategic communication is not unproblematic. Among as many as 22 challenges that

Paul (2009, 15) identifies are the need for leadership, improved coordination, a better leverage of the private sector, greater focus on measurement, updating doctrine and increasing training. From the UK perspective, the assessment is that 'what is needed is a strategic communications mindset or culture, integral to every department of state and at every level of national policy and strategy' (Cornish, Lindley-French and Yorke 2011, 40). Dennis Murphy (2010, 115), highlighting the practical gaps from the point of view of those who wear the "boots on the ground," adds streamlining measures of effectiveness to ensure a more rapid feedback from the field, emphasis on foreign language skills and a deeper understanding of cultural anthropology. As he poignantly writes elsewhere (Murphy 2009), however, perhaps the greatest obstacle to "doing" strategic communication is that its very notion is hard to grasp: 'an emergent concept with several definitions floating about, no doctrinal base and a lexicon that fails completely to convey the desired understanding' (Murphy 2009, 3).

Further to this last set of critiques, my argument is that the worst problems with strategic communication are not the practical ones related to its implementation, be they connected to political leadership or organization, or the wording of the concept. These only arise, as I am going to demonstrate, because strategic communication is fundamentally flawed *theoretically*. Strategic communication, in other words, will never work because it is founded on the wrong premises. They involve a narrow understanding of the very meaning of communication and the way this works, not just in the age of the communication revolution, but more generally, and not least in political and social contexts that are becoming increasingly polarized. These aspects are illustrated through empirical examples ranging from governmental efforts aimed at countering violent extremism (CVE), to public diplomacy, and measures to counter-propaganda from foreign countries, especially when it comes to dealing with (alleged) election interference and "fake news."

The analysis identifies two main errors in the way communication and its dynamics are currently approached. They are addressed in turn and contrasted to an alternative understanding of communication that draws on the philosophy of media by John Durham Peters (2015) and the sociology of Harrison White (2008) and Stephan Fuchs (2001). The reference to the work of these scholars who, although based in different fields and using slightly different terms, all argue for a relational, networked, material understanding of how meaning is created by individuals and groups through interaction at specific times and places, underlines the urgency in rethinking the way scholars, policy makers and practitioners conceive the very world in which they operate and how we all relate to one another.

Too much emphasis on the "soft" side of communication

The first problem with both understanding and implementing strategic communication is that, despite the broad consensus on the fact that also action communicates, the material dimension of communication is never taken far enough. In this respect, strategic communication is undermined by an inherent contradiction: it wants to be an encompassing coordination of all activities—words and deeds—of an organization, at the same time it needs to be *strategic*, which means it needs to be target oriented and specialized. This leads to perpetuating, along the "old" lines of thinking, the separation between "communication"— approached as an exchange of messages—and "practice."

A telling example is offered by measures for the countering of terrorism. Along the logic of strategic communication, they are widely regarded as comprising the addressing of the material causes of extremism, as well as the ideological components of it. The *United Kingdom's Strategy to Counter Terrorism* (Home Office 2011, 59), for example, apart from detailing the actions to be taken to strengthen communities and make them more resilient to the physical threat of extremism, also underlines that 'preventing radicalisation must mean challenging extremist ideas that are conducive to terrorism and also part of a terrorist narrative.'

When it comes to implementation, however, there appears to be a divide between "communication"—which tends to be approached as the spreading of messages and counternarratives—on the one hand, and seemingly more "material" activities, on the other hand. I am going to look at some examples more closely, before making the point that the distinction between these two dimensions is based on a narrow view of communication that does not acknowledge its true social and material nature.

"Communication" vs "practice"

In terms of "communication," one could think, for a range of international cases, about the Global Engagement Centre of the US State Department, the Research, Information and Communication Unit (RICU) in the UK, and the Hedayah International Centre of Excellence for Countering Violent Extremism set up by the Global Counterterrorism Forum (an informal group of 29 countries plus the European Union) in Abu Dhabi.

The Global Engagement Centre is the most narrowly "specialized" in so far as it is "charged with coordinating U.S. counterterrorism messaging to foreign audiences," which involves using "modern, cutting-edge technology" and "the best talent and tools throughout the private sector and government." Effectiveness in the 'information space' is said to be pursued through 'partner-driven messaging and data analytics' (US Department of State, n.d.). RICU was founded in 2007 and is based at the Office for Security and Counter Terrorism of the Home Office. Its stated aims are 'to coordinate government-wide communication activities to counter the appeal of violent extremism while promoting stronger grass-roots inter-community relations' (Institute for Strategic Dialogue, n.d.). Although the mention of "community relations" could leave more scope for "action," the activity of RICU so far has been focused on communication-specific activities: audience analysis, digital campaigns aimed at vulnerable targets, advising media on reporting that could affect the counterterrorism agenda and producing communication toolkits and manuals (ibid.). Finally, Hedayah, established in 2012 as an 'independent, multilateral center devoted to capacity building programs, dialogue and communications, in addition to research and analysis to counter violent extremism in all of its forms and manifestations' (Hedayah, n.d.), is the first center dedicated exclusively to CVE. CVE, in principle, extends well beyond messaging. According to the definition provided by the Department for Homeland Security, it

> aims to address the root causes of violent extremism by providing resources to communities to build and sustain local prevention efforts and promote the use of counter-narratives to confront violent extremist messaging online. Building relationships based on trust with communities is essential to this effort.
>
> *(Homeland Security 2017)*

Further to this, Patrick Lynch, director of Training and Capacity Building, stated in 2015 that 'CVE is about reducing the terrorist threat through non-coercive approaches that address its root causes' (Lynch 2015). The Center, however, when one more closely examines the contents of the training it provides, tends rather heavily to focus on the more explicit communicative dimension, especially on counternarratives. This is also underlined by the opening, in October 2016, of an online Counter Narrative Library that contains hundreds of examples of best practice (Hedayah 2016). Of course, this is not incompatible with addressing the root cause of terrorism, although it again stresses that noncoercive, nonmilitary approaches to terrorism tend to be associated to the dissemination of "soft," "immaterial" messages.[2]

On the other hand, examining the activities included in exit-, counter- and de-radicalization, as well as prevention programs across Europe (Butt and Tuck 2014; Korn 2016), one could see that communication is present all along, in different forms that range from social interaction to conversations and education, but this component is neither acknowledged as such ("communication" is never even mentioned) nor explicitly investigated, seemingly on the ground that these are "practical" programs. We can see, for example, how the "Tolerance" program developed in Kungälv in 1995 in Sweden involved 're-socializing activities' (Butt and Tuck 2014, 10). Another program established in 1998 in the same country, EXIT Fryshuset, comprises 'work with the families of neo-Nazis to enable them to support young people engaged in or involved with white supremacist groups' (13). To mention more recent examples, "Back on Track" in Denmark (from 2012), to support prison inmates who have been convicted of terrorism, trains them to become better in handling everyday situations, problems and conflicts (17); the "Violence Prevention Network" in Germany, for both far-right and religious extremists, brings together social work with civic education to challenge the anger of their political view and re-educate them to a democratic way of expressing one's grievances (22).

What these examples show is that "communication" tends to be approached, in a narrow sense, as the sending of messages, the spreading of information, possibly electronically and digitally. When "communication" figures in the description of an activity, this also appears to involve a disproportionate focus on the bites exchanged on the latest technological platforms at the expense of face-to-face communication and the way policy measures produce meanings through their very implementation.

Challenging "messaging"

The tendency to approach communication in counterterrorism as the sending back and forth of messages has already been criticized by Steven Corman, Angela Trethewey and Bud Goodall (2007). Tatham and Le Page (2014, 16), in their *NATO Strategic Communication: More to Be Done?*, underline how these scholars' "Pragmatic Complexity" model, despite its "exceptional" relevance to the North Atlantic Treaty Organization (NATO) strategic communication activities, is still little known. The "Pragmatic Complexity" model, based on the work of Niklas Luhmann (1995), starts from the consideration that 'messages are always interpreted within a larger, ongoing communication system' and that 'communication is the medium through which individuals and groups construct their social realities' (Corman, Trethewey and Goodall 2007, 7). Communication, in this perspective, 'is not an act of one mind transmitting a message to another mind. It is a property of a complex system in which participants interpret one-another's actions and make attributions about the thoughts, motivations, intentions, etc. behind them' (9–10). This means that there is no receiver who just sits "out there" waiting to be impacted by a sender's message and that the reaction of the receiver will be shaped by the interaction between the receiver and the sender with each other and the rest of the system. That is why the authors recommend, among other measures, to desist from wanting to control the message at all costs, since this is simply not possible (12); to consider instead disrupting the *system* of thinking of the adversary; and to expect and plan for failure, since it is not possible to entirely predict the effects of any communication activity.

Even Tatham and Le Page (2014: 19), however, in their report, after having drawn a distinction between the senior military officers 'who get "it" ("it" being the power and complexity of strategic communication) and those whose actions positively demonstrate that they do not,' lament that

> NATO StratCom currently resides in the PDD [Public Diplomacy Division] where it is oft [*sic*] interpreted as strategic public affairs, and where it is never informed by the research and analysis required to develop messaging to not only inform operations, but influence their outcomes.

(21)

Their rhetoric appears to diverge from what the principles of the model of strategic complexity they endorsed only a few pages earlier. This points to a general difficulty, even for those who "get it," to make sense of communication beyond the traditional sender-receiver linear dynamic.

Adding to the useful critique by Corman, Trethewey and Goodall (2007), it is thus worth even more explicitly pointing out the material and social dimensions that a true understanding of communication would require. This is why I next turn to the discussion of materiality.

The "hard" side of communication

Communication is much more material that we are used to think. According to Durham Peters (2015), media should be conceived as 'elemental': for him material reality, even nature, 'the background to all possible meaning' is a medium of communication (2). In addition to this, the human body is 'the most basic of all media' (6). Peters' provocative argument, which aims to radically challenge all our existing assumptions about communication, might sound abstract but, both simplifying it and making it more concrete here for the purpose of this discussion: communication is not always intentional and happens constantly between us and the environment—which we might call, "all that happens around us," policy, or context—through our senses, even if there is no one out there who wants to send us any message. Fuchs, drawing on Luhmann, writes on this point: 'All participants in interaction systems know that they are being perceived, know that others know this [...] In interaction systems, it is impossible *not* to communicate, and even the refusal to communicate is itself a communication of conflict' (Fuchs 1988, 122, his emphasis). In other words, we (or objects, like division walls or an embassy building, for example) can communicate through mere presence. The material infrastructure (whether manmade or natural) also affects, by having an impact on where our bodies can be located, what they can do and perceive, the creation and sharing of meaning.

What would this mean for countering extremism, though? As I explain more in detail elsewhere (Archetti 2012, 73–74), acknowledging the role that objects and infrastructure have in communication can help placing into perspective the current disproportionate focus on digital communication technologies, particularly the Internet and social media, often demonized as terrorists' weapons. Their contribution in enabling (or hindering) extremism should be looked at as part of a convergence of factors. Not only are terrorists able to operate thanks to a range of basic infrastructures—electricity, broadband, cheap air travel, trade agreements between countries that makes it possible to buy goods from foreign countries...—without which the Internet and social media would not be of much help. The messages distributed on the Internet also do not exist in an "online dimension" that is separate from the off-line material world. The most convincing part of ISIS's propaganda, in this perspective, is not the assumed persuasiveness of the group's messages—which some associate with the use of popular culture references or sophisticated visuals inspired by movies, music videos and video games (Lesaca

2015, for instance)—but to the fact that they are sent by an actor who, by de facto controlling a sizeable territory across in Syria and Iraq, is perceived as "winning." It has long being known that the best propaganda is the one that is rooted in reality (Taylor 1990, 15). I will return to the notion of "reality" later, but let's just take the term at face value for now. Would ISIS propaganda have attracted the same number of recruits—according to the UN' Secretary General (Ban 2015), they were over 25,000 from 100 different countries—if the groups had ever only existed as an online loose network of affiliated cells and individuals? It is impossible to know for sure, yet the fact that the number of foreign fighters has been decreasing in parallel with ISIS's loss of territory (The Guardian 2017) raises questions about the supposed "effectiveness" of their propaganda messages alone.

In addition to this, the inability to see the less "soft" and digital sides of communication processes means that many synergies are lost: social workers and teachers who are on the frontline of programs against radicalization are also *communication* experts, yet their experiences tend not to be systematically reviewed and examined. The extent to which useful local lessons can be learned and fed into the practices of those who deal with activities that bear "communication" in their title is thus limited. It also leads to a lack of attention toward the impact of policy. People might end up feeling offended, perhaps even humiliated by it, to the point that well-intentioned measures might produce exactly the opposite effect of what they were designed to achieve. The UK Prevent strategy is an infamous example in this respect. The singling out of Muslim communities as the targets of the program made sense in relation to the setting of clear strategic goals, but backfired in, effectively, defining these communities as the problem. On this point, Maina Kiai, the UN's Special Rapporteur on the rights to freedom of peaceful assembly and of association, even concluded that '[b]y dividing, stigmatising and alienating segments of the population, Prevent could end up promoting extremism, rather than countering it' (Gayle 2016). Alternatively, or in conjunction to this, taxpayers' money is wasted pursuing objectives that are ultimately unrealistic. A program to deradicalize homegrown Islamists that was launched in France in 2015 was declared two years later a "total fiasco." The fact that the deradicalization—approached here as the replacement of ideas with more "democratic" ones—of hardcore extremists is not feasible is known to researchers (Archetti 2014, 142; Khosrokhavar quoted in France24 2017) and practitioners (Korn 2016; Crowell 2017). Yet, large amounts of funding, ignorance about communication processes, and public relations needs might converge into misconceived projects. As one of the Senators who wrote a cross-party report on the program remarked:

> Deradicalization does not exist. They [the "pseudo-experts"] thought they could take someone and wash their brains. In fact, brainwashing doesn't really work and it's a dangerous myth. It's understandable that the government wanted to reassure society after the terror attacks. But it started with a false premise.
>
> *(Samuel 2017)*

Lack of engagement with context

A consequence of not taking materiality seriously is that strategic communication tends to be approached as if it was detached from social and political circumstances. This, in turn, means a general neglect of what would normally be referred to as "context." This, as I am going to illustrate, is the broader environment where communication takes place. It is a relational and constantly moving system that includes actors (governments, organizations, individuals, media organizations) but also technologies, material infrastructure, geography and time (when you do things matter). It must be stressed that, although I choose the term "context" because it is straightforward to grasp, it might not be the most appropriate term because it also suggests some sort of background, perhaps as inert as wallpaper. It implies a detachment and separation from the actors. It is important to remember, though, that actors are themselves part of context.

The failure to seriously engage with context (beyond perhaps a study of audiences' attitudes) translates into four further limitations to understanding how communication actually works. They will be addressed next by providing more theory background and through the examples of the efforts to counter Russian propaganda and the threat posed by "fake news." The first is an overall blindness to the role of relationships and networks in the production, exchange and understanding of meaning. These are overlooked by a focus—and excessive faith—in the reach and transmission affordances of communication technology. The second is a lack of understanding of media effects, particularly the tendency to assume that it is sufficient for propaganda material to be available for audiences to consume it and be influenced by it. A corollary of this tendency, which I will look at as a third point, is assuming that providing facts and "the truth" to audiences will necessarily lead them to adopt the sender's viewpoint. The fourth is the failure to understand that communication dynamics actually change in a polarized context.

Network blindness

The current panic, within public debate, about social media, particularly Facebook, in distributing "fake news" fuels fears that technology is undermining our democracy (Viner 2016; Madrigal 2017) by providing a platform through which disruptive forces, like hostile foreign countries, populist politicians or even teenagers churning out clickbait for money (Kirby 2016), can manipulate voters. Brexit and the election of US President Trump are seen as the outcomes of bad choices taken by a public that was fed the "wrong" information (see Cadwalladr 2017 for one example). Algorithms, the in-built filters that affect which updates will be shown on our newsfeeds, are blamed for contributing to the creation of information bubbles and, since users end up in echo chambers where few or no alternative worldviews exist, political polarization (Del Vicario et al. 2016, for instance). Claims abound that we live in an age of post-truth politics, where facts no longer seem to matter and it is increasingly difficult to tell truth from fabrication apart (Davies 2016). Indeed this is what foreign propaganda, from Russia for example, is said to aim to achieve in the West: a sense of confusion and uncertainty that will lead to political paralysis and distrust of our own governments (MacFarquhar 2016).

These are, of course, all questionable arguments. There are also indications that technology does not produce polarization (Boyd 2017b; Boxell, Gentzkow and Shapiro 2017) and that online ads did not play such a decisive role in the 2016 US election—Hunt Allcott and Matthew Gentzkow (2017, 1) find that 'for fake news to have changed the outcome of the election, a single fake news article would need to have had the same persuasive effect as 36 television campaign ads.' There are also enough political and social reasons to explain the result of the US elections without involving any online "trolling" by foreign powers (Cramer 2016; Electoral Geographies 2016). The former interpretations are nonetheless widespread—perhaps another instance of "fake news" or, as I will explain later, a version of "reality" that fits within the worldview of some elite groups.

These interpretations also neglect the role of networks in shaping our identities and, as a result, our interests and view of the world. Harrison White (2008), in this respect, conceives society as entirely constituted of relationships constantly being negotiated. Identity, who we are, is thus 'produced and sustained within interacting relational networks' (Bearman and Stovel 2000, 74). This also means acknowledging that social reality is made up of the stories, or narratives, that are attached to these relationships and in fact support their very establishment. As White (2008: 20) puts it: 'a story is a [social] tie placed in context.' A family, a party, a terrorist groups or a football team are networks of individuals bound by different narratives about who they are, why they are together and what they are trying to achieve. This affects the way the members of the network relate to the world outside and how they interpret it. In this sense, constellations of relationships also affect our cognitive horizon.

The practical implication of this network-based understanding of reality is that "information bubbles" are not created by algorithms, but by social networks. It is actually not clear the extent to which algorithms feed information that fits into our already existing views. Algorithms, in fact, are designed with purposes that might change depending on the platform they serve—the aim is usually to make the user spend as long time as possible online (Bucher 2017). This does not mean that algorithms do not play any role. However, even if they really fed us mostly information that is in line with our existing worldview, they would only be *amplifying* the bias of our own social networks. Regardless of algorithms, in fact, the narrative that sustains a social network acts, for all practical purposes, as an interpretive filter to any event or content one comes across, indeed even affecting whether these will be noticed at all in the deluge of all that happens and the information available. It is thus the network, not the algorithm, that is the ultimate source of any interpretation bias: all networks are, to greater or lesser extent, information bubbles.

For the purposes of strategic communication, this means that the answers to the questions "How do we break an information bubble?" or "How do we replace an extremist/Russian/populist narrative?" are not purely matters of distributional reach and selection of the appropriate technology or message—not, in alternative terms, an issue of changing the algorithm, pumping out more content, or targeting the "right" narrative more precisely to users through the harvesting of "big data."

To truly break an information bubble, one needs, first, to change the network that supports it: in other words, give alienated individuals opportunities or demonstrate they are not "class B" citizens in the case of countering extremism; provide Russian-speaking Latvians with stakes that make it more costly to protest, when it comes to protecting them from the alleged influence of Russian propaganda: Ieva Bērziņa (2016, 11), in an investigation of the possibility of social destabilization in Latvia, finds for example that '[p]eople who have stable work and an income, who have something to lose and are satisfied with their material circumstances are less likely to protest, take part in demonstrations and to seek change in [the] existing political system.'

Imagined media effects

The second obstacle to the realization of strategic communication is a lack of understanding of media effects, particularly the tendency to assume that the mere existence of propaganda material equals consumption by audiences and influence on them. An example is the concern, visible through a range of alarmist news headlines, that 126 million users *might* have *seen* Russian government-related ads during the past US election (Byers 2017). In the context of NATO, as I observed at the organization's 2016 Information and Communicators Conference, this happens to such an extent that Russian propaganda, particularly the country's TV broadcast across the Baltic countries, is seen as a source of concern even in the presence of evidence that indicates that it is mostly aimed at a domestic Russian public and foreign audiences are not entirely buying into its worldview. In the case of Estonia, for example, ethnic Russians living in the country do not even *like* watching Russian news because 80% of it is about events in Ukraine (Luik 2016). My point is not to dismiss the Russian threat. It is important to remember, however, that effect, such as persuasion to think and act in a way desired by the originator of a message, cannot be simply inferred from the content of the communication.

Fuchs, further to this point, explains how networks have an effect on the interpretation of the content the individuals who belong to them come across. More specifically, he argues that networks "process" anything that heads their way:

> A closed network cannot digest anything "raw," as it were [...]. One might liken this to metabolism and immune systems in organisms; an organism

dissembles and rearranges that which it feeds on, and expels or neutralizes threats to its self-preservation [...] By analogy, how networks react and respond to what it occupies their attention and becomes their work is decided by their own blueprints.

(Fuchs 2009, 354)

This means that no meaning, whether expressed by words or actions, is ever received in the same form as it was sent. If one gets it at all, that is.

This means, first, that strategic communication cannot exist—at least in a country that is not tightly centralized and authoritarian—in the form of complete coordination across all activities of government because those tasked with implementing them in each department will never agree on them. If they do, messages and actions to be communicated will all mean something different to each of them. Even if the messages and actions were perfectly coordinated, they could never be *heard* consistently by all audiences.

As for the implications of the empirical cases discussed here, I am not arguing that we do not need to worry about interference attempts by foreign countries and that Russian propaganda has no effect. But when it comes to using strategic communication to respond to it (if we indeed *need* to do that), it means first acknowledging the possible limitations of what the adversary is doing, as well as ours. One simply cannot predict what the effects of any persuasion activity are going to be a priori. As Rosa Brooks noted in a statement to the US Congress on the evolution of strategic communication and information operations since 9/11 (2011, 36, her emphasis):

> Our strategic communication efforts involve throwing a whole lot of spaghetti at a whole lot of walls, and hoping some of it sticks [...] If it doesn't stick, it's not necessarily because it's badly made. [...] Strategic communication is, in a fundamental sense, an *aspirational* concept. We are never going to get in [*sic*] 100% right; there are always going to be too many variables, many of them beyond our control.

This applies to public diplomacy as much as to countering extremism and foreign propaganda. It should also serve as a counterbalance to the tendency to assume that "our" enemies always get it right—Brooks reminds us, for instance, the (wrong) post-9/11 belief that Bin Laden had "out-communicated" the West (37). Again it does not mean there are no effects. But pretending we know them by extrapolating them from content or erring on the side of caution by assuming the worst-case scenario, is only fueling panics and might in fact lead to an escalation of conflict (Veebel 2016).

A corollary of this tendency, which I will look at next, is assuming that providing facts and "the truth" to audiences will necessarily lead them to adopt the sender's viewpoint.

Truth is not obvious (to those outside your network)

Neither truth nor facts are self-evident. The whole sociology of science is engaged in showing that what we tend to agree upon as facts and scientific truths are in fact the outcome of processes, sometimes battles, where some interpretations come to be seen as natural and taken-for-granted while others are discarded. Fuchs, in this respect, explains that no statement can either be confirmed or falsified in isolation from a wider structure of meaning: 'The meaning of a term comes from its position and role in the network of related terms that make up the overall structure' (Fuchs 2009, 350).

A social network is the source of such structures of meanings, which constitute the 'reality' of that network: 'It [network] decides for and by itself what it considers as possible falsifiers and exceptions, and how it will deal with them, if at all. The reality it builds up is and remains its own' (Fuchs 2009, 354). Truth, in this perspective, is made up of the core beliefs of the network: 'a reality that cannot be imagined any different from what it actually and naturally is and must be' (2009, 357).

This raises some questions about the nature of "fake news." The expression tends to be used to refer to very different phenomena: it might be misleading information that has been circulated for the purpose of deception, or a label applied to reporting one does not like (Stephens 2017). It might also well be, however, the truth from the perspective of the "reality" of a different network. In an age of political polarization, this is to be expected. In fact, contrary to the claim that fake news is a new phenomenon enabled by technological platforms, rumor has always been endemic to conflict (Bloch 1921).

The practical implication of these considerations is that it is not enough to circulate the "right" information to change anyone's mind. The "problem" of fake news is not going to be solved by introducing fines for media companies (Miller 2017), since it is not the technological platforms fake news originates from. Sure, social media might be a convenient sharing tool, but the fact that a piece of news circulates only indicates the existence of a common view of the world among those who share it, supported by belonging to a common network. Fact-checking and media literacy training are not solutions either (Boyd 2017a). Both fact-checking and learning how to "spot" fake news are unfeasible without a broader set of standards against which to measure the accuracy of a fact (i.e. the extent to which it fits "reality") or the "quality" of a piece of information. Again, these reside in networks. In other words, what looks "true" to an individual who belongs to a liberal network might be false by the standard of a "populist." This is precisely what is happening in alternative media consistently and widely claiming that the liberal media is 'lying' (Figenschou and Ihlebæk 2017). According to the arguments of Fuchs' sociology, this is not purely a claim to discredit the liberal media, but contains some, for lack of a better term, truth.

Polarization changes the game

When polarization becomes extreme, the possibility of mutual understanding decreases. This happens in the case of extremism, but also when Republicans and Democrats, or supporters of "Brexit" and voters for "Remain" start living in separate realities. Geographer Christophe Guilluy (2014) convincingly explains how French "populism," far from being the result of electoral manipulation by any nationalist party, is in fact the outcome of a major political re-alignment along new social, cultural and territorial "faultlines." These follow the divide that runs across social classes and towns between the "urban" France, which enjoys the economic benefits of globalization, and the "peripheral" one, where the "popular classes"—who constitute as much as 60% of the country's population—have been squeezed out and excluded. His argument is easily applicable to contemporary political developments in most Western countries.

Material segregation, in turn, increases the isolation of networks, which also means increasingly sealed bubbles of information, as well as lifestyle, and more and more divergent views of the world (Belam 2017). That is why, just like trying to change the mind of an extremist is a waste of time (Archetti 2015, 55), it is important for strategic communicators to recognize that the possibilities for persuasion in a polarized environment are severely limited. In fact, the more polarized an environment, the less communication as simple injection-of-ideas-in-the-ether is going to achieve. It does not matter how good or convincing, in principle, an argument about the benefits of the free circulation of people inside the European Union—which might look self-evident to an academic or a banker—is going to be. That argument will sound equally self-evidently bad from the perspective of a seasonal worker whose livelihood might be jeopardized by the influx of foreign labor. For the seasonal worker to at least consider the possibility that free movement might have a positive side, this must in fact exist, in this case by ensuring that the benefits of European integration and globalization are enjoyed by more sections of society than its elite.

Conclusions

The conclusions of this analysis are threefold: strategic communication as a complete coordination of words and deeds across large organizations is unrealistic; it cannot be approached in isolation from the political and social context; although strategic communication can be a useful tool, its "power" should not be exaggerated, especially in the context of increasing political polarization.

Strategic communication requires a different understanding of communication than the shooting of messages at targets. The acknowledgment that "action" also sends a message is a good starting point, but it cannot be taken further—no matter how good the leadership, organization or coordination of any communication activity is going to be—until the material dimension of communication is taken more seriously. This also involves engaging with the political and social reality we live in. Why are mostly technological platforms or messages from dark forces operating on the Internet and social media blamed for the current political developments when there is evidence of deep fractures within our societies? Are perhaps researchers, policy makers and communication practitioners also trapped in the bubble (which supports a questionable worldview treated as truth) of their own transnational elite networks?

The strategic communication project as it is now conceived cannot possibly lead to more effective governance. To the contrary, the unrealistic expectations about the role of communication and technology in addressing the pressing issues of our time are obfuscating the understanding of the very roots of these problems. It is not some rhetorical silver bullet that is going to solve the polarization at the root of todays' conflict and extremisms. It is more inclusive networks and more equality.

Notes

1 For a collection of definitions by officials, academics and practitioners, see Paul (2011, 185–191).
2 For more examples, see Ferguson (2016) and Ministry of Foreign Affairs (2017). Notice also the presence, in the UK CONTEST strategy (Home Office 2011, 73–76), of a separate chapter on "Counter-terrorism and the Internet."

PART II
Countering violent extremism

6

THE DEMOCRATISATION OF HYBRID WARFARE AND PRACTICAL APPROACHES TO DEFEAT VIOLENT EXTREMISM IN THE DIGITAL AGE

Alicia Kearns

Governments and military organisations globally are grappling with the changing nature of influence: the democratisation of information and truth as the next stage in the development of hybrid warfare and violent extremism.

The Digital Age has ushered in a new battle space and rhythm, with skirmishes taking place in new, often transient, communities – online, in the media and in our homes – often without a word spoken aloud. But the battle continues to be fought over the same territory: the truth. The definition of, acceptance, and embracing of a specific, and absolute worldview. One that breaks down the false constructions, dichotomies, histories and false semblances of unity and peaceful coexistence our enemies claim we have created. The difference in the Digital Age is the soldiers. For the actors in the battle are no longer solely states, the media, or well-financed terror or organised crime groups, it is all of us: because we are all now agents of influence.

In this new world, how do governments and international organisations identify threats and opponents, and empower us, their new foot-soldiers – to rally to their benefit? It is the latter that poses the biggest challenge, and opportunity, since in the era of fake news and the quest for 'truth', such organisations must recognise that power rests more with this democratised diaspora, rather than with media conglomerates and world leaders.

This chapter considers how the Digital Age has transformed the ability of violent extremists to radicalise, recruit and carry out acts of terror. Specifically, how the democratisation of narrative control has aided the spread of violent extremism and created a new generation of agents of influence. Because whilst the battle remains the same: the dominance of one 'truth' over another, it is the Digital Age which has given individuals the ability to become arbiters of truths, above and beyond traditional power and information transference structures. This gives individual violent extremists more opportunity than ever before, but it also creates an entirely new brigade of counter-extremism soldiers: you and me. Across the world individuals have, to lesser and greater extents, embraced their new position as arbiters of truth and information, but not yet harnessed this opportunity to challenge violent extremism and protect their communities.

Eight practical approaches are then proposed to tackle this new battle rhythm and the democratisation of agency to aid practitioners. These are not exhaustive, nor applicable in countering all cases of violent extremism, but offer some feasible and practical solutions for governments, organisations and individuals seeking to counter violent extremism (CVE).

Convergence of violent extremism and hybrid warfare

No definition for hybrid warfare has as yet been adopted universally, it is often used interchangeably with 'grey zone', 'full-spectrum' or 'asymmetric warfare'. One of the first references is by Hoffman, who defines hybrid warfare as an 'adversary that simultaneously and adaptively employs a fused mix of conventional weapons, irregular tactics, terrorism and criminal behaviours in a battle space to obtain their political objectives' (Hoffman 2009, 15).

For the purposes of this chapter, hybrid warfare will be defined as the sustained and persistent strategic deployment of all potential instruments of influence: economic, informational, military, cultural, cyber, diplomatic, intelligence, criminal and civil society – at all levels – to achieve a specific world order or strategic intent. Within this definition, there is no attempt to define a battle space, because with true hybrid warfare no space is off-limits. Hybrid warfare is also not defined as being part of an overt, or declared, war: it is now deployed concurrently in peace and war time. Finally, actors are purposefully not defined, since the most effective enemy is the one who deploys forces actively against you, without your realising that you are under attack, or indeed, even at war.

Whereas previously hybrid warfare was conceptualised as a small component of traditional war efforts, now we must pivot to see traditional kinetic warfare itself as a part constituent of a much broader, multifaceted strategy of influence. This is not a monumental change in perspective, but it is still one sorely lacking. Hybrid warfare is no longer an esoteric afterthought, rather the whole lens through which influences and counter-influences must be focused, organised and fought.

The vast majority of discussions around hybrid warfare, and the actors undertaking it, focus on the actions of governments. However, looking back over the past 50 years, non-state actors, specifically terrorists, are as likely, if not more, to be deploying hybrid warfare against their enemies. Then President of the US, Barack Obama, stated in an interview on CBS' 60 Minutes in 2014 that Daesh otherwise known as the Islamic State or the so-called Islamic State was 'a hybrid of not just the terrorist network, but one with territorial ambitions, and some of the strategy and tactics of an army'.

Non-state actors, and particularly terrorists, have the freedom – due to their rejection of societal norms, values and international rule of law – to fully embrace hybrid warfare and test out its limit and its potential. The absence in most terror groups, of bureaucratic hierarchies and agreement protocols that often slow governments, coupled with limited accountability, and willingness to trial new approaches, allows them to be nimble and effective in deploying these tactics. It is therefore terrorist groups who are increasingly embracing and testing hybrid warfare in their efforts to assert new 'truths'.

Hezbollah is the most frequently cited example of a non-state actor that has adopted hybrid warfare tactics. The terror organisation balances several sets of personalities to enable it to lever as many instruments of influence as possible. It purports to be simultaneously a government and an insurgent group, a military and a political movement, a protector of the culture of its people; and a legitimate media and publishing house. Similarly, the terrorist group Daesh has adopted aspects of hybrid warfare in its attempt to create its so-called Caliphate. Although Daesh successfully occupied a large territory through traditional military means and terrorist tactics, it spent a large amount of its time focused on other efforts to achieve its aims and legitimise itself, employing propaganda, criminality, irregular forces, asymmetric attacks, financial crime and cyber-attacks. In this way, it was more effective and efficient in achieving its aims, than had it solely relied on traditional military opportunities.

The battle for 'truth'

In an era of industrialised hybrid warfare, the most potent weapon is truth. It is the greatest capital that is traded between nation-states and the highest calling terrorists offer to followers. Truth goes to the heart of what we as individuals, groups and constituent members of society believe and therefore determines to whom we pledge our allegiance. Weaponised truth is as effective, if not more effective, than traditional diplomacy, violence or kinetic activity for state and non-state actors. Of course, the 'truth' is now, or arguably always has been, of less countenance than 'the accepted truth'. The challenge we now face is that the definition and acceptance of narratives of 'truth' no longer rests with established, predictable parties; but rather these competing definitions are churned by a plethora of diverse actors – with the truth under constant reinvention and reinterpretation.

Terror groups push the limits of the most potent of all hybrid warfare weapons: to control information and to be the author of 'truth'. This has become the most fiercely fought battle in the Digital Age and is never more evident that in the violent extremism space. The Digital Age offers limitless information, sources and perspectives – and whilst the vast majority of the population benefit from the plethora of information, there are undoubtedly those who experience heightened uncertainty, characterised by a lack of trust in the world itself, in themselves and in their ability to act and rely on the knowledge they themselves hold. Giddens (1990a) terms this a loss of 'ontological security', in this state it is argued that individuals will attempt to attain information and knowledge in order to arm themselves against uncertainty.

Individuals who have been radicalised typically demonstrate an acute need for clarity and certainty as reassurance. Terrorist narratives offer exactly this – cognitive closure – a shortcut to a conclusion that is more or less rational, and this enables the individual not to have to question, challenge or deploy any critical thinking skills, or at least they believe that they already have. The average terror narrative can be undermined through debate and deconstruction – but individuals vulnerable to radicalisation are not seeking high levels of debate or investigation. Quite the opposite, they respond strongly to dogmatic, reductionist, uncompromising and binary world views which provide a sense of security in their simplicity. This reflects Penrod's (2001) work on the concept of uncertainty and how the need for confidence and control becomes of importance to individuals – and terrorists know it.

A loss of trust in the media and long-standing/traditional bastions of information has resulted in individuals seeking out those who provide the 'truth' – a worldview and normative framework they can understand, relate to and embrace without challenge. Beck (1992) put forward the idea of 'reflexive modernisation', where individuals embrace the concept of authoritatively guiding their own actions, diminishing the relevance of more traditional establishments or organisations. You then see individuals seek out information, experiences and relationships that confirm and consolidate this 'truth' to justify their cognitive bias and avoid any engagement or confrontation with, information, experiences and relationships that challenge this, often binary, normative framework. This is a direct response to the high levels of doubt and suspicion which now imbue information. In this circumstance, terror groups offer themselves up as the defenders of the truth, attempting to liberate communities and individuals from the suspicious and corrupt narrative webs in which they have been supposedly entrapped by malign governments, nation-states and organisations.

CVE efforts need to mobilise communities and prevent silence from being filled by far-right, Salafist takfiri jihadist or any other violent extremist narratives. It is not that there isn't a space, and indeed a need, for some counter work, just that the balance is wrong. Governments and organisations need to progress and proactively disseminate the narrative that sets out what they are doing, and why – in order to help counter violent extremist narratives, because in the absence of proactive outreach, conspiracies and untruths spread.

The primary occupation of actors of hybrid warfare and terrorism has become ensuring that their accepted truth is triumphant. Competing narratives are disseminated using all available communication platforms and networks: social media bots and troll farms, website and media platforms, nongovernmental organisations (NGOs), civil society organisations and advocate groups and individuals. Fake news is a well-blunted tool of hybrid warfare, made increasingly powerful with the democratisation of communication. The search for truly credible sources outside traditional media, which is suffering from the lowest levels of trust potentially since the advent of mass media, has made the propagation of narratives as part of hybrid warfare an easier task. The quest for 'truth', specific to the digital and informational age, is leading people to take on becoming generators and producers of news and content; this creates more opportunities for individuals to be agents of influence within hybrid warfare. We are seeing the mass export of narrative control to the masses. Information is often, therefore, the most highly prized, cost-effective and powerful weapon in hybrid warfare.

The creation and propagation of disinformation has become, or arguably has always been, a key method of warfare deployed by terror groups. As with states, the intention is not always to spread false information or to breed confusion, but to establish and cement doubt; on a specific issue or circumstance, or in the possibility of 'truth' actually existing. The most effective disinformation campaigns take existing vulnerabilities and expose them, creating or amplifying conspiracy theories. Organisations and governments must determine whether responding to all violent extremist and terror narratives is in their best interests. When organisations respond to terror narratives, they can risk further cementing the doubt the terror group seeks to imbue and that the government becomes a 'cut-out' for the terror group's intent.

The entrenchment of hybrid warfare, or rather its assimilation to simply war, may also create a 'get-out-of-jail-free' clause for violent extremist and terror groups. When they lose militarily, and the territories they once occupied are liberated, as was seen with Daesh, they continue to exercise influence and find a raison d'être: namely, non-military hybrid efforts such as criminality, terror and undermining legitimate governing structures through the creation of unrest within communities. These tactics can be perpetuated with such meagre resources, it is near impossible to fully eradicate all of these efforts. Therefore, traditional military defeat does not pose an existential threat to these terror organisations – their attacks therefore require a fully multifaceted response in order to be effectively nullified.

Over the coming years, non-state actors will continue to embrace hybrid warfare, and governments will attempt to become more effective and capable of both countering and engaging in hybrid warfare. We have begun, and will now increasingly see, the democratisation of hybrid warfare and its investiture in the masses.

So how do governments and organisations begin to tackle violent extremism in the Digital Age?

Tackling the impact of the democratisation of hybrid warfare in violent extremism

The Digital Age gifts terrorists and malign actors with the ability to enter the minds and hearts of a populace. To sweep at pace across an ecosystem, with very little effort, expertise or costs – but to great effect.

Digital technologies have fundamentally changed the dynamics of conflict, most dramatically they have greatly equalised the playing field. Never before has it been so easy to reach so many, so quickly and with so little cost. The entrenchment of, and access to, mass media and disruptive technology enables terrorists to break out of their echo chambers or closed communities with whom they have long-standing relationships and who previously would have provided their support base.

The information and Digital Age enables terror groups and malign non-state actors to more easily, swiftly and greatly recruit, finance, resource and activate their intentions. In this way, the dynamics of warfare are able to shift away from resting with states and international military organisations, to that of even small, weak, poorly resourced or niche organisations in the most remote parts of the world – enabling them to force project internationally. Indeed, there is good evidence that governments in Europe are funding radical political groups at grassroots level in order to leverage these movements' influence, obfuscating their own involvement and furthering their geopolitical aims – yet another tactic of hybrid warfare.

The Digital Age has significantly increased societal threats as the Internet and social media platforms have facilitated individuals to seek out and find those who hold views they find attractive, but that those in their real-world communities reject. Individuals are now able to seek out, locate and explore the most heinous of views with other lone individuals across the globe. This then enables individuals to legitimise their views by finding the few others with similar views and gaining acceptance. Coupled with the perception in this age, that speed of contact, equates to strength of feeling, these individuals celebrate one another's perverse views. The ability for terror groups to be permanently available, and permanently sympathetic – waiting for a vulnerable individual to make contact – plays a key part in their ability to recruit new members.

To orchestrate such tactics, the barriers to entry are now extremely low – a malign individual needs little more than a laptop and an Internet connection. This has brought an end to the days of more physical techniques of communication that are not only labour or capital intensive such as leaflet drops, whisper campaigns or hiding messages in bread rolls – but often leave a considerable trail of evidence to incriminate the perpetrator. These subversive actions could be discovered, tracked and uncovered, but with the Internet and the advent of end-to-end encryption, social media platforms and greater digital literacy, discovery can be more easily eluded and identities obfuscated.

This is inherently beneficial for terror groups. The reduced footprint of recruiters – as a result of encrypted platforms and the Digital Age as a whole – enables terror recruiters to reach in to the minds of potential recruits in multiple countries, at the same time, without their parents, friends or loved ones having any awareness. The time lapse on social media also enables recruiters to construct the identity they feel recruits would best respond to, as face-to-face recruit makes it more difficult to construct an entirely false recruiter identity, or more difficult to maintain a pretence. The recruiter is able to swiftly ensconce themselves in the target community and operate with far greater freedom than they would in the real world. Equally once terror groups task their followers – swiftly, discreetly and without cost using social media – the terrorists themselves require little to carry out their attacks. Again, the Internet is used to research their target. Weapons can either be sourced online, or may even be a computer itself (in instances of cyber-attacks).

Hybrid warfare, particularly acts perpetrated by non-state actors, is greatly facilitated by the ease and immediacy of online communication. This allows terrorists to pursue increasingly innovative methods to increase their range and their influence – at a fraction for the cost, effort and risk of more traditional military means.

Here are eight ways in which organisations can further effectively CVE in the Digital Age:

1. End copy-cat counter approach
2. Reactive narrative teams
3. Native narratives
4. Credible voices
5. Non-securitised engagement
6. Deployment of everyday foot-soldiers
7. Take a steer from hybrid warfare
8. Embedding strategic communications into institutional responses

End copy-cat counter approach

Governments rightly identify, analyse and assess the communications approaches taken by terror groups in order to effectively design mechanisms to stop them from propagating their messages and using communications to achieve their desired outcomes, to understand their pull-on recruits and to identify the terrorists' targets. Too often however, organisations create duplicate programmes to counter the violent extremists, or focus on the platforms terrorists exploit rather than designing solutions to render terrorist efforts inert.

There is an ongoing preoccupation with the efforts of social media companies to counter hate and violent extremism on their platforms. Whilst it is true to say that such platforms can and should, do more, it is better to focus efforts on the underlying causes and tools driving recruitment and dissemination of extremist narratives.

A straightforward example is how to tackle terrorists on the platform Twitter. The long-standing focus has been on removing users' accounts. This often descends into an endless cycle of 'whack-a-mole' with new accounts promptly spawned – with little chance of social media platforms, or those reporting, keeping up. All this achieves is temporary respite and may drive terrorists and their recruiters further underground, on to more encrypted and more difficult-to-track platforms. Intelligence collection relies on the use of more mainstream channels to light up the activities of terrorists, sometimes even their locations can be inadvertently disclosed by terrorists or other malign actors carelessly posting content whilst their locator services are enabled. Intelligence gathering is key for the long-term defeat of this violent extremism, so in instances where terrorists freely reveal themselves, it may be counterproductive to raise their guard or push them underground. Therefore, a different approach is needed.

We need to step back and explore how terrorists utilise platforms – not just their existence on them. Different terrorist organisations and groups within them use individual and specific hashtags to communicate with one another. Instead of cracking down on the accounts, a solution might be to instead flood their hashtags with counter-narratives, or more accurate (and readily verifiable) information. You can infiltrate them with counter-messaging, messages that undermine the credibility of the group and confidence of its followers, and start to seed your own messages. This may only achieve effect with just a few followers, but those individuals have their own online and off-line networks, and doubt you seed will begin to spread. Alternatively, if terrorists are falsely claiming success in a particular area: flood the hashtag with images of the reality showing opposing forces in control. Even without a silver bullet to refute their prime narrative – it is to possible to at least flood their hashtag with redundant chatter – making it difficult to for them to unite and gather momentum.

There is a risk in the age of social media that the ability of a terror group to repeatedly organise themselves and communicate with one another on a specific hashtag will be seen as a failure by government to properly monitor, and shut down, a terror groups ability to manoeuvre. Individuals and organisations countering violent extremism need to balance up the desire to castrate the group from communicating and potential media reporting and criticism that the extremists are able to communicate, with the potential benefits, intelligence and opportunities that arise by not curtailing their hashtag use or communications portal. This often requires a decision to ignore substantial criticism from the media and others for a 'failure' to remove them. The balance sits in an assessment of the significance of those individuals taking part in the discussion on that platform or via a specific hashtag. Identification of channels and conversations streams used by terrorists and violent extremists presents an opportunity for intelligence collection; not just identification of members, details on plans and efforts, but also for intelligence on how the groups communicate. But moreover, it presents an opportunity to intercede in a more insidious and effective manner. If CVE organisations, social media platforms and governments identify a communications channel, it may be better to attempt to infiltrate the group, and cede narratives and messages that breed discontent, confusion and ultimately defections or internal strife, than immediately, as a matter of course, remove them from the platform.

As organisations countering violent extremism often jump on hashtags being deployed by terrorists, terrorists do just the same. This has seen some organisations freeze and believe that they should stop using the hashtag or platform. Do not stop if violent extremists begin to use your hashtag – there is a reason for it. Either you have irritated them sufficiently with your output that they felt the need to jump on to your efforts to counter them or subsume them – you've achieved a goal of distracting them from their goals, forcing them to become the rebutters. This is a measure of effect. Or, they've sensed an opportunity to spread their messages using you as a channel. Each situation is of course unique, but I for one do not plan to be driven off a hashtag by terrorists. Should your hashtag or platform come under attack, take a moment to review the circumstances, and decide how best to respond. In this situation, you are continuing to get your information out, and now a number of their members, followers and potential recruits are seeing it too – they have opened up an additional audience for you – and you may well get through to them should you adapt and respond.

A note on social media platforms. The democratisation of technology, information and hybrid warfare has seen the advent of social media platforms. Currently, the majority of social media channels are putting significant efforts in to resisting classification as publishers. This will become even more acute in the coming years, but it is high time that these platforms recognise that every second they facilitate individuals to be publishers, and that protecting the online communities they create is a responsibility. When an individual or organisation signs up to platforms such as YouTube, Snapchat, Facebook and Twitter, they agree to adhere to a certain set of principles and rules, which generally cover the same concepts of respect, tolerance and non-acceptance of threats of abuse or violence. As such, these platforms are issuing editorial guidelines to users, and when these are not upheld, the platform has a responsibility to remove the content and not in the sclerotic or arbitrary manner too often displayed.

Reactive narrative teams

The immediate aftermath of terror attacks is a peak period for recruiting 'fanboys', supporters and current or future terrorists. Individuals will often search online for information about the individual who has carried out the atrocity, the organisation to which they are affiliated, the cause to which they pledge their allegiance and their rationale for carrying out the atrocity. During this information-seeking period, individuals are essentially hand-raising, they want to learn more and are seeking to understand the rationale for the act of terrorism – an ideal time for extremists to identify potential recruits and attempt to radicalise them. Without the Digital Age, individuals would be unable to be so quickly or easily identified, at such great distances by violent extremists online – now a single comment can allow terrorist recruiters access to the mind of a vulnerable individual.

The most effective CVE initiatives are activated when individuals are cognitively most receptive to an intervention. The immediate aftermath of a terror attack, or an incident of consequence such as the liberation of a city from a terror group, ideally meets this brief. Organisations should pre-prepare materials, very few specifics are required, that can be released through preexisting official and unofficial channels on social media using the hashtags being deployed by recruiters, interested groups and the general public. Additionally, to reach as many vulnerable audiences as possible, counter efforts should use the main hashtags used by terror groups when communicating in general within their posts.

Some organisations have begun to embrace this approach, but ideally beyond simply pushing out pre-approved messages and rebuttal lines, organisations should use these opportunities to engage in meaningful discussion with individuals asking questions or seeking more information. This quick response requires organisations to have on-call, skilled communicators ready to engage.

Potentials obstacles to this approach will likely be raised by organisations fearful of what individuals undertaking conversations on their behalf might say in their attempt to redirect an individual, but this can be managed by creating conversation trees which cover most of the topics or questions likely to come up, and then training individuals and giving them the authority required to carry out conversations. Ideally, these individuals would be psychologists or social workers expert in working with radicalised individuals. Governments and large organisations may also baulk at the need to give sufficient authority to the individuals and organisations carrying out these conversations – this must be given.

Timely engagement with individuals reaching out for information about the motives and actions of terror groups can effectively dissuade them from seeking more information, adopting any sympathy or becoming active supporters of violent extremists as it reaches them during a period where they are not just receptive to, but actively seeking, information. Additionally, many will be open to critical thinking and assessment of narratives they engage with during this time.

Native narratives

Most counter terror campaigns are just that – focused defensively on countering terrorists' narratives and tactics. Governments and international organisations typically spend over 90% of their efforts countering terrorist groups' output. However, this runs contrary to most military doctrines which discourage forever fighting on the back foot.

So how have we become stuck on this back foot? The majority of counter-terrorism communications strategies identify the core narratives of the enemy and then create counter-narratives that can be reproduced across a multitude of platforms and spokespeople which expose the reality of that narrative or seek to undermine it. Responding to the terrorists' narratives and arguing in the arena they construct, on the issues they want to discuss, their battleground? It is the responsibility of governments and organisations to frustrate and impede terror groups. We need to drag the enemy, kicking and screaming, in to the arenas in which we're comfortable or control, which undermine and eviscerate the false claims, conspiracies or twisted interpretations on which their narratives sit.

One of the strongest measures of success is moving a terror group's propaganda machine away from pushing out materials focused on their own priorities and editorial schedule, to having to create products and narratives to rebut and counter your claims and narratives. Take Daesh, which claimed it was militarily invincible, and that it is a provider of a legitimate and fully functional state. To counter these claims, organisations can and should push out evidence of how Daesh is losing territory and fighters as well as evidence that its claims of statehood are lies. These are factual issues, not complicated and debatable issues of religion or ideology. The goal is to be sufficiently effective that the terror group has to issue comment and products to counter your claims. In so doing, they are also inadvertently spreading your claims or evidence of the reality, but more importantly they are no longer setting the agenda. But to counter them, we must also move beyond rebutting their core narratives as these are not native narratives, but important counter-narrative efforts.

The next step towards creating native narratives is to identify the terror group's vulnerabilities and to expose them. To relentlessly distribute narratives and communications products that expose, highlight and drive home falsities, internal disputes, failings, and expose how groups twist information, history or religious belief for their own benefit. The goal is to force the terror group or violent extremists to again devote their efforts to rebutting your narratives. As these groups will label governments as the enemy, liars or not to be trusted, governments sometimes believe that they will not be perceived as credible if these narratives and products are issues by government accounts. This fails to remember that there is, on some cognitive level, a belief that democratic, Western, governments must be telling some element of the truth. It is crucial that governments do not forget that whilst for many audiences they may not be the most credible, they must continue to proactively distribute factual information. Simply by telling the truth, you are forcing the terrorist to be deterred from their primary effort, and by responding to you, they are spreading your factual truths, as well as their rebuttal. This is half-way towards creating native narratives.

A true native narrative helps establish and maintain trust with those communities with whom an organisation works and supports. Too often the narratives pushed out by organisations and governments are ultimately in response to an issue or to justify actions. Effective countering requires a concerted, planned and regular release of materials and creation of opportunities which help embed within the community the organisation's overall goals, the efforts they are taking to keep the audience safe and CVE, and why this approach is being taken. This requires first an understanding of how your organisation is perceived by the community/audience, the rationale and beliefs underpinning these views, and the specific manner in which they receive (and trust) information about your organisation and the manner in which they describe it – a top-line target audience analysis. Too often when managing issues of national security, audience analysis is only undertaken on vulnerable audiences – failing to recognise why an organisation works as it does: to keep its communities safe.

The next step is to use this insight gained to devise a unifying narrative and key messages which are then embedded in every engagement, media interaction, stakeholder activity or social media output. Too often organisations forget that their every output, be it programmes they are running in-country, a reactive media statement, speech, tweet, music video, Snapchat filter, graffiti or TV programme, can be designed to help deliver behaviour change – greater understanding of your native narrative and, therefore, greater trust in your work and counterterrorism efforts. Whilst some organisations design overall narratives for their departments or teams, these are usually put to one side and rarely incorporated in to daily output, let alone converted in to a programme of proactive outreach scheduled to deliver and embed said messaging.

A potential risk to this approach is that the native narrative may create a new series of topics for the terror group to criticise the organisation over or create new critical conversations about you or your organisation. However, even if they believe that have identified a new angle to attack or undermine you, they are automatically on the back foot, as they are attacking you on a topic or action that you have chosen to make a public point of discussion, and you will be better placed to win the narrative. Additionally, your narrative will have been issued first, and therefore the audience is more likely (psychologically) to believe it, over the counter-narrative of the terrorists.

Violent extremists will often seek to proactively drive a wedge between their targets for radicalisation and community organisations/governments. By proactively deploying a native narrative, your audience will have received, internalised and understood why you seek to deliver specific efforts, to what effect and in whose interest efforts before the violent extremists seed division. By pushing out this narrative (ideally first), the extremists will have to work that much harder to undermine it. Organisations working to CVE must move to a model of deploying native narratives if they wish to defeat terror groups and keep communities with them.

Credible voices

As previously detailed, control of narratives is no longer top-down, resting in the hands of just a few powerful groups, the media and governments. This democratisation empowers individuals and civil society groups to better combat violent extremism and the narratives that underpin it.

The use of credible voices in CVE messaging efforts has become a primary area of investment for governments and counterterror organisations. Governments make considerable efforts to identify the most credible voices within audiences and communities at risk of being radicalised. However, the definition of credible has been limited to religious or celebrity voices; and even then the celebrity's religion is often a decisive factor. This raises the question as to whether religious voices are best placed to CVE and what other alternative may also be utilised.

When looking at why people commit violent extremist actions, we seek to establish the trigger of an action and its motivation. With violent extremists, the core motivations frequently lead back to issues of human security, attractiveness of criminality, safety, enfranchisement, shelter, food and opportunity. This reveals the basis of most human decision-making: generally, we make decisions based on self-interest, protecting ourselves and our families. The English Defence League is a far-right, ostensibly non-religious group in the UK responsible for encouraging extremist, and often violent, views – and employing numerous familiar tactics of hybrid warfare. Joel Busher (2015) identified is his ethnography of the extremist group that members primarily identify themselves as victims, members of the 'true' British society who have become victims of a 'two-tier' system of British justice, victims of a militant 'other' which in most case they have defined as Muslims. Recruits form bonds of friendship around this perception of being alienated, mistreated by the system. Any failures or issues in their personal circumstances, be it employment, relationships or, more widely, are a result of this attack on them which the institutions of government are either ignoring, or actively colluding with against them. The enemy is clearly defined. This fact pattern underscores the need for governments to not simply condemn extremism, but to further nullify narratives of alienation and collusion – and instead provide positive information that keeps individuals enfranchised within society. This same approach can be applied effectively in most cases of extremism.

This isn't to say there aren't solely religious motivations for some. Undoubtedly, we must continue to empower religious credible voices and give them the skills to challenge hate and division wherever they encounter it, but we must understand who truly influences those vulnerable to radicalisation, and empower them. Focusing on faith or religious justifications to stop violent extremism will always bring its challenges, because by its nature, religion is about interpretation. Beyond that challenge, there is a more fundamental issue: the violent extremists we seek to impede and undermine are terrorists first, and supposed members of religions or organisations second. If one assesses the motivations of individuals for joining or supporting violent extremist groups, more often than not they boil down to a history of, or inclination towards, criminality, violence, extreme and obsessive tendencies, and a desire for fame whether manifested as infamy or revenge. Or alternatively issues of human security and provision for themselves and their families.

The goal in CVE is to create more barriers to entry and to insert more opportunities for critical thinking. Therefore, credible voices constitute those who can create barriers to criminality and violence, as well as those who can build barriers to adoption or utilisation of religion as an excuse or motivation for violence. For too long, governments have focused too heavily on employing primarily religious voices for credibility – particularly when tackling Salafi takfiri extremism. Alternative credible voices within networks may include the following:

Responsible citizens

Following the terror attacks witnessed in recent years, numerous individuals have raised their voices and reported individuals of concern. In this hand-raising action, some of these good citizens are marking themselves as individuals willing to step up, who are capable of identifying individuals at risk. These are the credible voices, acting out of concern for our communities who need to be empowered to go in to their communities and hold meaningful conversation. Governments and CVE organisations should not overlook such individuals becoming credible voices – witnesses who become actors empowering their own communities and in so doing protecting them.

Community opinion nodes

These are individuals within a community who play an active role in shaping the opinions of others. If we consider each community or geographic area of concern individually, we will identify individuals who have the ability to shape opinion or drive debate. This may be the local children's football coach, a local radio presenter, a school bullying champion or the manager of a local recording studio. These voices will be able to hold discussions and initiate critical thinking in a less hostile environment. Crucially relationships are not defined by an individual's risk of radicalisation – resulting in better outcomes and trust.

A potential limitation of this approach is the inability of non-religious voices to debate or counter highly nuanced religious points made in support of violence or extremism. However, often the most effective counter-extremism campaigns do not counter proposed religious authorities or religious perspectives, but instead focus on discussing the key motivations of humans, such as safety, enfranchisement, shelter, food and opportunity, or basic human decency and community, which inextricably underpin much of the radicalising narratives deployed by extremists.

Non-securitised engagement

Governments, international alliances and peacekeeping organisations need to normalise the holding of conversations around human security issues, particularly terrorism and violent extremism, with the communities they protect. Currently, public CVE debates (if held at all) take place largely in the context of counterterrorism programmes (for example, 'Prevent' in the UK) and take place almost exclusively with identified as 'at-risk' audiences. Positing anti-radicalisation discussions in such stark terms as national security – so-called 'securitised' engagement – tends to be divisive, alienating and counterproductive. This is particularly the case in the aftermath of a terrorist atrocity when a knee-jerk response can aggravate already inflamed sensitivities. Instead, governments should look to pursue 'non-securitised' engagement, whereby conversations are not held solely due to thinly veiled security concerns – but instead form a reassuring pattern of information and support within all communities.

The foremost role of government is to keep its people safe, now whilst this takes many forms, protecting them from violent extremism and terror attacks is one of the most pertinent. Governments need to break down the walls that have been constructed around national security – barriers originally put in place to limit public concern in periods where information was strictly controlled by governments and the media, and prior to the Digital Age. In an era where information abounds at the click of the button, communities and individuals perceive an absence of information and engagement as aloof, and for some, demonstrative of malign intent.

It is commonly accepted that governments are not credible in the CVE space. This is unacceptable, governments should not be written off as having no credibility when in fact it is security services and instruments of government, that have the most credibility of all when it comes to identifying, understanding and tackling threats to keep our nations safe. It is the role of communicators in government to re-establish credibility, and to do that through meaningful engagement. This is not to advocate that one-to-one engagements to de-radicalise an individual are best undertaken by civil servants or politicians wearing government name tags, nor that government representatives should insert themselves into communities and attempt to have the same credibility. Instead, governments need to hold meaningful dialogue with all its communities and not just those identified as at risk of radicalisation. Governments must stop running from, or dismissing, their own credibility and recognise where they are credible, owning those platforms and opportunities.

Amongst communications professionals, the notion that the general public poses a short attention span is an unhelpful and antiquated mantra. This has resulted in decades of government communications efforts focused on top-down and elusive statements. These serve to end, rather than enable, discussion, or more crucially, critical thinking. In this way, governments have increasingly isolated themselves from meaningful debate and opportunities to explain government motivations, policy decisions and strategic intent; and in so doing reduced the potential for populations to engage in critical thinking around our national security agendas. This vacuum allows radicalising narratives to take root. Critics of this argument might state that on national security the issues are too complicated, too nuanced and too critical to our safety for the general public to be encouraged to debate and reflect upon. However, personal security is a key quality of a nation and is rightly an existential preoccupation. It is these common concerns around human security, and an absence of persuasive or relevant input from a government, that can lead people to seek out further information elsewhere. It is in these alternative channels where the spark of hatred, alienation, racism or extremism can be lit.

Governments need to normalise conversation with the public – particularly those who are disillusioned – about all policy areas, especially home and foreign affairs when tackling violent extremism. A tangible example is that of social media: government accounts will experience a high demand from users for answers to legitimate and fairly worded questions about government policy and actions. The general public, academics and even politicians will proactively seek out government-controlled social media accounts to request information or clarification. These channels gain considerable credibility through this two-way dialogue, and this is an incredibly effective tool to reinforce government narratives not through repudiation but by information. Such channels are not designed explicitly as de-radicalisation tools; however, their effectiveness is indisputable, simply by engaging with individuals who predominantly want to be simply recognised, or afforded the courtesy and the respect of a response. Yet very few governments have recognised the true power of digital diplomacy to effect behaviour change, and still treat social media as a vanity mirror.

Similarly, governments should take greater steps towards working with special interest (for example, Black, Asian and Minority Ethnic, free sheets, foreign language, special interest) and local media outlets and online channels. These media enjoy greater levels of trust than many national media, but may not have the resources to comprehensively cover complex matters of government policy. Indeed, it is a sad fact that minorities may be some of the more likely to experience social marginalisation (for example, poverty, homelessness; or a lack of access to housing, work or health care) – and therefore, it is all the more reason for governments to support and engage more, not less, with media who have their ears. Sadly, too many governments take the exact opposite approach, such as preventing their departments responsible for policing or prison services from engaging with media representative of those communities most disproportionately represented in police engagements or prison. Through these channels, not only can governments release informative content – for example, countering the many misnomers around drones (Remotely Piloted Air Systems and Unmanned Air Vehicles) –, but in the long term, greater levels of trust and cooperation between publications and governments will mean the government is solicited for background guidance or fact-checking on less contentious news stories – offering a trusted and credible outlet for the government's non-securitised messaging.

More broadly, a fundamental issue remains that for too many governments view communications as a one-way road and solely for the creation of publicity: the chance to put a bow around an already concluded and delivered policy. Communications are best delivered with two-way engagement between governments, their respective departments and either publications, trusted agents of influence, communities or individual members of the public. Additionally, by holding ongoing engagement with communities, outside periods of specific concern, governments and authorities will be able to form more positive lines of communication enabling them to quickly hold dialogue with them at times of crisis, and be more positively received. The main potential risks arise from poorly planned and conducted engagement with the public, or ineffective preparation of the individuals who will be engaging with them.

On matters of CVE and terrorism issues, governments need to enfranchise individuals to become everyday amplifiers of non-radical narratives. Without information and engagement, malign actors can pervert public discourse – gaining the upper hand in their hybrid war. Empower the public with information, provided in a genuine space of meaningful engagement, and they will become your foot-soldiers, tackling warped narratives without your tasking and defeating extremist narratives.

Deployment of everyday foot-soldiers

Hybrid warfare will become increasingly democratised; the process has already begun. As such, we need to move analysis and discussion beyond a narrow focus on state and increasingly non-state actors, to look at the role of the global population: individuals as agents of influence.

Today, anyone can become an actor and contribute to hybrid warfare efforts. Individuals can now more easily create and rally civil society movements with malign intent, expose information, hack platforms or disrupt individuals' lives, boycott goods and services, create media platforms and leak information or spread mistruths. These are just some of the tactics individuals can deploy. But it is the use of information in hybrid warfare that has become the most democratised.

The rationale for hybrid warfare by states and non-state actors is easy to understand, but what would motivate individuals to become agents of hybrid warfare? The motivation will most likely rest not only in the desire, or for some the innate need, to hold and propagate the 'truth', but in the desire and ability to effect change in some meaningful way. Ownership of action and immediacy of impact is high thanks to the Digital Age, and carrying out an action which you control, and seeing an immediate and (often significant) impact from it, is something which many may feel is absent from their lives – an ability to influence the world and effect change. Individuals are increasingly seeking opportunities to establish and project their identities, and gain social currency for doing so, through social movements.

Further to this context, it has now become mainstream for individuals to be content producers, and, in this way, arbiters of 'truth' and information. Social media platforms, particularly YouTube and Snapchat, thrive solely on the decision of individuals to create, consume and share content. Individuals are being continually encouraged to be online authors, and whilst many choose to stick to a specific area of expertise they already have, many will feel inclined to share their views and summations on contentious news or content. It is, therefore, vital that governments and CVE organisations do more to spread accurate information about their efforts and goals and to win the general public to their side. This requires a step-change towards proactive media output, rather than rebuttal units or the lacklustre release of press notices. Government press offices are prone to employ dated methods and formulaic releases even when attempting to be proactive. Genuine proactively requires a strategic, sustained and planned communications schedule with meaningful engagement online and off-line, in person and through the media (as directed by the consumption habits and trusted channels and networks of the target audiences), to achieve genuine effect and meaningful attitudinal and behavioural change. News stories, opinions and perceptions are now bottom-up and that requires a drastic re-thinking in communications.

Some recent examples of individuals electing to undertake hybrid warfare include hackers attacking and driving Daesh off open-source platforms and areas of the dark web. This action is broadly welcomed, as it limits Daesh's ability to communicate and it prevents individuals from being able to view and share Daesh propaganda. These individuals have chosen to assist in the global effort to defeat Daesh and become hybrid warfare actors. The motivations could be solely to help defeat a terror group, or potentially an attempt to show that Daesh's prop-aganda, Internet and hacking abilities – despite being praised by the media – are actually still substandard to that of their own.

We will see blurring between terrorist and violent extremist groups and state actors. But we will also increasingly see the inability to distinguish, or heavy blurring between, non-state actors, and individuals who have elected to carry out terror attacks. Take most recently and notably the terror group Daesh. The media and academics hotly debate and anticipate whether a terrorist attack had been formally directed by the terror group, or whether the individual, or group, were simply foot-soldiers who took it upon themselves to follow the terror group's narrative and well-known intentions and carry out an attack without for-mal direction. Terrorism can now operate under a franchise model: terror leaders curate content, provide branding and direct strategic communication; but it is the individuals who open new branches, take the vast majority of the risk, and ultimately serve the deadly product. With such agency in so many hands, gov-ernments must leverage the agency of regular citizens and other trusted agents of influence – in order to effectively counter the narratives proffered by terrorists.

Concurrent to the democratisation of authorship, as digital technologies fur-ther evolve, particularly those that mimic human interaction and responses cur-rently used for online shopping or help chats, hybrid warfare interventions will evolve to be undertaken by artificial intelligence and machines. The role of bots in hybrid warfare is well recognised: troll farms, supported by bots help spread disinformation, undermine credibility and swarm accounts in order to intimi-date individuals and organisations towards a specific strategic intent. The chal-lenge rests with Internet service providers and social media platforms to develop technologies that seek out and nullify bots, to prevent their being deployed as the cheapest warfare efforts. We may find we are already in a period where hybrid warfare requires less manpower and relies on automation, and this will only be-come more sophisticated and entrenched.

This period will be the most dangerous phase of hybrid warfare we have yet seen, as individuals are able to obfuscate their identities, objectives and backers (if any). However, the democratisation of hybrid warfare creates new opportuni-ties for state actors nimble enough to embrace them – namely, the ability to veil efforts, making them even more effective. If governments engage meaningfully with communities online and off-line, they are able to activate entire movements online. Communicating with the public around security issues: governments, international organisations and NGOs can form and deploy digital and at the kitchen table foot – soldiers to fight the daily online skirmishes for them.

Organisations and governments may worry that this approach has limitations in that it could leave them liable to be responsible for the actions of these foot-soldiers. But this is not the case. A more informed public can only strengthen the state of society. The information given to the public and communities must be accurate and provided in a manner that is accessible – that is the sole responsibility of organisations.

If governments have effectively engaged in non-securitised discussion and information sharing with their communities, then these individuals will be able to deploy effective counter-narratives for them. Whilst Western governments' bureaucracies and risk aversion may slow the process of activating supportive stakeholders and the general public, even a slight nudge towards more regular and meaningful engagement could create a sea-change in how individuals relate to, and support, their governments and see individuals and communities choose to activate themselves as narrative supporters and propagators, without request.

Take a steer from hybrid warfare

The democratisation of hybrid warfare is further blurring the lines between state and non-state actors, giving states increased deniability in the murky world of accountability and international scrutiny. The question of where the agency of individuals ends, and the inciting of actions by state or non-state actors begins, will occupy more of our security services' time and help malign efforts to achieve their ends.

For example, with the downing of Malaysian Airlines Flight 17, Russia was able to benefit from, and potentially capitalise on, its existing efforts to create proxies, deploy and support deniable forces, breed dissent and undermine the Ukrainian Government – all hybrid warfare efforts. Faced with these efforts, the average person, even today, may not feel confident saying with certainty whether the aircraft was shot down by Russian troops, or by Russian-backed troops, or by Ukrainians. This is despite the UK's Mi6 concluding that 'beyond any reasonable doubt … Russian military supplied and subsequently recovered the missile launcher' as reported in their annual report (2017).

One of the most effective uses of communications in hybrid warfare is to breed confusion. The Russian Government has successfully obfuscated who the actors are, created multiple narratives and conspiracy theories, and enforced strict message control from Russian outlets and spokespeople to ensure their version of the incident is repeated, and therefore hopefully accepted. As reported in McClatchy DC Bureau (2017), Bellingcat – a credible and well-recognised organisation which undertakes extensive online investigations using open-source materials – has successfully located and verified a recording of a Russian General ordering the missile's launch, corroborating numerous other elements of their research into the tragedy. These facts have secured far less media attention than warranted – this was due in part to the efforts of specific entities and governments – specifically Russia, to discredit the organisation for fear of its ability to identify, collate and evidence hybrid warfare efforts. The world's increasing awareness of hybrid warfare can be seen with individuals and governments actively (and falsely) labelling genuine organisations – such as Bellingcat and the White Helmets in Syria as reported internationally (Guardian 2017) –, proxies or fake NGOs to discredit the evidence-based information they are making available to the public. One of the greatest success stories in hybrid warfare may be Russia's successful insertion of the narrative that the West still holds a Cold War mentality, which 'preys upon a very Western sense of self-criticism and guilt' as Michael Weiss puts it in his 2017 article for the *Daily Beast*.

Challenges around finding conclusive, or convincing evidence, that groups who 'pop-up' with the goal of progressing a specific agenda are backed by or aligned to, nation-states will become increasingly difficult. These proxy groups – deniable forces – are perhaps the most desirable, as they can be argued to be operating without direction, albeit to the beat of an actor's drum. One of the biggest changes the Digital Age introduces is the increasing likelihood that groups and individuals will unknowingly be acting under a government or terror group's instruction. With implicit or even unknown and unsolicited state support, non-state actors see their foes conveniently vanquished, their channels clear and the objectives in sight. Our challenge remains to identify these invisible hands of influence in order to best nullify the treat that these malign forces pose.

The following example demonstrates how a simple tactic and how varied hybrid warfare tactics can be. In this example, a terror group recruits, establishes and funds a publicly non-aligned music group and then propagates its music imbued with their messaging. This musical group could achieve a significant following and attract supplicants at speed across the Internet, with little to no cost, without their enemy even realising that this musical group exists to further the terror group's goals. This demonstrates the importance of governments and organisations being attuned to these new threats and having the inventiveness and discretion to respond to them.

Organisations should include spreading disinformation about terror groups and breeding confusion in their efforts to effectively counter violent extremists. There are of course limitations, for example, governments are less likely to be able to spread disinformation; however, they can spread information which breeds confusion amongst violent extremists and their supporters.

Embedding strategic communications into institutional responses

Governments and international organisations have yet to fully adopt an operating model in which they can adequately respond to, and tackle, hybrid warfare and violent extremism. The importance of effective communications by government and strategic deployment of communications is paramount, but governments will need to adapt to a warfare where the desire to control information is increasingly redundant.

Governments are beginning to focus their efforts on developing full-spectrum responses to terrorist groups and networks, in recognition that the threat they face is hybrid in nature although the majority remain focused on hybrid threats arising from nation-states. However, they have yet to adequately adopt and deploy the masses and individuals.

There are also institutional changes required. Few militaries treat information operations as a specialisation; however, investment in this area is not only an effective tool on today's battlefields – it can also be an efficient (and indeed low-cost) strategy to neutralise the enemies of the future. If every battle is won or lost before it is ever fought – communications can provide a critical tool in preventing a battle entirely. Therefore, a fundamental re-think is needed about how governments, and indeed organisations across civil society should imagine the roles they play in tackling societal threats in the Digital Age.

Militaries need to review the role of the modern information operations officer. Too often existing resources and past threats play too great a role in determining tactics and approaches. To beat violent extremists, the arena of influence needs to be brought forward from the side lines of the battlefield. Operators require new tools, training and permissions to effect change at radicalisation touchpoints. Equally strategic communications needs to be incorporated into training operations – in recognition of the offensive role strategic communications plays. Whether it be incorporating the finding of enemy materials, the use of radio to discombobulate and spread disinformation, or the use of media stories to confuse the enemy.

Embedding the creation of opportunities for critical thinking is also vital. Violent extremists and recruiters deploy oversimplified stereotypes and target unreflective thinkers with false binaries and absolutist narratives that they hope will bounce around the target's echo chambers. Recognising that one of the most credible and meaningful CVE efforts is to create interventions that build resilience within individuals and communities by improving an individual's capacity for critical thinking. Fake news, and the awakening of the public to it, presents an opportunity to revive critical thinking skills as a core part of school curriculums. Analysis, assessment and debate need to be part of every child's upbringing and school education, within every class and specifically within citizenship and media classes looking at how people seek to influence us.

Conclusion

The democratisation of hybrid warfare has important implications for countering violent extremism, the majority of which are only just becoming apparent. Over the past decade, the Digital Age has given individuals the agency to wrestle control of information away from traditional institutions of power – the media and governments. We have now moved to the next stage in this evolution – to the democratisation of, and battle over, truth. Individuals no longer seek to solely liberate control over information, but to be the actors who root out, and own, the 'truth' – determining and shaping information in order to achieve their desired outcomes: a realisation that we are all agents of influence.

Organisations and governments will need to reflect on how best to adapt to this – this chapter puts forward suggestions around increased non-securitised engagement, a re-thinking of credible voices, the need for proactive narratives and potentially the most difficult of all – embracing Joe Public as an agent of influence in hybrid warfare operations against states and terror groups: enfranchising the public to become 'amplifiers' of non-extremist narratives, whilst retaining critical thinking. Hopefully, operators will find some of the unclassified suggestions within this chapter helpful.

Beyond what this means for institutions, there is a job for each of us as individuals. We each need to each make a conscious effort to step up and realise we are all credible voices within our own networks.

Responsibility for change sits, not only with media houses, Internet service providers and social media platforms and governments, but also with all of us as individuals and as constituents of our communities. Hatred, the key driver of terrorism and hybrid warfare, is nourished by everyday indifference, as divisive rhetoric is uncritically adopted by the neighbour next door, or ourselves. We each need to help build stronger and more cohesive communities, and change the standard of discourse at dinner tables, on WhatsApp and in shops and communities around the world. Not only to challenge violent extremism, but to include people who otherwise could be susceptible to the easy answers of hate.

We can overcome the divisions that exist, and start a conversation. We can build the empathy needed for people to realise that the divisionary worldview they have inherited or constructed has no place in our shared futures. We are each credible voices. In this way, the democratisation of hybrid warfare gives us all opportunity to be agents of positive change.

7

THE AESTHETICS OF VIOLENT EXTREMIST AND COUNTER-VIOLENT EXTREMIST COMMUNICATION

Ilan Manor and Rhys Crilley

Introduction

For more than a decade, foreign ministries have employed online platforms in order to combat violent extremism. The US State Department first migrated online with a desire to counter the online narrative of Al-Qaeda and disrupt its recruitment strategies. Presently, counter violent extremist (CVE) activities conducted on social media are still premised on the assumption that extremist recruitment and support is facilitated through the dissemination of simple, clear narratives, and that there is subsequently a need for counternarratives to draw people away from extremism. This chapter extends recent work by arguing that scholars of violent extremism and CVE should pay attention not only to narrative but also to the broader aesthetics of communication. We do so because within the CVE literature, there is currently a focus on language and narratives, and scant attention to other communicative media such as photographs, videos, and music. This is problematic for several reasons. First, in the Digital Age, communication is reliant upon a broad range of multimedia, and to focus only on linguistic narratives in CVE is to ignore a large part of the media ecology. Second, research suggests that aesthetic media such as photographs have more of an impact on audiences than words alone. Third, an attention to aesthetics allows for an exploration of emotions and how they are of fundamental importance to CVE. Here, we argue that narratives do not simply appeal to people because of their content, but because of how they resonate with their emotions. If extremist groups are able to elicit sympathy or inspire followers through the use of images, CVE must also offer compelling images that resonate emotionally with publics.

This chapter begins by offering an aesthetic understanding of communication and CVE in the contemporary media ecology. This framework advances the study of CVE beyond a qualitative analysis of narratives and toward a focus on how people interpret, make sense of, and feel emotions toward the world. Here, we build upon important work that has found that aesthetic media such as images are integral to people's understandings, emotions, and beliefs about events and issues in world politics (Bleiker, 2001; Williams, 2003; Hansen, 2011).

We then focus on analyzing the narratives and images published by the CVE Twitter channel @Coalition, which is a collaborative channel operated by member states of the Global Coalition against Daesh. This CVE channel is an important case study for several reasons. First, @Coalition differs from most CVE channels as its content represents the policies and actions of both 'Western' and majority Muslim countries (such as the United Arab Emirates, Qatar, and Jordan). As such, the narrative disseminated on @Coalition with regard to the Muslim faith, and Daesh's self-proclamation as an Islamic state, may differ from narratives disseminated by Western Ministries of Foreign Affairs (such as that of the British Government @UKAganistDaesh). Second, as this channel is spearheaded by the US State Department, UK Foreign Office, and the United Arab Emirates Sawab center, its messaging may be viewed by Muslim social media users as more authentic, leading to higher levels of engagement and a greater willingness to share @Coalition content. Third, @Coalition is meant to complement the Global Coalition's off-line activities which include military and financial operations. The channel's stated goal is to combat Daesh propaganda by exposing the group's false claims and presenting a positive, alternative, future for the region. Thus, unlike other CVE channels, @Coalition's narrative may focus on debunking Daesh myths rather than combating Daesh online recruitment efforts. However, given that the content shared on this CVE channel must represent the views of all Coalition member states, the scope of the narrative and diversity of content disseminated on this channel may be limited when compared to CVE channels operated by individual Ministries of Foreign Affairs.

This chapter analyzes content shared by the @Coalition during two time periods: December 2016 to January 2017 and the month of April 2017. Our analysis is informed by work on narrative and aesthetics, and during the first stage of analysis, we categorized all tweets published by the @Coalition based on their subject matter. Then, we identified recurring themes in @Coalition tweets that articulated the Global Coalition's online narrative. We then analyzed the images accompanying @Coalition tweets through an aesthetic framework that focuses on who/what is represented (content), how they are represented (composition and technical aspects), and the broader cultural connotations of this content (i.e., resonance with culturally significant iconography/narratives). Finally, we analyzed the relationship between images and the text that accompanies such tweets. This enabled us to identify the manner in which images are used to construct and project a narrative on this CVE channel.

Importantly, CVE activities conducted on social media may benefit from adopting a dialogic approach that not only disseminates narratives and images but also tailors such content to the feedback of online audiences. Thus, during our analysis of content from December 2016 and January 2017, we also include a quantitative analysis so as to identify the types of images that elicit the highest rate of user engagement (the number of comments, likes, and shares). This analysis provides a tentative step toward understanding how and why social media CVE activities elicit emotional responses from online audiences.

Finally, we analyze content shared on the @Coalition channel during April 2017. This second analysis explores whether the CVE channel refrains from using images that elicit negative reactions from followers, or increases the use of images that resonate positively with followers. This analysis offers an understanding of how 'listening' to social media followers can increase the potential efficacy of CVE activities. In total, some 500 tweets and 250 images or videos are analyzed as part of this chapter. Our research is driven by two questions: how does the @Coalition use aesthetics in their online CVE activities? And, how do audiences interpret and respond to this? Prior to answering these, we now engage with the current literature on radicalization, violent extremism, CVE, and narrative, in order to demonstrate how it can, and needs to begin to explore the role of aesthetics.

Radicalization and violent extremism: the role of narratives

Since the mid-2000s, the concept of radicalization has been the focus of much attention from policy makers and academics interested in how to prevent acts of terror. Despite this, there is little consensus on what the term means, what radicalization involves, or what to do about it (Kundnani, 2012; Schmid, 2013; Sedgwick, 2010). Once succinctly described as 'what goes on before the bomb goes off' (Neumann, 2008: 4), the literature on radicalization is diverse, suggesting that various factors lead to people becoming radicalized to the extent that they commit violent acts. Some theories of radicalization argue that religious beliefs and theology are the root causes of radicalization (Laqueur, 2004; Gartenstein-Ross and Grossman, 2009), others suggest that it is driven by charismatic leaders (Hoffman, 2006), whereas others point toward the role of individual or group psychology and social networks (Sageman, 2004, 2011), other scholars point toward the role of the media (Hoskins et al., 2011). These theories have been critiqued for a variety of reasons, namely that they problematically place attention on Muslims as suspect communities, assume that radical thought leads to violence, and fail to recognize that radicalization is an inherently complex process involving multiple factors of which there is no single universal root cause (see Kundnani, 2012; Schmid, 2013; Sedgwick, 2010).

Recently, scholars have shifted from focusing on singular root causes of radicalization and have instead drawn attention to how a variety of factors constitute a 'violent radical milieu' (Conway, 2012), which in turn shape how and why people commit political violence. Maura Conway defines these as 'specific social environments whose culture, narratives, and symbols shape both individuals and groups, and the social networks and relationships out of which those individuals and groups develop and emerge' (Conway, 2012, p. 12). In recent scholarship, two factors (1) the Internet and (2) narratives, are often, if not always, deemed to be important in these violent milieus.

First, the Internet is often seen to play a fundamental role in contemporary acts of terror. The Internet enables violent extremists from all political persuasions – from far-right organizations, to Jihadi Salafi groups – to communicate with other like-minded people through forums, social media, and private messaging services, while also being able to utilize these technologies to produce and widely disseminate their propaganda (Awan, 2007; Conway, 2016; Meleagrou-Hitchens et al., 2017; Ramsay, 2010). Even so, some scholars suggest that the Internet may be 'auxiliary to preconditions, antecedent behaviours and root causes [of violent extremism]' (Meleagrou-Hitchens et al., 2017: 1246; see also Githens-Mazer and Lambert, 2010). Indeed, more research is needed to determine the Internet's exact role in radical violent milieus (Conway, 2016); however, it is increasingly the case that scholars recognize that 'the question is no longer *if* the Internet has a role to play in contemporary violent extremism and terrorism, but the more pertinent issue is determining its level of significance in contemporary violent radicalization processes' (Conway, 2016: 81).

To this end, there is a growing consensus in the academic literature and the policymaking world that one of the most significant roles that the Internet plays in contemporary radical violent milieus is in enabling violent extremists to disseminate their narratives directly to audiences (Ashour, 2011; Braddock and Horgan, 2016; Briggs and Feve, 2013; Ferguson, 2016; Halverson et al., 2011; Leuprecht et al., 2010; Schmid, 2014). Indeed, as Braddock and Horgan note,

> Although terrorist groups use a variety of communicative strategies to encourage audiences to adopt their ideologies, the development and diffusion of narrative content comprised of themes consistent with the group's ideology is one of the more ubiquitous.
>
> *(Braddock and Horgan, 2016: 385)*

In the UK, military doctrine formulated in 2012 suggests that al-Qaeda's success is partly down to the simplicity of their narrative that can be distilled down to 'the West is at war with Islam' (Ministry of Defence, 2012: 2–12). Such sentiments were reflected by Barack Obama in 2015 when he suggested that 'this narrative becomes the foundation upon which terrorists build their ideology and by which they try to justify their violence' (Obama, 2015). Subsequently, it is clear that 'narrative is now at the forefront of concerns about terrorism, or violent extremism, and "counter-narrative" is frequently advanced as a principal means of preventing terrorism/violent extremism' (Glazzard, 2017: 3).

In particular, work on CVE has assumed that confronting and challenging the narratives of violent extremists should be a primary strategic objective. Yet despite a growing concern with using counternarratives to prevent violent extremism, there have been surprisingly 'few attempts to offer theory-based guidelines for their construction and dissemination' (Braddock and Horgan, 2016: 382). Those that have been offered in recent years remain focused on theorizing the psychological persuasive nature of narratives (Braddock and Horgan, 2016) or their literary form (Halverson et al., 2011; Glazzard, 2017). Undoubtedly, these works provide important insights; however, they provide a limited understanding of narrative and its utility for CVE as they fail to explore the extent to which the narratives of violent extremists and those of CVE practitioners are aesthetic, rather than linguistic. In the following section, we now articulate an approach to CVE that is not only attuned to narrative but also to the broader aesthetics of communication.

Going beyond linguistic narratives: aesthetics, multimedia, and emotions

Recent work in the area of CVE suggests that counternarratives are important because they can 'contradict the themes that fuel and sustain terrorist narratives, and by extension, discourage the support for terrorism they foster' (Braddock and Horgan, 2016: 381–382). In this regard, the work of Braddock and Horgan draws upon a psychological approach that is focused on understanding how narratives can be used to persuade (2016: 383). Subsequently, their work and their recommendations for effective CVE remain focused on the linguistics of violent extremist narratives and how they represent core themes (Braddock and Horgan, 2016: 387). While this work provides a guide for analyzing violent extremist narratives and for creating counternarratives, it is rather reductive because, as Andrew Glazzard argues, it focuses only on the capacity of narratives to change minds and 'by mining narratives for their themes and messages, little attention is paid to how those themes and messages are presented' (Glazzard, 2017: 8).

Glazzard himself provides a thoughtful and convincing critique of the psychological approach to counternarratives and draws upon literary theory to provide a rich account of violent extremist narratives and how they can be countered. In his discussion of other work on narratives and CVE, Glazzard suggests that scholars and practitioners often 'miss the affective and aesthetic dimensions of narrative that are fundamental to its appeal' (Glazzard, 2017: 11). His approach then draws upon the work of prominent literary theorist Mieke Bal to go beyond an analysis that focuses on the themes of narratives and their ability to persuade (2017: 14). Instead, Glazzard suggests that 'by seeing terrorist propaganda as aesthetic texts, we can understand that they may work in ways other than by ideological indoctrination, or simple persuasion' (2017: 15). This, according to Glazzard, is important as it helps us recognize that (1) narratives not only persuade, but can inspire; (2) narratives shape culture, which, in turn, shape ideology; and (3) the appeal of narratives are more complex and subtle than the messages they contain (2017: 16). Together this suggests that 'if counter-narrative is to rise to the challenge, it means using the aesthetic and affective resources of storytelling, and not just making appeals to reason or to self-interest' (Glazzard, 2017: 16).

Despite Glazzard's intervention that begins to explore the aesthetics of CVE, his work remains focused on narrative in linguistic form and while it begins to suggest that emotions and affect are important in understanding how narratives resonate with audiences, he does not demonstrate or theorize how this is so. Here then, we wish to make several interventions into the work on counternarratives and CVE. Both the psychological and the literary approach to CVE remain limited for understanding and challenging the violent radical milieus of the Digital Age. This is because, first, communication is reliant upon a broad range of multimedia, and to focus only on linguistic narratives of violent extremists and how to construct linguistic counternarratives for CVE is to ignore a large part of the media ecology. Scholars working in international relations have long drawn attention to the importance of aesthetics, visual media, art, and music in all aspects of global politics and political violence (Bleiker, 2001, 2009; Moore, 2006; Moore and Shepherd, 2010). While scholars are right to suggest that violent extremist groups like al-Qaeda and ISIS have utilized narratives to great effect (Braddock and Horgan, 2016; Glazzard, 2017; Schmid, 2014), research suggests that these narratives have been effective because of their aesthetic form – whether that be in the form of 'powerful, emotional images' (Farwell, 2014: 50), music and nasheed, or other multimedia forms (Ramsay, 2015: 63–68). Indeed, in her work on radicalization in Denmark, Manni Crone draws attention to how it makes little sense to focus on linguistics and narratives in the current media ecology. She notes,

> aesthetic technologies currently sidetrack traditional intellectual technologies of the self as the Koran, the fatwa or Islamist doctrine. In contrast to intellectual technologies that primarily work through the intellect and make use of linguistics, aesthetic technologies are 'assemblages' in which speech, visualities, sound and materialities interact in ways that produce specific 'frames' of violence.
>
> *(Crone, 2014: 292)*

Hence, it is essential to understand how violent extremist narratives are communicated beyond the realm of words. The way in which these narratives are communicated is not superfluous. Rather, the visual, aural, and multimedia forms in which violent extremist narratives take is of fundamental importance to their effectiveness.

This is especially pertinent because research suggests that aesthetic media such as photographs have more of an impact on audiences than words alone. Visual media have long been considered vital to the conduct of war (Butler, 2010; Hariman and Lucaites, 2007; Mirzoeff, 2011; Virilio, 1994), and according to the aesthetic philosopher Jacques Rancière, visual media provide a distribution of the sensible that shapes what is and is not politically possible (2006: 12–13). Even scholars who are skeptical of the primacy of images in the communication of political violence and war recognize that understanding aesthetic media and images is of importance, suggesting that 'it is not merely a question of image or larger narrative, but how the two are composed together' (O'Loughlin, 2011: 84). Research on ISIS is unequivocal in its recognition that images of both brutal actions and everyday life in the self-proclaimed caliphate have been a vital component to the groups recruitment and military strategies (Farwell, 2014; Friis, 2015, 2017; Leander, 2017). Consequently, in the contemporary media ecology, it is imperative that any analysis of violent extremist narratives or CVE is attuned to the importance of visual media and attempts to 'understand when, how and why images mesh or jar with narratives' (O'Loughlin, 2011: 89).

Further to this, an attention to aesthetics allows for an exploration of emotions and how they are of fundamental importance to the efficacy of violent extremist narratives and CVE counternarratives. Here, it must be noted that narratives do not simply appeal to people because of their content, but because of how they resonate with their emotions (Solomon, 2014: 729). Glazzard suggests that violent extremist narratives draw upon 'affective resources' (Glazzard, 2017, p. 16), and recent scholarship on 'affective investments' (Laclau, 2004, 2007; Solomon, 2014) can help further the understanding of how emotions are important in violent extremist narratives and CVE counternarratives. According to the discourse theorist Ernest Laclau, when scholars analyze discourse and narrative, they focus on the 'form' in which it is expressed (Laclau, 2007: 326), rather than paying attention to the 'forces' of discourses and narratives; that is, their affective and emotional registers that make them appealing to audiences in the first place (Laclau, 2007: 111). As Anna Leander has recently argued in the context of ISIS, violent extremist narratives have, at their heart 'affective, creative, diffuse, and individual processes' (2017: 13–14), and it is imperative that we attempt to understand how violent extremist narratives have an emotional appeal with audiences rather than simply analyzing their content.

A framework for analyzing the aesthetics of violent extremism and CVE

The above discussion has several implications for how we study the propaganda and narratives of violent extremists and also how we create effective counternarratives for the purpose of CVE. In line with recent research, we suggest that an analysis of violent extremist messaging and propaganda should begin by focusing on narratives. Understanding narratives as meaningful, temporally structured frameworks of representations that grasp together 'into one whole and complete story multiple and scattered events' (Ricoeur, 1984: x), we can begin to see the utility in both the psychological approach and the literary approaches to violent extremist narratives and CVE. We can then compliment these approaches by analyzing the aesthetics of violent extremist and CVE messaging. Here, the analysis should begin with an exploration of a narratives core themes using content and discourse analysis (Braddock and Horgan, 2016: 386), and this can and should be supplemented with an exploration of a narratives structure and constituent parts, such as focus, ordering, rhythm, and frequency (Glazzard, 2017: 14), and 'what was done (act), when or where it was done (scene), who did it (agent), how he did it (agency), and why (purpose)' (Burke, 1969: xv).

Following this, we need to explore how narratives are expressed in multimedia forms. This requires an attention to visual aspects, the role of music and speech, as well as other sensory signifiers. Here, visual analysis should pay attention to both what the content of an image literally depicts and how that content has broader cultural significance (Barthes, 1977a, 1977b). This can build upon the thematic and content analysis used to analyze the narratives and should include an exploration of who is shown in images, what they are doing, what else is included in the image, and what technical aspects are featured (such as colors, framing, and perspective).

While how to study emotions remains a source of debate within academic circles (Åhäll and Gregory, 2015; Hutchison, 2016; Ross, 2013a), it is clear that in the Digital Age 'online media facilitates political formations of affect' (Papacharissi, 2015: 9). Here, we suggest that Emma Hutchison provides a clear way of theorizing and studying emotions in the context of violent extremism and CVE. She argues that scholars should study emotions by analyzing how they are expressed in media, because

> the internal, ephemeral nature of emotions precludes the possibility of understanding them through any other means than their instrumental display. Emotions become manifest through the media—the words, visual images, and gestures—in which they are expressed.
>
> *(Hutchison, 2016: 4)*

Therefore, analysis of violent extremist propaganda and CVE counternarratives should explore how emotions are expressed in the words and multimedia forms that are produced and shared by violent extremists and those attempting to counter them. Further to this, in the Digital Age, we can complement such an analysis by exploring how people online feel about the narratives presented to them by analyzing how their online comments express emotions.

BOX 7.1: QUESTIONS FOR ANALYZING NARRATIVES OF VIOLENT EXTREMISTS AND COUNTERNARRATIVES OF CVE

Narrative

What are the themes of the narrative?

What are the constituent parts of the narrative? How are they drawn together in a plot?

Multimedia

How is the narrative communicated in a multimedia form?

What are the specific issues of these multimedia, aesthetic forms (visual, aural, music, etc.)?

Emotions

How do the narrative and its aesthetic communication express emotions?
　　How does that expression of emotions seek to appeal to relevant audiences?
　　How do people respond to the narratives presented to them?

Such a framework for analysis can both be used to provide an insight into violent extremist propaganda; however, it can also be used to analyze CVE messaging. We now apply this framework to the case of the Coalition's attempts to counter ISIS/Daesh propaganda. We do so because while there is ample research into the propaganda of ISIS (Farwell, 2014; Friis, 2015, 2017; Leander, 2017), there is little scholarly attention paid to attempts to counter and challenge this propaganda. In what follows we apply our analytical framework to the content published by the Coalition on Twitter. Doing so enables us not to simply draw out the utility of our framework but also to critically evaluate the Coalition's CVE messaging, and to suggest, in the final section, how an attention to aesthetics can potentially make for more effective CVE.

The @Coalition Twitter channel

According to the website of the Global Coalition against Daesh, tackling Daesh propaganda is 'critically important' to the Coalition's efforts. The Coalition website specifically states that Daesh's employment of social media to spread its hateful message facilitates acts of terror. The goal of the Coalition's online communication is, therefore, to oppose Daesh's narrative and undermine the appeal of Daesh ideology. This is to be achieved by (1) undermining Daesh's claims to statehood, military success, and religious ideology and (2) presenting a positive alternative future for the region. The Coalition's online communications are spearheaded by the US State Department's Global Engagement Center, the UAE-based Sawab Center, and the UK Government.

As part of its online activities, the Coalition launched the @Coalition Twitter channel in March 2016. To date, the channel has published 4,600 tweets and has attracted a following of more than 36,000 Twitter users. The account tweets solely in English, which suggests that it aims to reach a broad audience as a means of publicizing Coalition activities and achievements. Furthermore, the channel is rich with multimedia. During December 2016 and January 2017, 56% of all tweets were accompanied by multimedia ranging from infographics to animations and videos.

In this chapter, we sought to analyze the narrative disseminated on the @Coalition Twitter channel and to explore the role of multimedia and emotions in this narrative. Moreover, we aimed to investigate the Coalitions' willingness to engage with its online audience. To do so, we employed a three-step methodology. First, we used thematic analysis to identify recurring themes in @Coalition tweets. These themes were viewed as the building blocks of the Coalition's online narrative. Our thematic analysis followed the roadmap offered by qualitative researchers (Boyatzis, 1998; Clarke and Braun, 2014) who define such an analysis as a method of identifying overlying themes within a research corpus. Our sample consisted of 324 tweets published during the period from December 2016 to January 2017. Next, we analyzed multimedia used in each theme so as to explore the aesthetic and affective dimension of the Coalition's CVE narrative. Finally, we employed quantitative analysis so as to identify the extent to which the Coalition tailors its online communication to audience feedback. This included recording all instances in which the @Coalition channel responded to comments posted by Twitter followers, supplied information requested by followers or interacted in any form of two-way communication with followers. In addition, we measured follower engagement levels with Coalition tweets in order to identify which messages best resonate with Twitter followers in terms of the number of comments, likes, and retweets. We then analyzed 250 tweets published in April 2017 as a means of assessing whether the @Coalition channel made more frequent use of messages that had formerly resonated with audiences, and refrained from using messages that had been poorly received by audiences.

Notably, we chose to examine tweets published between December 2016 and January 2017 for three reasons. First, this time period saw the expansion of the Coalition and the joining of another Muslim country, Libya. Second, this time frame saw a major military campaign against Daesh in Mosul. Third, this time frame included several joint exercises between coalition forces. Thus, we assumed that this time period would produce a robust research sample that would enable us to analyze the Coalitions' narrative and use of social media.

Analysis of the @Coalition narrative

Between December 2016 and January 2017, the @Coalition Twitter channel published 324 tweets. Of these, we analyzed the 183 tweets that included images, infographics, animations, and videos. As part of our thematic analysis, we categorized all tweets based on their subject matter. For instance, a large number of tweets focused on depicting the horror of life under Daesh. In addition, we found tweets that focused on the hypocrisy of Daesh leaders and their brutal punishments inflicted in the civilian population. Thus, a 'Horror of Life under Daesh' and a 'Hypocrisy of Daesh Leaders' categories were created. Once all tweets were categorized, we grouped them into broader themes. For instance, the 'horror of life under Daesh' and 'Daesh hypocrisy' categories were both grouped into the broader theme of 'Exposing Daesh Lies'. In total, we identified four broad themes which comprise the core of the Coalition's CVE narrative.

The first broad theme identified was that of 'A Better Alternative Future'. Tweets comprising this theme focused on three central issues. The first was the lives of children in liberated areas who, thanks to Coalition efforts, were returning to schools and rebuilding their lives. The second issue was that of offering hope to areas still occupied by Daesh or areas recently liberated, and the third issue comprising this theme was that of liberation as a long-term process (Figure 7.1).

The second broad theme identified in our analysis was that of 'Exposing Daesh Lies'. Tweets in this theme focused on five issues. The first was the hypocrisy of Daesh leaders which was manifest in their lavish lifestyle, their acceptance of bribes, their willingness to deny health services to civilians, and their trade in alcohol and cultural artifacts. Other tweets depicted the horror of life under Daesh, including summary executions, forced domestic violence against women, brutal punishments for attempting to flee Daesh territory, and Daesh's looting of shops and homes. Third, these horrors were communicated through testimonials of people who survived Daesh brutality or lived in Daesh held areas. Such tweets were dubbed as 'voice from the streets', and in one notable example an Iraqi survivor stated that Daesh had 'cloaked itself in religion but it has no religion. Something this wrong should be broken'. The fourth issue of this theme was Daesh recruitment of children and their brainwashing of children as part of military training. The final issue concerned Deash's destruction of cultural heritage sites in areas under their control (Figure 7.2).

The third broad theme we identified was that of 'Debunking the Myth of Daesh Military Success'. Tweets comprising this theme consisted mostly of maps depicting Daesh's territorial losses as well as satellite images depicting Coalition gains. Other tweets included videos of briefings by US official pertaining to

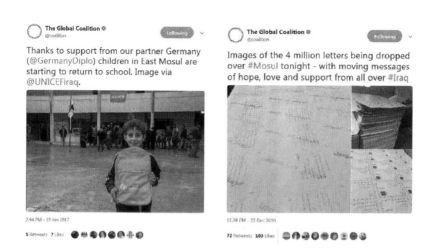

FIGURE 7.1 'A Better Alternative Future' @Coalition Tweets.

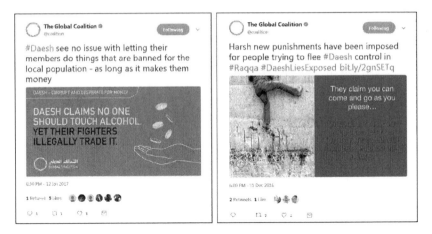

FIGURE 7.2 'Exposing Daesh Lies' @Coalition Tweets.

FIGURE 7.3 'Debunking the Myth of Daesh Military Success' @Coalition Tweets.

Daesh military losses or infographics stating that Daesh was losing 'Huge areas in hours'. This theme also included tweets that depicted the military successes of Iraqi forces, namely, its conquering of Mosul, a Daesh stronghold (Figure 7.3).

The fourth and final broad theme we identified was 'A War *for* Islam'. Tweets comprising this theme depicted the Coalition as a collaborative effort between Muslim and non-Muslim countries as opposed to a Western invasion of Muslim countries. The tweets in this theme focused on four issues, the first of which was the training of Iraqi soldiers by Western militaries including the armies of Italy, Spain, and Slovenia. The second issue was joint task forces of Western and Muslim states, the third issue focused on the active involvement of Muslim countries in Coalition efforts including Libya's joining the coalition, the UAE's support of reconstruction in liberated areas, and Kuwait's humanitarian aid to

FIGURE 7.4 'A War for Islam' @Coalition Tweets.

displaced Iraqis. The final, and most prominent issue comprising this theme, was that of humanitarian aid. These tweets focused on aid delivered to Iraqis by specific Coalition actors, including Germany, the European Union, Japan, and Denmark alongside UN agencies such as UNICEF (Figure 7.4).

These four broad themes constitute the pillars of the Coalition's CVE narrative which infers that 'the coalition is liberating, rehabilitating, and reconciling areas affected by Daesh'. By liberation, we refer to the Coalition's debunking of the myth of Daesh military success and territorial expansion. Indeed the Coalition went to great efforts to depict its military gains and portray Daesh as being on the retreat. Importantly, the liberation of Iraq was depicted as being spearheaded by Iraqi forces. By rehabilitation, we refer to the depiction of life in liberated areas and the return to normalcy. Yet we also refer to the recognition that the road to rehabilitation is a long one given the horror of life under Daesh. In other words, there were no 'Mission Accomplished' images on the @Coalition Twitter channel. Additionally, the Coalition attempted to unmask Daesh and portray it as a barbaric, corrupt, and hypocritical terrorist group that shares nothing with Islam. Finally, by reconciliation, we refer to the depiction of the Coalition as a new relationship between the West and Muslim countries, one that stands in contrast to the previous decade of Western invasions of Muslim countries. This collaborative relationship was made evident in joint training exercises, joint task forces, and Western humanitarian aid to Iraqis. In summary, we find that the Coalition's CVE narrative was a direct rebuke of Daesh's narrative of a war between Islam and the West and its self-proclaimed status as an Islamic state stretching over entire regions of the Middle East. In order to understand how aesthetics were important to the projection of this narrative, we now analyze the multimedia used in Coalition tweets and explore how they communicate the Coalition's narrative in aesthetic, rather than linguistic form.

The aesthetics of the @Coalitions CVE social media activities

The Coalition's CVE narrative focuses on liberation, rehabilitation, and reconciliation. One tweet that exemplifies how the liberation and rehabilitation elements were communicated in multimedia form was published on December 30; one month after Libya joined the coalition (Figure 7.5). In this image, the raising of the Libyan flag may be regarded as an act of renewed independence, one made possible thanks to the Coalition's aid in defeating Daesh. The flag is also symbolic in that it bares the half crescent of Islam, while the image bares the color green which is also associated with Islam. The image thus suggests that it is the Libyan flag that truly represents Islam and not Daesh's flag. Moreover, by incorporating the colors and symbols of Islam, the Coalition may be signifying that it is fighting in the name of Islamic values and not against Islam. At an implicit level, there is a demonstrative element to the image as the protagonist seems to be standing tall and firm while proudly waving his national flag. Thus, the image also resonates with the hopeful spirit of the Arab Spring that swept through the region, and Libya, in 2011. However, while the Arab Spring saw citizens rise against tyrants, today they are rising against the tyranny of Daesh.

Importantly, this image is one of hope rather than fear. It dwells on the future of Libya rather than its past, a future in which Libyans will be free to rebuild their country. If anything, this image is one that evokes a positive emotional response as it inspires the viewer to think of a better tomorrow. It is through the use of Islamic symbols, and the reference to the Arab Spring, that this image communicates both the reconciliation and rehabilitation elements of the Coalition's narrative.

FIGURE 7.5 Visualizing Liberation.

On January 6, the Coalition published another image that resonates with the rehabilitation and reconciltaion elements of its narrative. The image (Figure 7.6) is a collage that depicts three separate scenes: a boy marching ahead of Iraqi sol-idres, citizens joyfully gathered around Iraqi soliders, and an Iraqi solider being embraced by a woman. The image depicts the Iraqi army as the people's army; an army that is celebrated by Iraqis. Notably, while the caption relates to military actions, the images are of interactions with the civilian population. Thus, the image signifies that the Iraqi army is a liberation army, one whose triumph lies not merley in defeating Daesh but in giving hope to thousands of Iraqis.

The collage's most prominent image is that of a child marching ahead of Iraqi soldiers. This image may have been used as a contrast to Daesh propoganda which often depicts children as soldiers. The image suggests that unlike the bar-baric Daesh, the Iraqi army fights for children, not with them. Moreover, the composition of the image suggests that the Iraqi army is fighting for the future of Iraq, a future symbolized by a child marching toward rehabilitaton. The im-age implies that it is the Iraqi army that is leading the charge against Daesh, not Western militaries, and the image serves to evoke emotions of hope and optimi-sim as the collage is made up of joyous celebrations (Figure 7.6).

Understanding how the Coalition communicates its narratives requires an attention to aesthetics. In the above discussion, we have hopefully gone some way to demonstrating how the core themes of the coalitions' narratives were commu-nicated through aesthetic multimedia. In addition to this interpretive analysis, we now turn to a quantitative analysis in order to identify which forms of Coalition

FIGURE 7.6 Visualizing Rehabilitation and Reconciliation.

CVE content elicits high levels of online engagement. We also turn this analysis to tweets published by the Coalition in April 2016 in order to tentatively explore how the channel may have tailored their CVE content based on follower feedback.

Understanding audience engagement with the aesthetics of CVE

Our first task here was to identify which form of CVE content elicits the highest level of follower engagement. To this end, we analyzed the average number of favorites, retweets, and comments garnered by two kinds of tweets: those that include multimedia and those which do not. Using a sample of 324 tweets, we found that tweets containing multimedia elicit the highest level of engagement in terms of favorites and retweets. However, there was no discernable difference in the number of comments. These results can be seen in Figure 7.7.

Next, we analyzed which multimedia content garnered the highest and lowest levels of engagement in terms of favorites and retweets. This was achieved by identifying tweets that garnered the most retweets and favorites as well as those that garnered the least retweets. Results suggest that tweets which elicit positive emotions are those that are likely to be best received by audiences. The @Coalition tweets that received the highest number of retweets were those dealing with letters of hope airdropped on areas still under Daesh control ($n = 72$); tweets depicting children returning to school in liberated areas ($n = 31$); tweets depicting civilians embracing the Iraqi army ($n = 30$); tweets depicting children returning to their homes ($n = 20$); and infographics attesting to Daesh's heavy losses of territory ($n = 22$). Overall, these tweets received an average of 35 favorites, 31 retweets, and 2.25 comments (Figure 7.7).

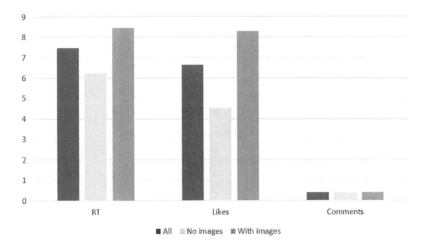

FIGURE 7.7 Average Levels of Engagement with @Coalition Tweets.

FIGURE 7.8 Images with Low Audience Engagement.

Conversely, we found that tweets which elicit negative emotions are negatively received by audiences. Of the tweets to gain the lowest number of retweets and favorites, two depicted children marching in Daesh uniforms (Figure 7.8, $n = 1$); one depicted the conditions in refugee camps ($n = 2$); one depicted an aid worker standing amid stacks of aid packages in a dimly lit room ($n = 2$); and another depicted the likely fate of those attempting to flee Daesh territory ($n = 2$). Overall, these negative tweets received an average of 1.12 favorites, 1.8 retweets, and 0.12 comments.

In summary, our results suggest that CVE content that includes multimedia, and which can elicit positive emotions, is likely to receive the highest levels of follower engagement. Follower engagement may subsequently pave the way for dialogue and relationship building. Moreover, a lack of multimedia and the use of images which elicit negative emotions can lead to reduced levels of follower engagement and, subsequently, a lack of ability to interact with followers in meaningful dialogue.

Our final analysis focused on the @Coalition's tailoring of social media content to follower feedback. To do so, we first recorded all instances in which the @Coalition engaged in any form of two-way interactions with followers, be it in responding to questions, supplying information, or answering follower comments. Our analysis found *no such instances*. The @Coalition did hold one Q&A session on December 19 during which followers could, for a limited time, query a US military spokesperson on Coalition activities. However, such Q&A sessions may be viewed as quarantined forms of engagement that fail to leverage social media toward relationship building (Kampf et al., 2015).

Next, we explored whether the @Coalition channel improved its audience engagement, by analyzing whether, in April 2017, they made frequent use of images that were well received by followers, and refrained from using images that failed to engage followers. To this end, we analyzed an additional 250 tweets published during April 2017. We found that the Coalition used similar images to

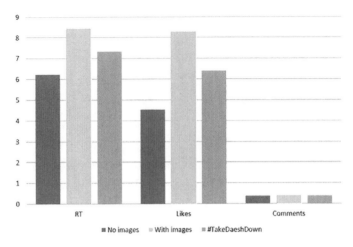

FIGURE 7.9 Average Levels of Engagement with @Coalition Tweets.

those published during December and January. Moreover, the Coalition made frequent use of images that can elicit negative emotions and multimedia that received a low number of retweets, favorites, and comments during December and January. As such, is appears that the @Coalition fails to take into account audience feedback and tailor its use of social media and multimedia content to follower feedback.

It should, however, be mentioned that during April 2017 the @Coalition published a host of tweets using the hashtag #TakeDaeshDown. These tweets invited followers to help fight Daesh propaganda by reporting abusive content to social media platforms, such as Twitter and Facebook. Such tweets may be seen as an attempt to offer Twitter followers opportunities for online collaborations, to involve followers in @Coalition activities, and to enable followers to better their societies. All these activities have been recognized as important forms of two-way interactions between organizations and their online communities (Taylor and Kent, 2014). #TakeDaeshDown tweets were well received by @Coalition followers when compared to tweets that included and did not include multimedia (Figure 7.9).

Conclusion

This chapter has demonstrated the utility of paying attention to aesthetics when analyzing violent extremist narratives as well as those CVE counternarratives. In the Digital Age, narratives are increasingly communicated through visual, aesthetic multimedia forms such as photographs, inforgraphics, and videos. Both those who wish to study and those who wish to produce CVE activities, it is imperative to recognize the aesthetics of communication. Through a case study of the Coalition against Daesh's twitter content, we have highlighted how the core aspects of the Coalition's CVE counternarratives were communicated through aesthetic, visual multimedia. By analyzing audience engagement with this content, we also found that it is aesthetic content that is more likely to elicit audience engagement. Therefore, we suggest that future online CVE counternarratives should, first, be communicated through aesthetic media. These should serve to summarize aspects of the narrative being communicated and should resonate, symbolically, culturally, and emotionally, with the audience that is being sought. Second, this content should invoke positive emotions in order to gain high levels of engagement. Third, those conducting CVE activities should listen to and tailor their content to their audiences, and engage with dialogue rather than simply publishing content. With all of this being said, this chapter has only provided a foundation for thinking about the aesthetics of CVE, and there is subsequently a need for further research – across a variety of cases and contexts – in order to understand both how violent extremism is reliant on aesthetics and how aesthetics can be used to effectively challenge and counter violent extremism.

8

VIRTUAL VIOLENCE

Understanding the potential power of ISIS' violent videos to buttress strategic narratives and persuade foreign recruits

Sean Aday

Introduction

Even though terrorism predates the mass media age, in many ways it is a tactic perfectly suited to it. Television, and now social media, allow terrorists to not only spread their strategic narratives to millions globally, these media are especially well suited to conveying the vivid spectacle of terrorist attacks (Livingston 1994). Since the rise of al-Qaeda (AQ) in the 1990s, and especially since the catastrophic attacks of 9/11, television and digital media have been important transmitters of terrorist group's strategic narratives. Many of these messages utilize gory fear appeals in an effort to accentuate their broader narratives regarding the religious righteousness of their cause, their claims about Western imperialism, and, recently, claims that ISIS is a model of good governance.

Of the many types of terrorist messages spread through mass media channels, the ones that have received the most attention and caused the most alarm are those that traffic in extreme violence and show cold-hearted, graphic executions. Policy makers, pundits, and others frequently claim that terrorists, be they AQ or ISIS, are "winning" the war of ideas – and indeed getting the upper hand in the more traditional wars the West has been waging against these groups for more than 20 years – in part because of the assumed effectiveness of these violent videos. In the US, for example, policy makers have responded to these videos in several ways, including creating high-profile (if under-resourced) organizations within the State Department tasked with combating the online messaging of terrorist groups. Indeed, presidential policy itself appears to have been affected by these videos when President Obama abandoned a more deliberate approach to developing a plan for the US in Syria following the release of videos showing the beheading of American journalists James Foley and Steven Sotloff, an example of what in the CNN Effect literature would be known as a policy accelerant (Gilboa 2005, Livingston 1997, Robinson 1999, 2002).

Somewhat typical of the history of reactions about media influence, these reactions by the press, policy makers, and the public rest on two untested (in this context) assumptions: that media are powerful and that media power is often negative. Indeed, contemporary concerns about the power of these videos is reminiscent of early 20th-century arguments, now debunked, that media exercised a kind of hypodermic needle effect on audiences, injecting their message to a passive audience unable to resist its power (Gitlin 1978). Violent terrorist videos, for instance, are said to be powerful recruitment tools, swaying impressionable viewers, especially young people around the world to join the fight. (Interestingly, another potential effect of the videos perhaps more consistent with their intent – to shock the West into overreacting and getting drawn into expensive, bloody, draining wars with no end – is rarely discussed.)

What is missing from most of these arguments, however, is any theory of what the causal mechanism for the videos' power might be, or, for that matter, any evidence of their "effectiveness." This leads to policy responses that are effectively akin to shooting wildly in the dark. For example, in response to what was perceived to be a slew of powerful, violent ISIS videos spreading online, the White House created the Center for Strategic Counter Communication (CSCC) at the State Department in 2011 and in 2015 tasked it with countering ISIS's strategic narrative with a more persuasive one of its own. Yet the Center did not base their strategy, or their countermessaging, on any evidence about (1) whether ISIS videos were effective and if so why; (2) what an effective message from the US would look like; (3) what the audience characteristics were for the target audience that might (a) make them potentially susceptible to ISIS videos, yet (b) still be open to a US countermessage; (4) any serious post hoc analyses of impact or effects; or, finally, (5) much of any a priori strategic thinking. Instead, due in large part to the Center being underfunded and understaffed and yet tasked with defeating ISIS online immediately, the small, overworked team was left throwing darts blindfolded. Unsurprisingly, these efforts – especially a campaign with the hashtag #thinkagainturnaway that included gory images with sarcastic commentary – were largely pilloried in the press (Kaczynski 2014, Mazzetti & Gordon 2015).

This chapter takes a different approach. It analyzes characteristics of ISIS execution videos through the lens of prior research on the effects of vivid and violent media messages in order to better answer several questions: (1) Is there reason to think these videos are, in fact, persuasive? (2) If so, why and with whom? And finally, (3) What are the implications of this for thinking about effective countermessaging? As an analytical strategy for answering these questions, this chapter compares ISIS execution videos to those produced earlier in the century by AQ and its affiliates, notably al-Qaeda in Iraq (AQI), to illustrate key differences that the literature suggests might make ISIS videos more persuasive with a wider array of persuadable audiences.

Specifically, this chapter argues that the pop culture motifs/frames in most ISIS violent videos are effective with a wider audience of potentially persuadable foreign fighters (especially in the West) than the typical AQ execution videos, because:

a   By priming a mental model of entertainment media, they create more of an emotional distance between the viewer and the violence than AQ execution videos (and potentially other ISIS execution videos that mimic the AQ videos) that employ a news/documentary format.

b   Although the violence would still be too vivid/graphic for most people, for persuadables fluent in violent video games and/or similarly themed entertainment media the videos may prime mental models that are (i) pleasurable and/or (ii) efficacious.

c   Put another way, in the same way that research shows that some people chose to engage with, and enjoy, violent video games and violent entertainment media because they are seeking gratification for certain emotional and cognitive needs (e.g., catharsis, efficacy, excitement), these ISIS videos can be used to gratify similar needs precisely because they (i) utilize the same, familiar format and (ii) are thus not so shocking (to persuadables) to repel them.

d   AQ videos, on the other hand, employ formats that have been shown in vividness and violence studies to be repellent to many people, especially:

   i   Extreme gore
   ii   Close-ups
   iii   Auditory vividness (i.e., screaming)

e   Furthermore, by utilizing entertainment formats that prime efficacious and gratifying mental models, as well as create emotional distance and a sense of unreality to the violence, these ISIS videos may be more likely to activate <u>cognitive elaboration</u> in persuadable viewers (in the same way previous research has shown violent video games can for those receptive to them): this in turn makes the *messages* in the videos – for example, in the didactic songs, or *nasheeds*, that typically comprise the video's score – more persuasive.

f   Finally, other research has shown that for those who are drawn to violent video games and media, violent messages and aggression-oriented feelings and attitudes can be enduring in memory, implying that the same may be true for the messages in ISIS videos. Because these videos probably appeal to more people than AQ execution videos for the reasons stated above and elaborated on below, that should make their effects stronger and more enduring for a larger number of potential recruits.

In sum, ISIS videos' utilization of pop culture formats allows them to cast a wider net than AQ's violent videos because they (1) create more emotional distance between the audience and the violence and may have stronger, more enduring effects because they (2) prime preexisting efficacy-reinforcing mental models and (3) induce cognitive elaboration.

Characteristics of al Qaeda violence videos

The first execution video released by AQ was that of contractor Nicholas Berg in Iraq. The video is typical of the execution videos released by the group, especially by its Iraqi offshoot, AQI, whose leader until his death in 2006, Abu Musab al-Zarqawi, became infamous for his especially brutal tactics during the American occupation, so much so that he received letters from AQ leaders al Zawahiri and Bin Laden admonishing him to be less brutal, especially toward Iraqis, lest he create a backlash against the group.

The Berg video, like many others released by AQI, shows the victim kneeling and bound, wearing an orange jumpsuit similar to those worn by detainees in the US prison at Guantanamo Bay, Cuba (Figure 8.1). Behind him, a row of black masked AQI fighters stand at attention, while the one in the middle – later identified as Zarqawi himself – reads a lengthy manifesto that, among other things, condemns the Coalition for invading Iraq and Afghanistan and other alleged offenses, and makes the case for why AQ is fighting for a "true" interpretation of the Quran and why people should join it. This goes on for about 14 minutes and is similar to manifestos read by Osama Bin Laden in videos released to the media going back to the late 1990s. At the end of the reading, Zarqawi takes out a large knife, grabs Berg by the hair from behind, forces him to the ground and decapitates him. Berg can be heard screaming in pain and terror for several seconds before he dies.

This video, and others like it, has several important characteristics. First, the video is in a news/documentary format. In part, this might be because it was released before YouTube and during a period when AQ/AQI's dissemination strategy was a combination of uploading videos to the Internet (especially chat rooms and other venues) and distributing videos and DVDs to news organizations (especially but not limited to al-Jazeera). Still, this format persists even with some ISIS videos to this day.

Second, the video is quite pallid in its message and presentation for a long period of time and then suddenly *extremely* vivid and graphic, including,

FIGURE 8.1   Still from Nicholas Berg Execution Video.

importantly, vivid audio of Berg screaming. Third, these videos exhibited low production value, typically filmed with one camera, usually a relatively inexpensive camcorder with an attached microphone, adding to the resemblance to some news footage. Finally, these videos emphasized the group's leaders, usually in a lecture format. Even a video like that depicting the execution of *Wall Street Journal* reporter Daniel Pearl, recorded by AQ in Pakistan and employing some crude editing in of images of alleged persecution of Muslims by the West and Israel, largely fits this description.

Characteristics of ISIS violence videos

While some ISIS execution videos adopt the lecture-murder format of older AQ videos (e.g., that of journalist James Foley), many are quite different. First, they have relatively high production values, including lighting (e.g., filming during the "magic light" periods of the day, dawn, or dusk), multiple cameras, coverage from multiple angles, rehearsals and multiple takes, better line reading and even sometimes acting, slick graphics, scripts, and didactic music scores known as *Nasheeds* that are, in ISIS's usage, religious battle hymns aimed at not only worshipping God but calling others to join Islam and fight (Gråtrud 2016). ISIS places such a high value on these videos that they train their production teams (or employ recruits with prior production experience) and often pay them as much as three times what other fighters make (Miller & Mekhennet 2015). They often do not focus on leaders lecturing the audience, but instead use fighters – including children – and graphics to tell their story and make their claims.

But perhaps the most important aspect of ISIS videos for understanding their potential effects is their use of pop culture themes and motifs. Although commentators and policy makers often exaggerate how many ISIS videos traffic in gory images (one exhaustive study found only about 15% did), about 40% of them mimic in content, imagery, cover art, graphics, and action popular video games, movies, and television shows produced in the West (especially America) (Lesaca 2015). For example, covers of ISIS execution DVDs will be made to replicate posters for movies such as "American Sniper," or video game box covers such as "Grand Theft Auto." The videos themselves will often recreate scenes from those movies, shows, and games, especially first-person shooter video games like "Call of Duty," wherein an ISIS fighter has a Go-Pro or other small camera mounted on their gun sight as they chase and shoot their victims (Figures 8.2 and 8.3).

Many have posited that these videos, precisely because of their high production value and pop culture appropriation, are dangerously persuasive and potentially effective in recruiting foreign fighters and converts. As Byman and Williams (2015) put it,

> Which do you think is more likely to attract the attention of an 18-year-old boy dreaming of adventure and glory: a badass video with CGI flames and explosions, or a two-hour lecture on the Qur'an from a grey-haired old man?

FIGURE 8.2 Cover of ISIS Video Mimicking Call of Duty Video Game Cover.

FIGURE 8.3 Still from ISIS Execution Video Mimicking First-Person Shooter Video Game "Call of Duty".

Yet missing from these arguments is any theoretical or empirical reasoning underlying their assumptions.

Put simply, is there any reason to think these videos are, in fact, persuasive? The next section looks to past research on effects of casualty coverage and research on violent and vivid entertainment media to answer that question.

Lessons from casualty coverage research

Since Mueller's (1973) seminal research on public opinion and war, policy makers and many academics have assumed that Americans are "casualty averse," meaning that their support for war is roughly inversely related to rising casualties. This assumption has been modified or rejected by more recent work, demonstrating a variety of ways in which the public contextualizes casualties (Burk 1999; Dauber 2001; Gartner & Segura 1998; Klarevas 2002). These include the nature of the conflict and severity of the threat (Jentleson 1992; Jentleson and Britton 1998), partisan predispositions and elite consensus or dissensus (Berinsky 2007, 2009; Berinsky and Druckman 2007; Larson 1996), a kind of rational cost-benefit analysis (Lacquement 2004), and whether the intervention is seen by the public as being likely to succeed and as righteous (Gelpi et al. 2005/2006, 2009; Feaver and Gelpi 2004; Sidman and Norpoth 2012).

Still, others in academia and public policy have argued that media coverage of casualties, especially the vivid coverage that, theoretically at least, television could show, could have a negative impact on public support for an intervention. In the 1990s, the casualty aversion hypothesis formed the theoretical basis of the "CNN Effect," a strand of communication research that investigated whether in an era of 24-hour broadcast news, some vivid images might spur support for intervention (e.g., images of a famine), while others, notably casualties, might make the public risk averse.

The preponderance of CNN Effect literature, however, has found little evidence of direct effects on the public in line with the CNN Effect hypothesis (Gilboa 2005; Dauber 2001; Livingston and Eachus 1995; Robinson 1999). Significantly, however, policy makers' *perception* of the media's power to turn the public against an intervention by showing American casualties has been shown to sometimes lead them to adopt policies that avoid or limit American risks.

Interestingly, while we know a lot about casualty coverage – specifically that in the West (especially the US) it is rare and even more rarely graphic (Aday 2005, 2010a; Althaus et al. 2014; Carruthers 2000; Knightley 2004; Robinson et al. 2010) – we don't have many empirical studies of the effects of exposure to these images. Scholars have investigated the effects of overall casualties on public opinion and support for interventions, finding, for instance, that the evidence from the past 60 years of major military conflicts shows that public support for war in the US tends to increase as coverage of the war increases – and decreases as coverage decreases – regardless of casualty coverage or other variables (Althaus & Coe 2011).

More recently, a few studies have looked experimentally at the effects of exposure to casualty images. Grizzard et al. (2017), for instance, found that exposure to news footage of mass executions by ISIS led to heightened disgust and anger, and greater levels of moral sensitivity and support for anti-ISIS interventions. Yet other studies suggest that, although these images can have a pronounced effect on attitudes under certain circumstances (Gartner 2011; Pfau et al. 2006, 2008), these effects seem to be filtered through prior attitudes and predispositions and emotions. Aday (2010b), for instance, found evidence that news audiences reframe graphic images of dead American soldiers through the prism of their partisan predispositions. In his study, Republican-leaning study participants who read a story about a battle in the Iraq War with an accompanying photo of a dead American soldier were more likely to feel pride and see the dead American as a noble sacrifice. Yet Democratic-leaning subjects who saw the same story and photo were more likely to feel anger and see the death as a tragic waste. In a series of experiments, Gartner (2008, 2011) also found effects to be filtered through partisan predispositions.

In sum, then, the somewhat limited research we have on the effects of casualty coverage exposure has some lessons for understanding the potential effects of terrorist execution videos. Specifically, that people appear to process images, including violent ones, through the prism of their prior attitudes and predispositions. This implies that if one is sympathetic to the message or the messenger, then images that would be offensive or repellent to others might be seen in a more positive light. The implication for Jihadi videos is twofold: (1) alarmist worries that these videos will be widely appealing are undoubtedly misplaced, but (2) those predisposed, for whatever reason, to Jihadi messages not only may not find the images revolting, but may in fact frame them positively. On the first point, most people will see these videos in edited form on the news, in which the goriest images will be implied but not shown. This audience will be overwhelmingly comprised of those not predisposed to supporting the terrorists' message, and thus whatever gore is shown or implied will be processed through that prism and the corresponding message likely rejected or averted entirely.

The concern, however, is what the effects of these images will be on those who see the videos in their entirety online. Given that the nature of digital media exposure is one of self-selection, this is potentially concerning because it means that many of those most likely to see these videos are those that are already in some way predisposed to being open to the terrorists' message. Still, there is a major difference between the level of gore shown in news and thus experimental studies of exposure to casualty coverage (at least those that maintain a semblance of representational validity) and that shown in execution videos. The next question thus becomes whether there is reason to think these images will be repellent even to those open to terrorists' messages, or whether being predisposed to such a message will lead these persuadable audiences to reframe the gruesome images in a more positive light.

Lessons from vividness studies

Scholars have investigated the effects of vivid and pallid messages for decades, especially in terms of their persuasiveness (Frey & Eagly 1993; Nisbett & Ross 1980; Riddle 2014; Sherer & Rogers 1984; Taylor & Thompson 1982). Despite the face-value assumption that vivid messages should be more persuasive, in fact the results of these studies have shown that the relationship isn't always so cut and dry. Like casualty coverage (itself a kind of vivid message), effects are often contextual. Still, there are some general conclusions we can draw from this literature that are relevant to understanding the potential effects of terrorist execution videos.

First, prior research shows that vividness (sometimes operationalized as graphicness) can lead to greater *attention* to messages (Kelley 1989). Following exposure, attention has been shown to be the second of several steps in the process of message acceptance, attitude change, and, potentially, behavioral outcomes (McGuire 1968). A second important finding from this research, however, is that if messages are too vivid, they can lead people to look away and ignore the message. In particular, too much gore and aural vividness (especially screaming) have been shown to shrink the audience and the persuasive impact of a message (Riddle 2013). Finally, and related, if the vivid elements in the message are a distraction from the main message, then the message can actually be less persuasive than a more pallid one that stays true to its core message (Frey & Eagly 1993).

Hence, on the one hand, not everyone is affected by vivid messages. If they are too vivid, some of the audience is turned off and does not engage with the rest of the message. For example, an animal welfare group like the People for the Ethical Treatment of Animals that features pictures of animal cruelty in a campaign to entice the public to pressure members of Congress on some piece of legislation may find that those vivid images turn away potential supporters who in fact never attend to the campaign's message because they cannot get past the graphic imagery. The same has been found in studies of violent media and video games where participants find imagery too gory (McCauley 1998; Jeong et al. 2011).

On the other hand, not everyone is turned off by such images, which, like casualty images, may end up being contextualized by audiences. The question then becomes, who may be open to messages using these images? There are two answers:

1. **The choir**: The hardliners, or "partisans," who are drawn to the message in the first place and thus less likely to be put off by it. These are true believers predisposed to being receptive to the message and thus likely to filter the graphic imagery more positively through those predispositions.
2. **The persuadables**: People drawn for some reason to the message, but not yet hardliners. This is the group of interest because they can go one way or the other and there is presumably a greater number of them. However, because they are not yet hardliners, there is a greater likelihood that they may be turned off by extremely vivid graphic violence that only the choir can appreciate. Hence, to reach persuadables, violence will either need to be less vivid or framed in a way that reduces its shock value.

One way prior research suggests this may occur is by placing the violence in the context of entertainment. Of particular utility for understanding the potential effects of terrorist execution videos is Karyn Riddle's (2014) Theory of Vivid Media Violence (TVMV). When media violence scholars use the term "graphicness," Riddle shows that they are typically referring to two factors: (1) the amount of blood and gore in a violent scene and (2) the degree to which the violence is shown up close. Vivid material has been shown to incite strong emotional reactions, to be highly accessible and memorable over the long term, and perhaps most importantly to lead to cognitive elaboration (Riddle 2014).

Based on these findings, Riddle's TVMV has several propositions relevant to our discussion. First, she argues that people will pay more attention to messages and material that include what she refers to as "media violence vividness." Second, gender, age, and sensation seeking stand out as possible moderators of these effects, with women more likely than men to become disgusted by media violence and more likely to look away. Hence, these media are more likely to appeal to young men, who also happen to be the primary target audience of ISIS videos and also those most likely to view them. They also comprise the vast majority of foreign recruits. Third, media violence vividness will lead to stronger emotional reactions. For example, violent video games with images of blood and screaming (i.e., high vividness) create a higher sense of arousal in players compared to study participants who played games without those features. Still, overly graphic and gory violence has been shown to turn off audiences, meaning that these images may be highly arousing, but negatively valent. Fourth, this kind of media violence will, according to Riddle, increase the long-term *accessibility* of related thoughts in memory. For example, studies show that audiences can recall violence in R rated movies such as the *Saw* franchise (whose elements are recreated in ISIS videos) long after exposure.

Fifth, Riddle argues that media violence vividness will increase the complexity of mental models that develop after exposure. Mental models, which are similar to cognitive schema, are representations in memory used to make sense of the world around us and act as cognitive shortcuts for processing information (Roskos-Ewoldson et al. 2004). Scholars have studied whether media violence results in mental models for aggression, finding, for instance, that media violence can activate mental models for aggression, violence, and gore (e.g., Farrar et al. 2006; Krcmar & Hight 2007; Potter et al. 2002; Potter & Smith 2000).

Sixth, this violence will increase the likelihood that audiences will engage in cognitive elaboration, which refers to how thoroughly people process information when exposed to a message, and the degree to which they link new information to cognitions already in memory. In other words, the more vivid the material, the more likely that the audience will process that information in great detail. Studies show, for instance, that vivid messages lead people to elaborate more on the message's central argument than pallid messages do, and have those thoughts and attitudes remain in memory longer (Guadagno et al. 2011; Bushman & Geen 1990).

Lessons from studies of violent video games and violent entertainment media

Research on video games and violent media shows a few things that are important for this discussion. First, some people are especially susceptible to negative effects from exposure to violent images, especially those with family problems and/or a history of domestic violence; personality issues such as callous and unemotional traits, narcissism, and Machiavellianism; social rejection from peer groups; and those with access to guns and/or who have drug and alcohol problems. Effects (for some) include aggressive behavior and cognitions, decreased empathy, and increased psychological arousal (see, Ferguson & Colwell 2017).

Perhaps the most important potential effect, however, is desensitization to violence. Some studies show that long-term exposure to violent media can lead to desensitization, which is a lessening of cognitive, emotional, and behavioral responses to violent stimuli (Linz, Donnerstein, & Penrod 1988). Grizzard et al. (2016) found that repeated video game play led not only to greater habituation (i.e., less arousal) but also to generalization (the extension of habitual responses to novel situations). In other words, players became more numb to the violent action in the video games, and this extended to their reactions to a new, but similarly arousing video game. In another study that had some participants assume the character of a "moral" UN soldier and others an "immoral" terrorist, Grizzard et al. expanded on these findings by showing that repeated playing of video games led to a decrease in elicitations of guilt in the immoral condition. This also extended to real-world hypotheticals for those who had assumed the first-person "terrorist" character.

Thus, it is possible that one long-term effect of regular exposure to vivid violence, which permeates pop culture, is a general desensitization and that this can reduce feelings of moral responsibility not only in the game but also in novel situations. That is, violence in video games and entertainment media are so common as to have desensitized many viewers when they encounter violence in these and other domains that mimic those formats. Recent research suggests desensitization effects are a precursor to cognitive and affective outcomes. These outcomes include changes in knowledge structures such as increased belief that violence is normative, and decreased negative attitudes toward violence (Bushman and Anderson, 2009). A knowledge structure is any set of concepts in an associative network that have "become strongly linked together" (Buckley and Anderson, 2006) through experience.

In addition, it is important to recognize that prior research shows many positive effects of playing violent video games and watching violent movies for some people, especially positive emotions and efficacious feelings that may be transferable to the experience of exposure to videos that use similar motifs (Nabi 2009, Zendle 2016). In other words, the positive affect one gains from playing violent video games or watching violent movies can be activated by exposure to similar content in other domains. The cognitive mechanism by which this occurs is that of spreading activation in an associative network. In such a network, the mind is modeled as a set of discrete nodes that each contains a distinct concept and is joined together by associations (Collins and Loftus, 1975). This implies that for some people susceptible to ISIS messaging, the knowledge structure, in part reinforced by violent video games and entertainment media, is activated when they see the ISIS videos that replicate those modes.

Summary and discussion: why ISIS videos may be more effective than AQ videos

Past research on the effects of vivid and violent messages, especially in entertainment formats such as video games, movies, and television shows, offers many reasons to think violent ISIS videos that utilize these formats might be influential with a wider array of persuadable audiences than AQ execution videos. First, we know from the literature on casualty coverage effects that people appear to process such images through the prism of their predispositions. This implies that those selectively exposing themselves to terrorist online videos come to that experience receptive, at least at some level, to that message and may thus be more likely than the general public to accept the frame of the violence they see as justified.

Still, that does not in any way guarantee that this will occur. For one important reason, the violence in these videos is far more graphic and extreme than any found in Western news coverage of war casualties. Hence, the first hurdle violent messages must clear before they can hope to be persuasive is the likelihood of audience aversion. Prior research in other domains shows that overly vivid images, especially those that include visual and aural violence, can repulse audiences to the point that they do not choose to expose themselves to the rest of the message, or don't pay close attention to it. Given that, terrorist videos that utilize particularly shocking images and sounds of violence – such as the Berg AQ video described above – are likely to turn off all but the "choir" of already converted audience members.

Yet we also know from earlier work that vivid messages that don't cross this line can increase audience attention and be more persuasive. The question then becomes, are there reasons to think that ISIS videos that include violence and executions could achieve this goal? There are several reasons, suggested by prior research discussed above, to think they might.

First, and most important, videos that utilize pop culture formats – which comprise about 40% of ISIS videos featuring executions (Lesaca 2015) – create more emotional distance between the audience and the violence than, for example, videos that employ a news or documentary format, such as AQ execution videos. That is, by using familiar tropes, the gore looks like that found in a video game or a horror movie, and thus lacks verisimilitude and the same level of shock value. AQ videos, by contrast, look like news, which is real, and thus the violence is more real and more horrifying.

Second, the reason for this is that people's exposure to a steady diet of violent entertainment media has been shown to create a mental model that normalizes violence in these formats, and research shows that these mental models are transferable to other, similar domains. Hence, for those predisposed to being open to ISIS messages – evidenced by their selective exposure to these videos – we would expect many of them to have this "entertainment violence" mental model activated by the presence of familiar pop culture motifs. The violence, in other words, has a familiar kind of unreal quality to it that makes it more palatable and less likely to turn these persuadable viewers off from the rest of the message. In addition, prior research shows that violent entertainment media can actually be functional for certain viewers, satisfying a variety of needs, including pleasure, escapism, and, most importantly, efficacy (Nabi 2009). These feelings have also been shown to be transferable, meaning that some persuadable audiences may be especially susceptible to the underlying arguments in these videos of empowerment.

Third, because the violence in many of these pop culture themed ISIS videos is framed in a way that is more likely to accentuate the effects of vivid messages than the more shocking and aversion-creating AQ videos, we would expect these videos to lead to cognitive elaboration among many persuadable audience members. Cognitive elaboration has been shown to occur after exposure to vivid messages, including violent ones that activate attention rather than cross a line leading to aversion. It refers to the way these types of messages can induce audiences to devote more cognitive effort and resources to thinking critically about the entire message, and perhaps being more open to it. This is important in understanding the potentially disturbing effectiveness of these types of ISIS videos. If the violence was overly shocking, as with the AQ videos, only the choir would be likely to be able to stomach exposure much less pay attention to and accept the underlying message. ISIS videos, by contrast, frame the violence in a more palatable format that is vivid enough to open the minds of persuadables to the rest of the message, which is embodied in everything from the *Nasheed* battle hymns, to the dialogue spoken by fighters and narrators, to graphics that make explicit and implicit arguments about ISIS's key themes of brutality, victimhood, mercy, war, belonging, and apocalyptic utopianism (Winter 2015).

As an example, consider *Nasheeds*, the didactic music that forms the soundtrack of most ISIS videos. These are interesting messaging techniques that would be ineffective if audiences were too mentally busy being repelled by onscreen violence. Research by Lemieux and Nill (2011), for example, shows that people tend to be less critical of a message when its set to music and that music with aggressive themes can activate aggressive thoughts and feelings in audiences. Yet the key point here is that these communication effects can only occur if the audience is paying attention in the first place. But if they are, and if in fact they are attending to a message likely to lead to cognitive elaboration, then the implication is that the music's message – key to ISIS rhetoric – will be especially likely to be inculcated. If the violence was too vivid, by contrast, research shows it could draw attention away from the core message.

In sum, ISIS videos' utilization of pop culture formats allows them to cast a wider net than AQ's violent videos because they (1) create more emotional distance between the audience and the violence, and may have stronger, more enduring effects because they (2) prime preexisting efficacy-reinforcing mental models and (3) induce cognitive elaboration. According to Winter, the group's messaging focuses on six interconnected themes: brutality, victimhood, mercy, war, belonging, and apocalyptic utopianism. These, then, make up the components of the mental model created by exposure to ISIS videos for those who are predisposed to being open to their message.

Conclusions

Policy makers, pundits, and frightened and horrified people around the world have worried about the alleged power of violent terrorist media messages since at least the release of the Nicholas Berg beheading video in 2003. This fear is rooted in concerns about "powerful media" as a negative influence on weak, susceptible audiences that goes back more than century, and seems to return with heightened hyperbolism with the introduction of each new mass medium since at least the advent of radio in the early 20th century. Digital media, and terrorists' use of it, fanned the flames of these fears once again, leading world governments to spend millions of dollars combating these online messages and worrying about their effectiveness in winning wars of ideas, terror, or whatever the catchphrase of the day may be.

Of particular concern, especially in light of terrorist attacks in the West and rising numbers of foreign fighters flocking to Iraq, Syria, Libya, and other war-torn countries, has been the ability of these violent videos to sway vulnerable citizens of, especially, Western countries to join the terrorists' cause. The assumptions about the power of these videos have remained constant over the years, even as the videos' content has evolved. Critically, however, these assumptions have rarely if ever been based on any theoretical or empirical reason to believe that these videos are, in fact, effective.

Although it would be difficult to the point of perhaps being impossible to test the power of these videos on persuadable audiences experimentally or in some other empirical way that would help us answer this question more definitively, a large, long-standing research literature in the study of vividness and violent media effects provides a strong theoretical basis for assessing the potential effects of these messages. That literature makes a couple of points clear. First, the most shocking violence, the kind shown in videos like the Berg and Foley beheadings that are most likely to end up on the news, are probably the least likely to persuade all but the already persuaded. They are too vivid, and their graphic vividness is only accentuated by their news/documentary format.

There may be reason to be more concerned, however, about the pop culture themed violent videos produced by ISIS over the past few years. These videos, with their high production values and violence embedded in formats familiar to virtually anyone immersed in Western entertainment culture (which of course has a global reach and appeal), are likely to appeal to a wider array of persuadable viewers already predisposed to being open to the basic ISIS message of Western imperialism and Muslim victimhood and empowerment. In these cases, the violence is more likely to activate mental models of violent entertainment that create emotional distance between the viewer and the violence, are infused with potentially efficacious and positive affective responses, and are vivid in a way that leads to cognitive elaboration that makes the larger, underlying message of the video potentially more persuasive.

This is all the more disturbing when we consider the traits of many of those, especially in the West, who have joined or tried to join ISIS. In an exhaustive study of American recruits, Vidino and Hughes (2015) show that although there isn't the kind of common denominator that we would like to find that would help identify, target, and intervene before someone is converted or commits a lone wolf terrorist attack, there are some traits that are shared by more than a few ISIS recruits. Specifically, (1) a family history of domestic violence, as perpetrator and/or victim; (2) feelings of low efficacy and social isolation; (3) anger about perceived oppression of Muslims, especially in their home country and the West; (4) generally 18–35 years old, though many exceptions; (5) typically some interpersonal connection, be it online or with a real friend or family member who is in or sympathetic to ISIS; and (6) mostly men (though several cases of women who do not, contrary to Western media coverage, conform to gender stereotypical reasons for joining [Alexander 2016]).

In other words, these are often people who share some traits with many of those who are not only drawn to violent entertainment media and video games, but specifically (because many people fit that description) *do so to gratify specific needs for orientation/belonging and efficacy.* And these people are often the ones for whom violent media are not repellent, persuasive/effective in terms of message inculcation, and enduring in their effects, especially in terms of creation and priming of an aggression-laden mental model. This lends credence to the argument here that these videos – at least the ones that utilize the pop culture formats – may be more effective with a wider array of persuadable target audience members than, say, AQ videos or ISIS videos that don't employ these tactics.

There are several implications of this argument for thinking about combating ISIS's strategic narratives embodied in these videos. First and foremost, though, is the admonition to not exaggerate their power. While the argument here is that there are a host of theoretical reasons to think this specific kind of terrorist video may have a broader appeal, important caveats still apply. These include the fact that one has to be predisposed to the message in the first place, needs to be immersed enough in violent entertainment media to have already inculcated that particular mental model, and most likely needs to have this message reinforced through some interpersonal communication. This is, after all, consistent not only with the data on foreign fighters' experiences, but with the basic findings of media effects studies since the 1940s (Katz & Lazarsfeld 1955; Lazarsfeld & Merton 1948). In addition, it's important to note that claims that the terrorists' digital media strategy is "winning" the war usually coincide with periods when the particular group is ascendant. Yet we don't hear claims that the West is "defeating" ISIS online when the group is in retreat, as it is now. So while ISIS's video output has, like its recruitment of foreign fighters, dropped off precipitously in the past year, we know this isn't because of the West's digital counterstrategy, since there really wasn't much of an organized effort in that area during that time, especially with the Americans, who dissolved their flailing CSCC and replaced it with a Global Engagement Center (GEC) that is still getting off the ground. The reason ISIS's is "losing" the online war is simply because it's losing the actual war on the ground. To paraphrase an axiom from American politics, "It's the war, stupid."

This isn't to say, however, that policy makers shouldn't worry about and strategize to combat terrorists' online efforts. This chapter has demonstrated solid theoretical reasons to think some of these messages may have a broader appeal than other types of videos. Social messaging apps that traffic in a kind of virtual interpersonal communication and creation of terrorist opinion leaders within those networks have been shown to be dangerously effective and hard to counter, especially in Europe. The implications of this chapter's argument are that while we shouldn't exaggerate, much less panic about, the kind of violent videos that shock us, we should take some of them more seriously than others. That means, for instance, focusing on who is producing those videos and who is watching them. Other research, for instance, has shown that while it is common for online information bubbles to form that traffic in fear, misinformation, and groupthink, there are important individuals within those networks that are not only influential within them but sometimes crossover to other online networks (Lynch et al. 2015). Most importantly, though, it means adopting community and culturally based approaches to countermessaging, including working with local and regional messengers and media that are credible with the target audience, as opposed to the clumsy, heavy handed approach of much of CSCC's efforts, branded as they were with the US stamp. Encouragingly, this appears to be the strategy of the newer GEC. Less encouragingly, there is little reason to think media coverage won't continue to exaggerate the power of these videos, and of terrorists' online output, or that policy makers won't feel pressured by that coverage to overreact and thus reinforce the terrorists' strategic narrative.

9

THE BATTLE FOR THE BATTLE OF THE NARRATIVES

Sidestepping the double fetish of digital and CVE

Akil N. Awan, Alister Miskimmon and Ben O'Loughlin

Introduction

Countering violent extremism (CVE) is hot; digital CVE is hotter still. As the US replaced the Center for Strategic Counterterrorism Communications with another new CVE hub, the Global Engagement Center, other Western governments have followed suit in building teams charged with countering the narratives thought to radicalise individuals and groups into violence. Officials seek to 'contest the space', and, whilst most evidence points to the role of off-line social dynamics in leading individuals to violence (Sageman 2004; Awan 2007; Conway and McInerney 2008; Neumann 2012; Vidino and Hughes 2015; Conway 2017), the space is often taken as digital.

Digital CVE is not just hot stuff, it is also a lucrative business, offering significant sums of funding to those who can lay claim to navigating this space. Consequently, a whole host of government agencies, think tanks, civil society groups and private companies are investing a great deal of time, money and effort into digital CVE initiatives. Our aim in this chapter is not to assess and pass judgement on the relative merits of individual CVE campaigns. Certainly, there are potential shortcomings of much of the work currently undertaken on digital CVE. These fall under three broad categories: there is a lack of clarity on the evidentiary basis behind the assumptions underlying CVE. Second, evaluating the effectiveness of CVE campaigns is extremely challenging, leading to a tendency by policy actors to overstate its effect. Finally, there is increasing evidence to suggest that the stated objectives of CVE are difficult to meet because they do not translate into obvious metrics (Elshimi, 2017).

If the push towards CVE is not working, or at the very least, cannot easily be proven to be working, and the premise itself is dubious or not based on an evidentiary basis, then what in reality, is taking place here? We contend, that we are instead witnessing a dual fetishisation of digital CVE.

What do we mean by dual fetishisation? To fetishise is to be excessively or irrationally devoted to an object or activity; to imbue an object with special, even magical qualities, ignoring its banal reality. The banal reality is that all media are new media at one point in time, whether cave paintings or digital. The banal reality is that CVE was COIN (counter-insurgency) a decade ago and previous acronyms in the decades before that. In fact, we are always in the middle: in the middle of developments in mediation and in the middle of the evolution of conflict, violence and its justifications. There are newer and older forms of media, and different actors and institutions adapt and use these forms and technologies of mediation with greater or lesser speed and skill (Hoskins and O'Loughlin, 2007; 2015; Chadwick, 2013; Grusin, 2015). Terrorism and counterterrorism, radicalisers and counter-radicalisers – all are just another set of actors within this history. And yet, all too often, newer media and newer terrorist groups and behaviours are treated as special, even exceptional: a dual fetish.

This chapter makes two moves against this framing. First, we argue this is a *radically unrealistic account of communication and persuasion* that ignores decades of research on radicalisation and a century of research on media effects. It is radical because it is almost wilfully counterproductive. The bureaucratic, target-driven goals of governments may manifest this grasping for a tangible, quantifiable mark of progress, but it also signifies amnesia towards prior COIN and other campaigns. Second and the main purpose of this chapter is *we propose a model of narrative contestation through which governments can address real-world concerns*. Our strategic narrative framework identifies convergence or divergence across narratives of the international system, narratives of identity and narratives of specific problems. By charting possible narrative alignment about how the world works, how we fit into that world and how that bears on current problems, we can identify how and why some radicalising groups may offer a coherent and compelling narrative and why counter-radicalisation offers a less coherent and compelling narrative for certain audiences. This can help explain why a certain problem definition or even worldview becomes meaningful to those open to radicalisation and violence. We illustrate this by comparing the drivers of radicalisation in Europe – with a focus on France and Islamist radicalisation – with the counter-narratives being offered by European leaders. Empirical analysis of the experience of radicalised individuals helps explain why those extremist narratives are persuasive and why certain states' narratives are less so. On that basis, policy actors could form convincing narratives – but this will not be easy.

Our analysis of Islamic State (IS) public communications and claims indicates strong narrative alignment that might have appeal to individuals within particular contexts within French society. By contrast, we find that narratives being projected against IS and in defence of European society are less coherent. It is important to recognise that analysing narratives projected is on only one part of a complex picture; identifying and explaining *the difference these narratives make* to the opinions and behaviour of individuals is another. Narrative reception is complex and requires much further research. This chapter and our analysis provide the rationale for that research agenda.

CVE: the problem of identifying its impact

One of the cornerstones of CVE is the use of public communication tools to dissuade the supporters of violent extremism. The State Department Center for Strategic Counterterrorism Communication's CVE efforts are best captured by their unofficial motto, 'contesting the space'. The maxim received endorsement at the highest levels including that of US President Barak Obama, who deployed the phrase in a speech to the UN General Assembly in 2014, stating that the war against extremism meant "contesting the space that terrorists occupy – including the Internet and social media" (Knowlton 2014).

Primarily, this has involved undermining extremist narratives, and propagating alternative and counter-narratives to them. The US State Department's Global Engagement Center, for example, states that it "shall lead the coordination, integration, and synchronization of Government-wide communications activities directed at foreign audiences abroad in order to *counter the messaging* and diminish the influence of international terrorist organizations".[1] One well-known example of this practice was the use of the Twitter account, @ThinkAgain_DOS by the US State Department's Center for Strategic Counterterrorism Communications, to send anti-extremism messages, until it was superseded by the Global Engagement Center in 2016.

On the face of it, this sounds like an eminently laudable thing to do and would be perfectly reasonable if it was, in fact, only the extremists' narratives that we had to contend with. Indeed, it would be entirely rational as a strategy, if it was the extremists' narratives themselves that had the potency and efficacy to radicalise individuals towards violence. Clearly, that is a preposterous idea, considering that hardly everyone who views, or even regularly consumes extremist material, is transformed into a jihadist automaton. Indeed, such a strategy would rest on a *radically unrealistic account of communication and persuasion* that ignores more than a decade of research on radicalisation and a century of research on media effects, propaganda and PysOps.

The historian of public diplomacy, Robin Brown (2014), argues that Western responses to these aspects of Russian projection and Putin's communication strategies can be characterised as 'propaganda panic'. We argue that the same can be said for many responses to IS and al-Qaeda before them. Brown argues that policymakers, journalists and commentators had fallen into a post–Cold War narrative of declining Russian influence. Thus, they were taken by surprise when in 2014 Putin began to pursue an assertive kinetic and communicative strategy towards Ukraine and those opposing Russian influence there. Propaganda has been an easy peg to hang blame for the situation, Brown writes:

> The attraction of 'propaganda' is that it appears to stand somewhere outside the normal responsibilities of politics or diplomacy and helps to insulate those in charge from an accusation that they weren't paying attention or that their policies have failed. The explanation can then be offered that it is the inadequacy of our propaganda/public diplomacy/ information efforts. The additional twist is that the people who have been responsible for the 'inadequate' response have been saying all along that their work is totally underfunded and so instead of coming out swinging at their critics gratefully pocket the increased appropriations.
>
> *(2014, no page)*

Tongue slightly in cheek and perhaps with "hybrid war" in mind, Brown notes how quickly commentators turn one situation into a broader category, "the rise of a new unconventional-hybrid-asymmetric-Mad Max – conflict threat" (2014, no page). But perhaps more telling is the assumption that if the West could out-propagandise Putin and Russia through better-funded, more sophisticated communication strategies, influence could be exerted in the region. A similar surprise has been evident in Western approaches to Islamist terrorism. The mythology of bin Laden in the caves of Afghanistan reaching into Western homes through the Internet to radicalise the vulnerable individual is one that assumes a juxtaposition of low- and high-technology environments as well as a geographical distance and a near-metaphysical shock that this distance is overcome. Equally, that mythology reinforces an assumption that such influence is possible and, therefore, must be countered. This in turn assumes that such counter-operations must also be able to exert influence. This is a series of missteps based on an initial false assumption.

The propaganda panic identified by Brown exemplifies the tendency of policymakers to imagine how influence works. After years of ethnographic study of UK military communications teams, Sarah Maltby (2015; see also 2012a, 2012b) argues that strategic communication policymakers fall into a trap of presuming that if they take full advantage of contemporary media systems, then they can exert more influence on the attitudes and behaviour of target populations. It is not simply that, as Brown suggests, policymakers tend to presume that there is a unified enemy with a coherent narrative that must be fought at all costs, fought by 'us' with our benign intentions. Maltby highlights the even more suspect assumption that influence activity by the West can cause the intended effect and that there is an audience waiting and open to narratives, whether IS's or the West's. A problem here is that policymakers trained in strategic communication by marketing and public relations experts are taught that 'the message' is transmitted from the source (them) to targets who receive what was transmitted and, allowing for the possibility of interference by noise, this will create behavioural effect in line with the message's content (Corman, 2009; cf. Carey, 1989). This transport metaphor is wholly unrealistic since there is never a beginning or end to communication, nor are 'messages' discrete packages with unambiguous content. Rather, there are perceptions and communications constantly reflecting between actors, often unintentionally, so that a more accurate metaphor would be a hall of mirrors (Archetti, 2017). The sense that 'targets' or audiences make of these communications is not the function of their position within a society. Rather, it depends on their social context and networks, who they talk politics with and how they think about how their opinion fits within broader public opinion.

Military and security policymakers seem to find intuitive sense in the notion that 'getting the message across' could make a predictable difference to attitudes and behaviours, and express fears that 'Islamic State are getting their message across better than we are'. This is an absolute misunderstanding of communication. Maltby cites the godfathers of communication theory and media analysis, Bernard Berelson and Paul Lazarsfeld, who in 1954 – a time of far fewer communication channels and a more controllable media environment – wrote,

> Some kinds of communication, on some kinds of issues, brought to the attention of some kinds of people under some kinds of conditions, have some kinds of effects.
>
> *(Berelson et al., 1954: 356)*

This is exactly our point about violent extremist materials in digital spaces: *some* content about *some* issues brought to the attention of *some* individuals living in *certain* contexts and consuming media in *certain* conditions, will have *some* kinds of effects. And yet, for states charged with security and order, they *must* be seen to act. They must act on and in communication spaces. Powers writes, "controlling information flows has become increasingly difficult, yet crucial, for state actors, and efforts at managing these flows are symbolic of the broader challenges that the modern era of globalization presents to state sovereignty" (Powers 2014: 239). The need to counter the narratives of IS is not simply about preventing the radicalisation of individuals, then; it is part of a broader anxiety about risk and connectivity in global society (Awan et al., 2011).

The role of strategic narratives

Cristina Archetti suggests that narratives in both terrorism research and for counterterrorism practitioners are *en vogue*. She argues, however, that, "…surprisingly little effort has gone into understanding the nature of narratives as well as their role in the phenomenon of contemporary extremism" (Archetti 2017: 218–219). Responding to Archetti's call, this chapter takes a strategic narrative approach to understanding the role of narratives in CVE. A strategic narrative analysis enables us to systematically explore how narratives are formed, projected and received. We contend that only by examining the processes of formation, projection and reception of narratives can we more fully understand processes, not only of how individuals become radicalised and how violent extremists influence others but also how CVE practitioners and analysts might understand the role of narratives and communication more generally in their activities. Strategic narrative also suggests a way to understand *what* is being communicated, by contending that narratives can be conceived as falling in to three categories: identity narratives, system narratives and issue narratives.

We define strategic narratives as the following:

> Strategic narratives are a means for political actors to construct a shared meaning of the past, present, and future of international politics to shape the behaviour of domestic and international actors.
>
> *(Miskimmon et al., 2013: 2)*

As we have already pointed out, strategic narratives come in three forms. Narratives of the international system generally point to who the main actors are and the rules, norms or regimes which underpin the structural order of the globe. As we will outline below, IS's system narrative straightforwardly captures the main points of divergence from the Western model of international order. Second, identity narratives point to the values and goals an actor has and along with the actor's system narrative, provide important context for the policy or issue narratives which the actor promotes. Each of these narratives – system, identity and issue – are linked, and coherence across each of these domains can lead to the creation of a compelling and influential narrative.

From the content of what is being strategically narrated, the narrative cycle of formation, projection and reception is vital to understanding how narratives move through the new media ecology and are crucially received, interpreted and remediated by individuals in many different ways. Understanding this cycle of communication is a key. Formation of narratives focuses on the process of creating a narrative and the role of key actors in this. Individuals, groups or institutions can all play a role in the formation of a narrative. External actors and events can prove disruptive in the formation process if the context for a particular narrative is changed. The process of projection of narratives focuses on how, particularly in a new media environment, narratives are projected and contested (Awan et al., 2011; Miskimmon et al., 2013). Reception is a crucially important process in strategic narrative research. Floor Keuleers (2015) stresses that people do not simply repeat elite narratives but reformulate them to fit their own life experience, hopes and fears. Reception has been studied in various ways, for example in public opinion polls or in focus groups. Central to reception of strategic narrative is the role of the individual and how they respond to the narrative they receive: "Reception happens in social contexts where narratives may be discussed socially as well as processed individually. Reception depends on the availability of specific mediums like radio or services like Facebook, and each medium offers different possibilities for communicating back" (Miskimmon et al., 2017: 9, Figures 9.1 and 9.2).

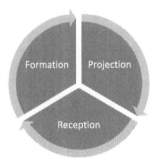

FIGURE 9.1 The Strategic Narrative Cycle.

FIGURE 9.2 Core Components of Strategic Narrative.

This chapter now moves to analyse IS strategic narrative and how they have been able to forge a relatively coherent system, identity and policy narrative to seek to advance their interests. We then seek to understand the reception of the IS narrative in terms of narrative resonance, and how this problematises existing efforts in CVE to project counter-narratives in to this space.

IS's narrative coherence

At the heart of IS's appeal is the alluring simplicity of its *System Narrative*, which is composed of two main strands. The first strand, which sits at the core of all jihadist narratives and originates with al-Qaeda, compels Muslim audiences to view contemporary conflicts through the prism of a wider historical global attack on Islam and Muslims by a belligerent 'Zionist-Crusader Alliance'. In response to this assault, the jihadists claimed not only to have awakened the *Ummah* (global Muslim community of belief) to the reality of their predicament but also claimed to serve as the sole and crucial vanguard, offering audiences the opportunity to reply to the enemy in kind (Awan 2012). As many commentators have recognised, this System Narrative has remained remarkably coherent and consistent over time (Scheuer 2008; Wright 2007).

Since June 2014, the second strand of the *System Narrative* – IS's own unique addendum to the already heady mix – claims that the caliphate has now been re-established, thereby restoring glory and honour to the downtrodden Muslims once again. The obvious corollary to the establishment of the caliphate was that it was therefore now incumbent on every Muslim to (i) make *hijrah*, or emigrate to the new caliphate; (ii) to make *bayah*, or pledge of allegiance to its leader and caliph; and (iii) to help defend and build this new utopian state. Hijrah is an important theme in Islamic literature and stems from the emigration of the Prophet Muhammad from Mecca around 632 AD in order to escape religious persecution and move to Medina, where he founded a religious community and burgeoning city-state. The establishment of the caliphate in June 2014, therefore, provided compelling alternative narratives to audiences: undertake your own hijrah (a journey that paralleled that of the Prophet Muhammad); escape the persecution in your own societies; live under Islamic sovereignty and law; help defend the burgeoning state and community; and ultimately restore the state to its long-lost glory (Awan 2016).

Both ideas, of jihad and Caliphate, are underpinned by the primary identity of all Muslims as first and foremost part of the worldwide *Ummah or community of believers* and not as residents or citizens of their countries of birth or residence. It is this radical interpretation of the religious community of believers as the sole locus of identity and belonging then, that IS's *Identity Narratives* are predicated upon. IS deploys the considerable weight of its media apparatus and social media presence to bolster and maintain these carefully constructed identity narratives. Awan (forthcoming) identifies three key media strategies from IS' extensive media catalogue that are central to its success in promulgating these identity narratives:

1. **Attachment** involves the reinforcing and strengthening of self-identity, by compelling audiences to see themselves as part of the in-group identity. Prominent examples include:
    *   Military training videos that witness the transformation of individual recruits into a fighting unit, by effacing the identity of the individual before fusing the identity of the individual with the broader fighting group.
    *   Nurturing fictive kinship through the vicarious identification with victimhood and grievance. Most jihadist testimony videos will follow particular tropes in which individuals cite altruistic motivations, such as the defence of their community, for their actions, invoking phrases like 'my brothers and sisters', 'our blood' or 'our children'. These are designed to nurture attachment to the group almost through blood bonds.
    *   Promoting in-group identities as redemptive, for example, by providing redemption from criminal or hedonistic pasts. Similarly, IS' social media canon is replete with imagery that promotes the identification with chivalrous warrior, hero, champion, winner or real men, providing redemption from impotent, marginalised or emasculated identities. These media outputs often very cleverly deploy popular culture references from films and videogame like *Call of Duty*, to sell these identities.

2. **Deracination/Deculturation** aims to weaken and delink individuals' identities from all other competing identities, whether they are national, ethnic, cultural or political in origin. Examples include:
    * Denying the legitimacy of modern nation-states, or geographical boundaries. These range from infographics and maps that erase current national borders and state demarcations, to viral social media campaigns such as #Sykespicotover, that accompanied the symbolic destruction of the historic Sykes-Picot border between eastern Syria and northern Iraq in 2015 (Awan and Dockter 2016).
    * Severing citizenhood by filming the ritualistic burning of original national identity documents in response to new members being issued IS branded passports.
    * Promoting a deculturated religion in Salafism which offers a 'pure' religious identity that is divorced from the cultural baggage of an ethnic or national religious affiliation.
3. **Polarisation** seeks to reinforce diametrical opposition between identities, highlighting how the self and the other differ. Examples include:
    * Dehumanisation of enemies, referring to them as dogs, pigs or monkeys, or through the use of pejorative sectarian insults.
    * Expressing loyalty to the believers and disavowal of others (*al-wala wal-bara*): Issue 11 of IS' English language magazine, *Dabiq*, shows happy multiracial brothers in arms alongside the concept of loyalty to believers and disavowal of disbelievers, juxtaposed against 'American Racism'. This is not just about dissaving those who are not of your faith, but about disavowing anyone who differs, including the recruit's parents and family.
    * Employing the practice of excommunication (*takfir*), which functions to keep the faith 'pure'. Following the Charlie Hebdo attacks in France in 2015, the February issue of *Dabiq*, wrote of polarising the world by destroying its greatest threat, the grayzone; that space in which young Frenchmen could be both Muslims and good citizens of the French Republic, without any inherent contradiction. IS anticipated that provocative terrorist attacks, like the ones in Paris, would goad the French towards overreaction and create a climate of fear and hostility, further alienating French Muslims from wider society. Western Muslims would then be forced to make 'one of two choices': between apostasy or IS' bastardised version of belief.

These narratives are immensely powerful, exhibiting remarkable coherence and strong *narrative alignment* across system, identity and issue narratives. However, these narratives, potent as they may be, are not, in and of themselves, sufficient to account for the radicalisation phenomenon, particularly amongst young Muslims in the West. Instead, we recognise that narratives constitute only one part in the complex array of elements that intersect to ultimately manifest as a move towards violent extremism.

Following Awan (2016), we conceptualise the role narratives play in violent radicalisation by viewing *Narrative* as one side of a triad, with the second and third sides representing *Context* and *Agency*, respectively. As we have seen, narratives propounded by extremist groups like IS are highly compelling, but it is the individual's *Context* (encompassing personal, political, psychological, social, political, economic and cultural spheres) that is central to whether this narrative resonates with the individual. In fact, the extremists' narrative is almost irrelevant unless it finds fertile ground to take root, which it achieves by resonating with individuals on a personal level, resonating with their everyday lives and lived experiences. Context is in fact the primary distinguisher between all of those who regularly consume extremist literature, say for academic, journalistic or other research purposes, but nevertheless manage to maintain scholarly distance, and a young 18-year-old who finds himself increasingly drawn to IS messaging. The final side in the triad representing individual agency highlights the fact that very few individuals whose context and circumstances intersect with a coherent narrative become de facto jihadist automatons, but rather individuals make decisions and choices. When all three elements of the triad intersect in this way, we witness *Narrative Resonance* (Awan 2016).

Narrative resonance

Let us turn to some examples of how IS narratives work to attain *narrative resonance*, by intersecting with structural conditions and the lived experiences facing some young Muslims in the West, and the challenges that this understanding then poses for digital CVE campaigns.

(i) Alienation & estrangement

A survey of public attitudes on Muslims in Western countries (Pew Research Center 2006; Ipsos Mori 2016), statements on Muslims by political leaders and an examination of Islamophobia within mainstream media outlets (Poole 2002; Poole and Richardson 2006; Allen 2010; Zempi and Awan 2017) illustrates just how toxic the popular and media discourse on Muslims has become in many parts of the US and Europe, often presenting Muslim minorities as an unwelcome presence.

France, who has exported the largest number of her citizens to the ranks of IS amongst European states (Van Ginkel and Entenmann 2016), is a particularly pertinent case study and illustrates the mechanisms through which narrative resonance might be readily attained. Within the public discourse in France over the past few decades, a growing Islamophobia, and increasing rejection of the immigrant, and the other, has permeated French political and social discourse around Muslims. This environment has led to, amongst other things, a large majority of French citizens holding unfavourable views of Islam – regarding it as 'intolerant' and 'incompatible' with French values;[2] a staggering public overestimation of

the size of the current and projected Muslim population in France;[3] the dese-
cration of gravestones of French Muslim World War II veterans (The Telegraph
2008); sartorial restrictions on Muslim women's dress and the linkage of dress
to violence – most visible with the forced undressing of French Muslim women
wearing burkinis by armed police (Quinn 2016); the advent of bestselling novels
like Michel Houellebecq's 2015 *Soumission*, which imagines a future France over-
run and ruled by Islamists. But perhaps most significantly, it has helped spur the
far-right Front National to victory in the 2014 European Parliament election and
significant electoral successes in the 2017 presidential election.

It is in this context that we might begin to understand how, for some French
Muslims feeling under siege and alienated in their own country, an alternative identity narrative might appear more appealing than a tainted national
one (for a literature review, see Mitts 2017). Groups like IS, that prey on this
kind of alienation, end up benefitting enormously. IS has shrewdly attempted
not just to capitalise on these feelings of alienation and identity crises, but
hopes to actively build on them by creating conditions in Western societies
that work towards these outcomes by eliminating the so-called 'grey zones'.
Moreover, IS wants to be perceived as a welcoming utopia, which is central to
its grand narrative. We tend to think of IS propaganda as primarily constituting
brutal violence, with grisly beheadings, burnings and crucifixions – what we
might refer to as the pornography of violence, which often deliberately targets
Western audiences and sensibilities (Awan 2016; O'Loughlin 2018). However,
the overwhelming majority of IS media content at the height of its output in
2015 – around 80% – was in fact centred around depictions of blissful civilian
life in the 'utopian' caliphate; state-building, identity and welcoming, joining
a community, escaping persecution and enjoying religious freedoms (Winter
2015; Awan forthcoming).

(ii) Socio-economic marginalisation

A second example of how narrative resonance is attained relates to socio-economic
marginalisation. Many of the individuals from France and Belgium who joined
IS or carried out attacks at home have hailed from the French *banlieues*, or other
ghetto like areas in and around Brussels. These environments are often characterised as providing a heady mix of unemployment, crime, drugs, institutional
racism and endemic cycles of poverty and disenfranchisement (Laurence and
Vaïsse 2006; Todd 2016; Packer 2015; Awan 2015). It is in these sorts of scenar-
ios that radical groups might potentially offer an escape from a bleak future, or
a criminal past. This is particularly striking in France where around 70% of the
prison population is Muslim, despite the fact that Muslims only make up around
7%–8% of the general population (Atran and Hamid 2015).

IS online propaganda shrewdly seeks to capitalise on these structural inequalities in its appeals. The jihadists offer redemption through the image of the
heroic warrior, with the individual reborn as some sort of avenging hero for the

victimised community. Following the Charlie Hedbo attack, IS's official radio station praised the 'Jihadi *heroes* who had avenged the Prophet', confirming the Kouachi brothers transformation from petty criminals and nobodies into heroes of Islam. The appeal to the valiant holy warrior or chivalrous knight is a recurring theme in jihadist literature, and the IS's propaganda machine has been busy pumping out material that shrewdly seeks to exploit these tensions. Recent social media propaganda included the telling phrases "Sometimes people with the worst pasts create the best futures" and "Why be a loser when you can be a martyr" (Awan 2016). In this context, IS's identity narrative offers, perhaps for the first time, a sense of being part of an elite group that compensates for the shortcomings of their own trivial existence and insignificance.

The West's counter-narrative response

Naturally, addressing issues like socio-economic marginalisation or identity alienation requires time, funds, effort and perhaps most importantly, political will. This applies across Western states seeking to CVE or radicalisation, and not least France. If, for example, the French government wanted to counter IS recruitment in France, the deeply troubling and disproportionate representation of Muslim men in French prisons would seem an obvious candidate to tackle. This is particularly pressing, considering that those prisons have long been recognised as incubators of radicalisation (Neumann 2010; Silke and Veldhuis 2017). However, this is not an easy undertaking and would demand institutional changes over the course of a number of generations to even begin to remedy – a prospect certainly outside the scope of any given French political election cycle. Similarly, any serious attempt to deal with the growing alienation of French Muslims from wider society would also require an urgent reappraisal of the shortcomings of France's national identity narrative, as enshrined in her motto, *Liberté, égalité, fraternité*, particularly when a significant proportion of her citizens feel they had been systematically deprived of these ideals and did not feel part of French society. In short, France would have to address a fundamental *narrative misalignment* between its System, Identity and Issue Narratives, and the resultant dissonance experience by some of her citizens.

In a European context, what counter-narratives are on offer? A more basic question is, what narratives do European states and the European Union (EU) tell about themselves and their role in the world? For if a vision of a bright future was on offer at home, there would be no alienation or dislocation that would push an individual to seek political alternatives at home or abroad. However, in recent years, there is a sense within Europe of multiple internal and external crises. Terrorist attacks in Paris and Brussels, followed by what German police labelled 'group sexual harassment in crowds' in Cologne on New Year's Eve 2015, have led to suspicion of existing citizens of North African or Middle East origin or migrants and refugees arriving in Europe. The conflation of refugees and migrants with terrorism and essentialised cultural difference contributes to the rising electoral popularity of far-right groups and leaders, as well as symbolic outbursts such as the cover of Polish magazine *wSieci* in February 2016, depicting a white woman draped in the blue EU flag being clutched at by dark hands coming in from outside the frame (Sherwood 2016). Finally, Brexit not only registers as a symbolic loss of one EU member but alters the balance of power within Europe, creating uncertainty about which path Europe is taking.

At a *system narrative* level, in recent years, the EU and European states have often reneged on former claims that world order was following a path towards universal values. The European Council has proclaimed that the EU foreign policy, through which it has traditionally sought to diffuse norms of democracy, the rule of law and human rights in regions surrounding the European area, is no longer promoting universal values. The European Council has stated that it "will take *stabilisation as its main political priority…*recognising that *not all partners aspire to EU rules and standards*" (European Commission and High Representative of the Union for Foreign Affairs and Security Policy 2015: 2, italics added). In other words, if authoritarian leaders in the Middle East and North Africa 'arc of instability' wish to reject democracy and human rights, the EU will no longer view this as a high priority problem to overcome. This signalled a pragmatic turn; still a nod to universal values but a recognition that these values are not always shared and, as crises intensify in and around Europe's borders, stability is the priority value to realise. The EU's chief foreign policymaker, High Representative Mogherini, has spoken not of a civilisation united by shared human rights and values but an "alliance of civilisations" (Mogherini, 2016: no page). If the system is no longer one of shared values, then this in turn creates a different European identity narrative: its values are no longer superior because they were forged through Enlightenment reason, but rather they are simply a local, contextual set of norms that others are free to turn away from. This has the potential to diminish the EU's historical identity narrative, the future direction of the European integration project, and sets potential limits on its persuasive power in international affairs. And France, as source to many of these once-universal values, faces this identity crisis most acutely.

Looking to policy narratives in Europe, it is not just the number of urgent policy dilemmas European states face – migration, post-financial crisis economic uncertainty, terrorism, Brexit and illiberal democracies – but the difficulty of addressing such challenges. As the Polish social theorist Bauman wrote, power has escaped politics:

> Having leaked from a society forcefully laid open by the pressures of globalizing forces, power and politics drift ever further in opposite directions. The problem, and the awesome task that will in all probability confront the current century as its paramount challenge, is the bringing of power and politics together again.
>
> *(Bauman 2007: 25)*

Bauman's argument speaks to our earlier claim that communication is at the heart of a wider anxiety about control for state policymakers in the 21st century. Any 'propaganda panic' is because control of communication is both important in itself for managing problems of radicalisation but also important because it characterises the dilemma of achieving control of multiple global flows – of people, arms, ideas and germs. This means that the quest for a more coherent narrative entails formulating a wider set of responses to these problems of how to govern in the 21st century at all. Again, this explains why states feel the need to *do something* even when there is no theoretical or evidentiary basis that it will work, including digital counter-narrative operations. For the larger challenge is too large for most policymakers to address.

These fundamental theoretical challenges concerning power and control, tied to long-standing issues and immediate real-world issues of stagnation in wages and social mobility and conflictual identity politics, are central factors that explain why a positive narrative about the future of life in Europe is not easy to articulate. And a narrative of mere stability or consolidation, of 'getting through the crisis', is hardly inspiring or appealing to young people. In short, whilst the IS narrative is fairly consistent, the EU and European leaders have trouble offering an inspiring or coherent narrative or offering hope for a better future.

These difficulties go some way towards explaining why CVE is so often fetishised. It is relatively cheap, when compared to say overhauling the French prison system. Crucially, it allows governments to be seen by anxious publics to be proactively *doing* something. Digital CVE will be picked up security correspondents and technology journalists and can act as a public signal of taking the matter seriously. CVE also caters to the bureaucratic, metric-driven goals of government public diplomacy and international communication. Government agencies inevitably need to specify targets, and how they might measure achievement of those targets, and so are often grasping for tangible, quantifiable milestones or mark of progress.

Twitter's 2015 'takedown' policy, which removed all IS-supporting accounts, is one widely cited example of success in the CVE field (Conway, Khawaja, and Lakhani 2017). However, what is often not acknowledged is that compelling a social media company to remove extremist material and accounts from its platform, has serious consequences for freedom of expression and censorship,[4] and often simply forces the group and its supporters to migrate to other social media platforms – in IS's case, primarily to Telegram.

However, even more problematically, other CVE campaigns which seek to contest the space by producing media content containing counter-narratives have used social media views, likes and even page impressions as proof of concept and efficacy. The biggest problem with this sort of metric for success is the constituency of the audience: if you are proverbially preaching to the choir, it hardly matters if your campaign goes viral. The other major problem is that such metrics are always incomplete because persuasion is qualitative and multifaceted. The inability to measure soft power is another example in international affairs; hence, we argue for analysing the role of strategic narratives, who can be evidenced, rather than attraction (see Roselle et al., 2014).

Moreover, CVE campaigns such as these can also circumvent proving their efficacy. There is little evidence to suggest that online CVE campaigns work. The problem is that it is impossible to prove a false negative; it is impossible to prove that you prevented someone from becoming a terrorist through some counter-messaging CVE campaign or other action. As long as advocates of these campaigns can use metrics as proxies for efficacy, they can also claim some measure of success.

These campaigns fetishise messaging. However, if we are faced with a young economically, socially and politically marginalised man who is buying into extremist messages like, "Sometimes people with the worst pasts create the best futures. criminal" and "why be a loser when you can be a martyr", why should we assume that removing or contesting the message would have any tangible impact, when nothing has been done to change the reality of the individual's predicament?

In light of all these problems, *we have proposed a model of narrative contestation through which governments can address real-world concerns.* Our strategic narrative framework that identifies alignment across narratives of the international system, narratives of identity and narratives of specific problems can help explain why a certain problem definition or even worldview becomes meaningful to those open to radicalisation and violence.

Conclusion

This double fetish of CVE comes at a cost: the 'battle of the narratives' becomes conceptualised and practiced as the quantitative online dominance of 'our' content over 'theirs'. Rather than admitting how intractably difficult persuasion is, and rather than responding to the real-world concerns of those persuadable by radical narratives – political disenfranchisement, socio-economic marginalisation, personal identity crises and xenophobia – the mass takedown of pro-IS accounts on Twitter in 2015 is instead considered a mark of progress. It is easier to simply stopping information from IS reaching individuals in the name of counter-radicalisation rather than exploring why the narrative of IS might be attractive and even persuasive. The enemy is extremism and extremism must be stopped, not the causes of its appeal.

Countering IS communication narratives cannot refute lived experience, particularly when that lived experience resonates with the narrative. Fighting the digital battle can be a small part of fighting the war, and an even smaller part of the politics of ensuring coherent and secure identities for all citizens as well as the prospect of a good life. As potent as the narratives of violent extremists may be, they are not, in and of themselves, sufficient to account for radicalisation as a phenomenon, particularly amongst young Muslims in the West. Narratives constitute only one part in the complex array of elements that intersect to ultimately manifest as a move towards violent extremism.

Today, IS is teetering on the brink of its demise, and Western governments have evinced relief that its reach over potential audiences has been drastically diminished. However, our analysis warns that unless these real-world concerns are taken seriously and addressed holistically, these very same issues will no doubt be taken up and mobilised towards the messaging of whichever extremist group inevitably emerges next.

Notes

1 www.hsdl.org/?abstract&did=791347 and www.state.gov/r/gec/
2 An Ipsos Mori survey published in 2013 found that 74% of French citizens view Islam as "intolerant" and "incompatible" with French values (Le Bars 2013).
3 A 2016 Ipsos Mori survey found French respondents were by far the most likely to overstate their country's current and projected Muslim population. The average French estimate for the current size of the Muslim population was 31%, compared with the actual percentage of 7.5% (Ipsos Mori 2016).
4 In 2016, for example, a prominent Arab Spring Iyad el-Baghdadi had his Twitter account suspended after administrators mistook him for the leader of the so-called Islamic State (BBC News 2016).

CONCLUSION

Rethinking strategic communication in the Digital Age

James Pamment and Corneliu Bjola

This concluding chapter outlines some of the issues that are awakened by this volume. It begins with a discussion of some important challenges for future research and practice, before discussing policy considerations and the way forward.

Challenges

Establish an interdisciplinary theoretical basis

As this volume demonstrates, the problem of disinformation may be approached from any number of academic disciplines. In the rather eclectic approach that we have adopted here, perspectives bridge International Relations, Political Science, Media & Communication Studies, Strategic Communication, Cognitive & Behavioural Psychology, and Diplomatic Studies. Still, one may wonder how several other related branches of academia might be added. For example, Law, Sociology, Economics, Philosophy, Computer Sciences, Pedagogics, Gender Studies, Middle East and Eurasian Studies, Intelligence Studies, Neuroscience and their related sub-fields could all have warranted their own chapters.

The challenge is not simply to bring these scholars and insights together, but to establish common grounds to develop consolidated theories. Traditional research funding is not well tooled to promote this. It is typical for research on disinformation and countering violent extremism (CVE) to take many years to produce, often falling behind the technological innovations that keep information operations a step ahead of both governments and the general public. Research is developed in siloes, by people who are rarely experts in more than two or three closely connected fields. New kinds of platforms are needed to generate new kinds of knowledge: in this case, the challenge is to find ways of supporting open-ended dialogue between scholars and practitioners of multiple disciplines, nations, experiences and agendas without any specific expectations of process or outcome. A consistent lobby upon research financiers is necessary to create conditions conducive to such debate.

Find a balance between threats and vulnerabilities

Most studies of information influence activities and CVE fall into one of two camps: either focused on the threat, or on the social vulnerabilities that are being exploited. A focus on threats tends to emphasise linguistic, socio-cultural and doctrinal knowledge of specific actors and their intentions and goals, whereas a focus on vulnerabilities attempts to understand domestic societal systems and how they can best be prepared to ensure resilience. Clearly, both are necessary. The question is, how can their insights be brought together in a way that avoids accusations of exaggerating or pathologising the threat (e.g. in the accusation of Russophobia), or of using an analysis of societal vulnerabilities as a pretext to cracking down on domestic freedoms (e.g. from governmental surveillance) or restricting democratic discourse.

Part of the solution may be found in dividing roles. Imagine the case of an arsonist at loose in a city. Clearly, there is a role for the police and criminal psychologists in investigating, tracking and capturing the criminal, through seeking to understand their motivations and patterns of behaviour. But there are also important roles for the rest of society: in establishing a competent firefighting service; in updating routines for fire drills, alarms and general readiness; in replacing and possibly legislating against flammable materials; in educating the public in both threats and risks; in creating information-sharing channels with authorities; and in establishing best practice that can be shared between actors. The challenge is to develop both approaches whilst finding an appropriate balance that is not toothless in relation to a given threat, but that predominately *raises the threshold of societal resilience* to any similar or unanticipated threats. After all, apprehending one arsonist does not remove the risk of fire.

An added dimension here is the counterfactual argument that information operations have not occurred *here*, so why should we dedicate resources to it? The counterfactual position suggests that the threat is either exaggerated or irrelevant to a specific society. Rather, governmental interest in the disinformation agenda is about stamping down on certain societal groups or increasing surveillance powers. Dedicating resources to societal resilience may awake domestic criticism if the attack never occurs; yet, those efforts may contribute to dissuading a hostile actor from focusing on that particular market. Finding a balance between threats and vulnerabilities, therefore, also entails developing models for evaluating impact. Impact must in these cases include potential threats that *did not happen* as an effect of awareness- and preparedness-raising; something that will provide a conceptual challenge going forward.

Adapting the experiences and knowledge from counterterrorism to counter influence

Western states' knowledge of CVE has been enriched over the past two decades through experiences of dealing with Al Qaeda and ISIS. Counterterrorism (CT) is hence a relatively well-researched and established field of inquiry for both academics and practitioners. Counter influence (CI), as an approach to containing and countering information influence activities, is far less well established. This is, in part, because the Russian invasion of Ukraine and interference in Western elections is a relatively recent phenomenon, and the knowledge base of digital and hybrid methods is in continual flux (even if the techniques themselves hold historical continuity). A major challenge for the CT community is to ensure that their knowledge and best practice is adapted to this new and challenging context, without expecting such knowledge to be directly applicable to these problems. Alicia Kearns' chapter in this volume is one example of how this can be achieved.

Moving from identifying to countering

A common feature of the burgeoning field of disinformation studies is a focus on identifying the nature of the challenge we as a society face. This is important work. The threat of hybrid war, grey zone activities and information influence campaigns is significant and needs to be raised to decision makers and the general public alike. However, it often appears that so much energy is expended on making the case that the threat exists, that suggestions for containing and countering the threat are de-prioritised. As the field matures, it will be increasingly important to accept that the grounds for CVE and information influence activities are indeed real and established and that efforts to mitigate their effects should form the centrepiece of the field of inquiry. Of more than 1,000 reports and articles published in the past few years, work that takes *countering* as its point of departure is less than 1 percent (Pamment et al. 2018). This must become the norm.

Reinterpret the history of (new) public diplomacy

By around 2008, a handful of major volumes had established the core tenets of the 'new' public diplomacy, including the relatively young digital dimension (Melissen 2005a; Cowan & Cull 2008; Welsh & Fearn 2008; Snow & Taylor 2009; see also Pamment 2012). The importance of building coalitions of like-minded actors who could act as multipliers of key messages, of facilitating collaboration between government and nongovernmental actors, of co-creation of content and shaping engagement, became a consensus amongst scholars and practitioners alike. A decade later, it seems that the new public diplomacy also underpins the techniques used by hostile actors in undermining democratic processes in foreign countries. The coalitions of actors include extremist political groups who might be financed and otherwise supported by foreign intelligence agencies. Nongovernment actors such as the St Petersburg troll factory echo government messaging with the support of networks of biased news platforms and multipliers in the blogosphere. Contents such as memes are created and circulated by individuals and groups engaged in specific political agendas that can be stoked by disinformation. Engagement is the key principle.

This is a significant problem for scholars of diplomacy, public diplomacy and digital diplomacy that prompts a reinterpretation of what these terms really mean. Is public diplomacy what *we* do, and propaganda what *others* do? Is it still public diplomacy if disinformation is part of the content? If we accept the premise that it is the techniques that characterise public diplomacy, we should also accept that their use is prevalent in the disinformation space. Public diplomacy supported by information operations has been used, for example, in Ukraine to shift the global public's perspective on what constitutes war and peace. Disinformation has been used against the Syrian Civil Defence Force, popularly known as the White Helmets, to influence the global public's understanding of what constitutes humanitarian intervention. Similar techniques have been used in the MH17 and Salisbury poisoning to systematically undermine and ridicule legitimate investigative processes. New public diplomacy techniques are being used to engage global publics, but instead of creating a progressive, enlightened global civil society, they are being deliberately manipulated in order to sow division and discord, as part of a wave of nationalism sweeping the globe.

A broader history of public diplomacy is required; one that acknowledges its role in shaping foreign societies' development as a form of soft power (Pamment & Wilkins 2018). Hostile states will argue that Westerners have meddled in their societies for centuries, influencing their elections, institutions and citizens through public diplomacy techniques mixed with diplomatic and economic levers and occasional coercion. Digitisation has simply provided a more level playing field, at least temporarily, in which digital platforms may be exploited at a relatively low cost. As the wealthiest countries dedicate increasing resources to closing the exploits in their systems and shaping societal resilience, one wonders where this leaves developing countries. It is conceivable that this period of high-profile influence campaigns within Western countries is the prelude to something far more disruptive to the developing world, which could have far-reaching consequences for global security.

Attribution, proxies and domestic politics

As the Mueller inquiry shows, a major challenge remains the attribution of information influence activities to specific actors. It is a time-consuming and costly process (both economically and politically) even for a country like the US. Open-source intelligence (OSINT) actors such as Bellingcat perform vital work in revealing the techniques by which disinformation circulates. Here, civil society has an important role to play in managing and correcting disinformation in the public sphere, free from the concerns for maintaining secret sources and methods that intelligence agencies must negotiate. Yet OSINT can only go so far. At the end of the day, it is national intelligence services that are best placed to credibly identify, expose and/or counter the sources of threats to national security. This is made especially complicated when foreign actors make use of domestic proxies to achieve their goals.

In this respect, information influence activities mirror the techniques of public diplomacy, in which a foreign government will often partner with local actors to influence policy decisions. Disinformation may have a hostile foreign actor at its source, but disinformation will in many cases be circulated by local representatives of civil society and political groups whose interests overlap, often innocently, with those of the hostile actor. The Cold War phrase 'usual idiot' is unhelpful here, since those domestic interest groups have both the legitimate right, and often legitimate intentions, to pursue their goals in the public sphere. Scholars and practitioners working in this field should be acutely sensitive to the risks of the general debate into disinformation, fake news and CVE creating the premise for more restrictive public debate. Our role here is simple: to protect the open and free debate from false information deliberately seeded into the system of opinion formation in order to undermine national security.

The result is that attribution is one of the biggest challenges the community faces. Not necessarily because it is difficult: indeed, between civil society OSINT actors, private sector intelligence actors and national secret intelligence services, the disinformation space should be well covered. Politically, however, the costs can be complex and problematic, with potentially profound risks to the democracy these actors are trying to protect. For example, if domestic interest groups come under the purview of intelligence services simply because a foreign troll tweeted out a similar narrative, democratic opinion-building is undermined. Attribution, proxies and domestic politics are an interconnected challenge that requires significant debate and discussion to be resolved in a way consistent with Western values.

The ethics of countering digital propaganda

A connected problem is that for many democratic countries, combatting digital propaganda comes with a serious ethical dilemma: how a state can react to acts of disinformation without losing the moral ground that it seeks to protect? Moral authority constitutes a critical resource in the fight against propaganda because it ensures that an actor can have its arguments treated with priority by others and thus build support for, and deflect challenges to, certain objectives that it favours, as long as its behaviour does not deviate from certain moral expectations. In the case of digital propaganda, an actor can maintain moral authority by making the case that it has been harmed, that it has normative standing to engage in counter-interventions, and that it does so in an appropriate manner. Failure to maintain moral authority could make an actor vulnerable to accusations of serving to amplify rather than contain disinformation and thus help to legitimise the claims of those intentionally promoting disinformation (Bjola 2018b).

At the same time, we should remain cognisant of the fact that in the Digital Age the instruments and mechanisms by which propaganda operates have undergone a serious transformation and therefore our ethical concepts must adapt as well in order to stay relevant. Algorithmic dissemination of content and the circumvention of traditional media filters and opinion-formation gatekeepers, makes disinformation spread faster, reach deeper, be more emotionally charged and, most importantly, be more resilient due to the confirmation bias that online echo-chambers enable and reinforce (Bjola 2018a). As some of the contributors to the volume have also indicated in their chapters, this raises some important questions about the role citizens as 'foot soldiers' play in the fight against disinformation (Kearns), the ethical redlines not to be crossed when tailoring the counter-narrative to the cognitive and emotional profile of the target audience (Bjola, Aday) or the moral imperative of addressing societal fractures as part of the counter-disinformation strategy (Archetti, Awan et al.).

Policy considerations

One of the major questions in this field is the lack of an overarching framework guiding activities and goals. What is the ultimate aim of countering disinformation? Does it include, for example, deterring actors from intervening in a society? Or is it enough simply to create robust institutions and to educate a public capable of sophisticated source criticism? One may argue that there is a lack of coherence in the desired end-state for relations between a country and a hostile state that is enacting information influence campaigns against it. Specific objectives are necessary that differ from those more general foreign policy objectives that countries pursue. The current literature suggests a small number of coherent policy approaches for (Western) countries to deal with the context of information influence. This list is far from exhaustive, but gives some sense of the range of approaches that might be considered. They are further elucidated in Pamment et al. (2018).

- *Civil society approach*: The civil society approach suggests that individuals and civil society should be empowered to resist information influence activities. Civil society is, therefore, expected to share the burden of raising awareness of citizens, educating for improved source criticism, identifying disinformation, and supporting a resilient, robust and reliable media system.
- *Facts first approach*: This approach suggests that fact-checking, debunking and deconstructing disinformation should constitute the core of countering information influence activities. The prevalence of this approach can be seen from the recent surge in fact-checking initiatives by both states, media institutions and civil society actors.

- *Collaborative approach*: The collaborative approach advocates for the establishment of more national and international networks to jointly increase our capacity to counter information influence activities by, for example, supporting information and experience sharing, establishing financial structures to scale up capacity development and improving coordination between like-minded actors and institutions.
- *Counter-narrative approach*: Counter-narratives are designed to provide alternative and believable frames of reference in order to prevent hostile narratives from gaining traction within a population. The counter-narrative approach suggests a focus on defining, formulating and perpetuating strategic narratives.
- *Counter-propaganda approach*: Reminiscent of the Cold War, the counter-propaganda approach advocates for tactical and strategic messaging conducted by state institutions to push back against unwanted messaging from hostile actors. It may be considered the attempt to directly counter information influence activities using targeted tactical and strategic messaging on a state level.
- *Raising the threshold approach*: Raising the threshold means dis-incentivising information influence activities by, for example, establishing resilient government structures with high legitimacy in society, actively pursuing and punishing the perpetrators as well as strengthening the population's vigilance and will to resist.
- *Ignoring approach*: In contrast to the counter-narrative approach, the ignoring approach simply seeks to minimise the reach of information influence activities by denying them attention and not engaging with them. This approach places faith in the democratic institutions of society and particularly the gatekeeping role of journalists, with the aim of disregarding information influence activities altogether (Hellman & Wagnsson 2017).
- *Regulatory approach*: Many issues related to information influence stem from the legal grey zone within which it operates. The regulatory approach advocates for minimising this grey zone by establishing clearer and stricter regulations.
- *Hard-liner approach*: Finally, the hard-liner approach suggests fighting fire with fire. This controversial approach includes measures such as, for example, imposing strict regulations to social media companies, Internet providers and media actors; and hitting back with proactive information influence activities, aggressive lawfare, kinetic operations and cyber operations.

Together, these approaches are suggestive of the kinds of relationships that countries may have to pursue with one another in the information sphere. Such approaches may have to become de facto constituents of foreign policy positions in the near future. Countries may have to choose different positions for different cases, which is suggestive of a far more complex organisational requirement for dealing with the threat than currently exists.

The way forward

Countermeasures are limited by the fact that they respond to somebody else's agenda. In this regard, the entire principle of countering information influence activities has a premise that is problematic, since the aggressor may appear to be setting the conditions under which a nation's democracy can or cannot properly function (Pamment et al., 2018). Without a clear vision and plan for what we want to achieve in this sphere, we are doomed to a game of cat-and-mouse, where an aggressor exploits a marginal technological advantage to create a short-term impact, whilst governments react by closing the loopholes after the fact. Such an approach does not appear sustainable, not least because elections seem to be an overt target of these activities. The way forward must be outlined in a clear and coherent long-term plan that explains more than the problems and solutions, but that also offers a vision of how relationships between countries and interest groups in an age of boundary-spanning disinformation should function. This is our primary recommendation for the field.

Our second recommendation is that governments need to work together with academia and society to create long-term platforms for mitigating these attacks on democratic discourse. This means bringing together different kinds of actors and giving them the space to make their contributions, at the same time as it means supporting short-term, tactical responses. In particular, the work of translating cutting-edge research into actionable policy advice is a challenge. Our third recommendation is to channel resources into *CI* methods. These should include truth trackers and OSINT analysts, communication techniques and organisational preparedness. This work should be supported by knowledge-sharing platforms that create a body of best practice shared between allies.

Finally, we recommend that the ongoing dialogue between governments, civil society and citizens on these issues emphasises democratic values and the importance of truth and transparency in the public sphere. In recent times, it appears that many high-profile politicians act as disinformers-in-chief. Trust in societal institutions – and hence in society – is difficult to sustain when presidents and prime ministers systematically undermine their own national institutions. Democracy cannot be promoted simply because it is under attack; we need to rediscover the value of finding common perspectives and interests in order to work together for peace and prosperity. Here, diplomats have a role to play. It may yet be that 'diplomatic thinking' (Sharp 2009) can provide solutions to intractable conflicts between competing worldviews.

WORKS CITED

Aday, S. (2005). "The real war will never get on television: An analysis of casualty imagery in American television coverage of the Iraq war." In P. Seib (Ed.), *Media and Conflict in the 21st Century* (pp. 141–156). Basingstoke: Palgrave.

———. (2010a). "Chasing the Bad News: An Analysis of 2005 Iraq and Afghanistan War Coverage on NBC and Fox News Channel." *Journal of Communication*, 60 (1): 144–164.

———. (2010b). "Leading the Charge: Media, Elite Cues, and Emotion in Public Support for War." *Journal of Communication*, 60 (3): 440–465.

Agarwal, A., Singh, R., & Toshniwal, D. (2018). "Geospatial Sentiment Analysis Using Twitter Data for UK-EU Referendum." *Journal of Information and Optimization Sciences*, 39 (1): 303–317. doi:10.1080/02522667.2017.1374735

Åhäll, L., & Gregory T. (2015). *Emotions, Politics and War*. New York: Routledge.

Ahmed, A.S. (2016). "WikiLeaks' Motivations Aren't What You Think." *HuffPost*. Available from: www.huffingtonpost.ca/entry/wikileaks-motivations_us_57a2575ee4b04414d1f365b1

Albright, J. (2016a). "#Election2016: Propaganda-lytics & Weaponized Shadow Tracking." *Medium*. Available from: http://bit.ly/2pD3Q3M

Albright, J. (2016b). "The #Election2016 Micro-Propaganda Machine." *Medium*. Available from: http://bit.ly/2qYWviJ

Albright, J. (2017). "Welcome to the Era of Fake News." *Media and Communication*, 5 (2): 87–89.

Alexander, A. (2016). "Cruel Intentions: Female Jihadists in America." *Program on Extremism*, George Washington University. Available from: https://cchs.gwu.edu/sites/cchs.gwu.edu/files/downloads/Female%20Jihadists%20in%20America.pdf

Allcott, H., & Gentzkow, M. (2017). *Social Media and Fake News in the 2016 Election*. Working Paper 23089. Cambridge, MA: National Bureau of Economic Research.

Allen, C. (2010). *Islamophobia*. Farnham, Surrey; Burlington, VT: Ashgate.

Althaus, S.L., & Coe, K. (2011). "Social Identity Processes and the Dynamics of Public Support for War." *Public Opinion Quarterly*, 75 (1): 65–88.

Althaus, S.L., Swigger, N., Chernykh, S., Hendry, D.J., Wals, S.C., & Tiwald, C. (2014). "Uplifting Manhood to Wonderful Heights? News Coverage of the Human Costs of Military Conflict from World War I to Gulf War II." *Political Communication*, 31: 193–217.

Anderson, M. (2016). "Social Media Causes Some Users to Rethink Their Views on an Issue." *Pew Research Center*, November 7. Available from: www.pewresearch.org/fact-tank/2016/11/07/social-media-causes-some-users-to-rethink-their-views-on-an-issue/ (accessed April 13, 2016).

Archetti, C. (2012). *Understanding Terrorism in the Age of Global Media: A Communication Approach.* Basingstoke: Palgrave.

Archetti, C. (2015). "Terrorism, Communication and New Media: Explaining Radicalization in the Digital Age." *Perspectives on Terrorism*, 9 (1): 49–59. Available from: www.terrorismanalysts.com/pt/index.php/pot/article/view/401/html

Archetti, C. (2017). "Narrative wars: Understanding terrorism in the era of global interconnectedness." In A. Miskimmon, B. O'Loughlin, & L. Roselle (Eds.), *Forging the World: Strategic Narratives and International Relations* (pp. 218–245). Ann Arbor, MI: University of Michigan Press.

Aristotle. (n.d.). *Rhetoric*, translated by W. Rhys Roberts. Available from: http://classics.mit.edu/Aristotle/rhetoric.1.i.html

Artime, M. (2016). "Angry and Alone: Demographic Characteristics of Those Who Post to Online Comment Sections." *Social Sciences*, 5 (4): 68.

Ashour O. (2011). "Online De-Radicalization? Countering Violent Extremist Narratives: Message, Messenger and Media Strategy." *Perspectives on Terrorism*, 4 (6): 15–19.

Assange, J. (2016a). "EXCLUSIVE: WikiLeaks' Julian Assange on Releasing DNC Emails That Ousted Debbie Wasserman Schultz." *Democracy Now.* Available from: www.democracynow.org/2016/7/25/exclusive_wikileaks_julian_assange_on_releasing

Assange, J. (2016b). "The Podesta Emails; Part One." *Wikileaks.* Available from: https://wikileaks.org/podesta-emails/press-release

Assange, J. Twitter Post. (October 25, 2017, 12:25 P.M.). Available from: https://twitter.com/julianassange/status/923226553428987904?lang=en

Asthana, A., Roth, A., Harding, L., & MacAskill, E. (2018). "Russian Spy Poisoning: Theresa May Issues Ultimatum to Moscow." *The Guardian*, March 13. Available from: www.theguardian.com/uk-news/2018/mar/12/russia-highly-likely-to-be-behind-poisoning-of-spy-says-theresa-may (accessed March 19, 2018).

Atran, S., & Hamid, N. (2015). "Paris: The War ISIS Wants." *The New York Review of Books*, November 16. Available from: www.nybooks.com/daily/2015/11/16/paris-attacks-isis-strategy-chaos/

Awan, A.N. (2007). "Radicalization on the Internet? The Virtual Propagation of Jihadist Media and Its Effects." *RUSI*, 152 (3): 76–81.

Awan, A.N. (2012). "Jihadi ideology in the new media environment." In J. Deol & Z. Kazmi (Eds.), *Contextualising Jihadi Thought.* London: Hurst & Co.

Awan, A.N. (2015). "The Charlie Hebdo Attack: The Double Alienation Dilemma." *The National Interest*, January 13. Available from: http://nationalinterest.org/feature/the-charlie-hebdo-attack-the-double-alienation-dilemma-12021

Awan, A.N. (2016). "The impact of evolving jihadist narratives on radicalisation in the west." In S. Staffell & A.N. Awan (Eds.), *Jihadism Transformed Al-Qaeda and Islamic State's Global Battle of Ideas.* London: Hurst & Co.

Awan, A.N. (Forthcoming). "Building identities within extremist organisations: The case of ISIS." In A.F. Lemieux & A.N. Awan (Eds.), *Mobilizing Media.* Oxford: Oxford University Press.

Awan, A.N., & Dockter, W. (2016). "ISIS and the Abuse of History." *History Today*, January. Available from: www.historytoday.com/akil-n-awan-and-warren-dockter/isis-and-abuse-history

Awan, A., Hoskins, A., & O'Loughlin, B. (2011). *Radicalisation and the Media: Connectivity and Terrorism in the New Media Ecology.* London: Routledge.

Baars, B.J., & Gage, M.N. (2010). *Cognition, Brain, and Consciousness.* Burlington, MA: AP, Elsevier.

Bakir, V. (2016). *Torture, Intelligence and Sousveillance in the War on Terror: Agenda-Building Struggles.* London: Routledge.

Ballhaus, R., & Bykowicz, J. (2017). "Data Firm's WikiLeaks Outreach Came as It Joined Trump Campaign." *Wall Street Journal,* November 10. Available from: www.wsj.com/articles/data-firms-wikileaks-outreach-came-as-it-joined-trump-campaign-1510339346

Ban, K. (2015). "Secretary-General's Remarks to Security Council Meeting on Threats to International Peace and Security Caused by Terrorist Acts (Foreign Terrorist Fighters)." *United Nations Secretary-General,* May 29. Available from: www.un.org/sg/en/content/sg/statement/2015-05-29/secretary-generals-remarks-security-council-meeting-threats (accessed July 10, 2016).

Barnett, M., & Martha, F. (1999). "The Politics, Power, and Pathologies of International Organizations." *International Organization,* 53 (4): 699–732.

Barojan, D. (2018). "#PutinAtWar: Social Media Surge on Skripal." *Atlantic Council's Digital Forensic Research Lab,* April 6. Available from: https://medium.com/dfrlab/putinatwar-social-media-surge-on-skripal-b5132db6f439 (accessed April 11, 2018).

Barthes, R. (1977a). "The photographic message." In *Image-Music-Text* (pp. 15–31). Glasgow: Fontana/Collins.

Barthes, R. (1977b). "The rhetoric of the image." In *Image-Music-Text* (pp. 32–51). Glasgow: Fontana/Collins.

Bátora, J. (2013). *"The 'Mitrailleuse Effect':* The EEAS as an Interstitial Organization and the Dynamics of Innovation in Diplomacy." *Journal of Common Market Studies,* 51 (4): 598–613.

Bauman, Z. (2007). *Liquid Life.* Cambridge: Polity.

BBC. (2007). "Bush 'involved' in CIA Leak Case." Available from: http://news.bbc.co.uk/2/hi/americas/7105001.stm

BBC. (2016a). "US Election 2016: Trump's 'Hidden' Facebook Army." *BBC.* Available from: http://bbc.in/2ftfkEF

BBC. (2016b). "Cologne Sex Attacks: Women Describe 'Terrible' Assaults." *BBC,* January 7. Available from: www.bbc.co.uk/news/world-europe-35250903 (accessed May 2, 2016).

BBC News. (2016). "Twitter 'Confuses' Man with IS Leader." *BBC News,* January 1, sec. World. Available from: www.bbc.co.uk/news/world-35210527

Bearman, P.S., & Stovel, K. (2000). "Becoming a Nazi: A Model for Narrative Networks." *Poetics,* 27: 69–90.

Beck, U. (1992). *Risk Society: Towards a New Modernity.* Thousand Oaks, CA: Sage.

Belam, M. (2017). "Sex, Slang, Steak: Views that Show Remainers and Leavers Are Worlds Apart." *The Guardian,* November 14. Available from: www.theguardian.com/politics/2017/nov/14/sex-slang-steak-views-leave-remain-worlds-apart

Bellingcat. (December 8, 2017). "Russian Colonel General Identified as Key MH17 Figure." Available from: www.bellingcat.com/news/uk-and-europe/2017/12/08/russian-colonel-general-delfin/

Benkler, Y. (2011). A Free Irresponsible Press: WikiLeaks and the Battle over the Soul of the Networked Fourth Estate (working draft, Harvard Civil Rights-Civil Liberties Law Review). Available from: http://benkler.org/Benkler_Wikileaks_current.pdf

Benkler, Y., Faris, R., Roberts, H., & Zuckerman, E. (2017). "Study: Breitbart-Led Right-Wing Media Ecosystem Altered Broader Media Agenda." *Columbia Journalism Review.* Available from: www.cjr.org/analysis/breitbart-media-trump-harvard-study.php

Berelson, B., Lazarsfeld, P., & McPhee, W. (1954). *Voting: A Study of Opinion Formation in a Presidential Campaign*. Chicago, IL: Chicago University Press.

Berinsky, A. (2007). "Assuming the Costs of War: Events, Elites, and American Public Support for Military Conflict." *Journal of Politics*, 69 (4): 975–997.

———. (2009). *In Time of War: Understanding American Public Opinion from World War II to Iraq*. Chicago, IL: University of Chicago Press.

Berinsky, A., & Druckman, J. (2007). "Public Opinion Research and Support for the Iraq War." *Public Opinion Quarterly*, 71: 126–141.

Bernays, E. (1928). *Propaganda*. London: Routledge.

Berntzen, L.E., & Weisskircher, M. (2016). "Anti-Islamic PEGIDA beyond Germany: Explaining Differences in Mobilisation." *Journal of Intercultural Studies*, 37 (6): 556–573. doi:10.1080/07256868.2016.1235021

Bērziņa, I. (2016). *The Possibility of Societal Destabilization in Latvia: Potential National Security Threats*. Riga: National Defence Academy of Latvia.

Bishop, M., & Goldman, E. (2003). "The Strategy and Tactics of Information Warfare." *Contemporary Security Policy*, 24 (1): 113–139.

Bjola, C. (2018a). "Propaganda in the Digital Age." *Global Affairs*, 3 (3): 189–191.

Bjola, C. (2018b). "The Ethics of Countering Digital Propaganda." *Ethics & International Affairs*, 32 (3): 305–315.

Bjola, C., & Pamment, J. (2016). "Digital Containment: Revisiting Containment Strategy in the Digital Age." *Global Affairs*, 2 (2): 131–142.

Bjola, C., Jiang, L., & Holmes, M. (2015). "Social media and public diplomacy: A comparative analysis of the digital diplomatic strategies of the EU, US and Japan in China." In C. Bkola & M. Holmes (Eds.), *Digital Diplomacy: Theory and Practice* (pp. 71–88). New York: Routledge.

Bleiker, R. (2001). "The Aesthetic Turn in International Political Theory." *Millennium - Journal of International Studies*, 30 (3): 509–533.

Bleiker, R. (2009). *Aesthetics and World Politics*. Basingstoke: Palgrave Macmillan.

Bloch, M. (2013 [1921]) "Reflections of a Historian on the False News of the War", translated by J.P. Holoka. *Michigan War Studies Review* 2013-051. Available from: www.miwsr.com/2013-051.aspx

Bond, D. (2017). "Russia a 'Formidable Adversary', Say UK Spymasters." *Financial Times*, December 20. Available from: www.ft.com/content/ff155500-e5a3-11e7-8b99-0191e45377ec

Boxell, L., Gentzkow, M., & Shapiro, J.M. (2017). *Is the Internet Causing Political Polarization? Evidence from Demographics*. Working Paper 23258. Cambridge, MA: National Bureau of Economic Research. Available from: www.brown.edu/Research/Shapiro/pdfs/age-polars.pdf

Boyd-Barrett, O. (2004). "Judith Miller, the New York Times, and the Propaganda Model." *Journalism Studies*, 5 (4): 435–449.

Boyd, D. (2017a). "Did Media Literacy Backfire?" *Points*, January 5. Available from: https://points.datasociety.net/did-media-literacy-backfire-7418c084d88d

Boyd, D. (2017b). "Why America is Self-Segregating." *Points*, January 5. Available from: https://points.datasociety.net/why-america-is-self-segregating-d881a39273ab

Boyatzis, R.E. (1998). *Transforming Qualitative Information: Thematic Analysis and Code Development*. Thousand Oaks, CA: SAGE Publications.

Braddock, K., & Horgan, J. (2016). "Towards a Guide for Constructing and Disseminating Counternarratives to Reduce Support for Terrorism." *Studies in Conflict & Terrorism*, 39 (5): 381–404.

Bradley, M.M., Codispoti, M., Cuthbert, B.N., & Lang, P.J. (2001). "Emotion and Motivation I: Defensive and Appetitive Reactions in Picture Processing." *Emotion*, 1: 276–298.

Briant, E.L. (2018). "Research on Leave. EU and Cambridge Analytica strategy published." *Digital, Culture, Media and Sport Committee Inquiry into Fake News.* Available from: www.parliament.uk/business/committees/committees-a-z/commons-select/digital-culture-media-and-sport-committee/news/fake-news-briant-evidence-17-19/

Briggs, R., & Feve, S. (2013). *Review of Programs to Counter Narratives of Violent Extremism.* London: Institute for Strategic Dialogue.

Brodkin, J. (2012). "FDA Whistleblowers Say Government Retaliated with Spyware." *ARS Technica.* Available from: https://arstechnica.com/tech-policy/2012/02/fda-whistleblowers-say-government-intercepted-gmail-yahoo-messages/

Brooks, R. (2011). "Prepared Statement. Testimony Before the House Armed Services Sub-Committee on Evolving Threats and Capabilities." In *Ten Years On: The Evolution of Strategic Communication and Information Operations Since 9/11*, published by the United States Congress, 32–45. Washington, DC: U.S. Government Printing Office.

Brown, R. (2014). "Counter-Propaganda: Do I Detect a Propaganda Panic™? Public Diplomacy, Networks, and Influence." *WordPress*, December 16 Available from: https://pdnetworks.wordpress.com/2014/12/16/counter-propaganda-do-i-detect-a-propaganda-panic/ (accessed December 20, 2017).

Bucher, T. (August 25, 2017). "Algoritmer i hverdaglivet og morgendagens medieforskning?" Presentation at "Morgendagens medievitenskap?" Seminar. University of Oslo.

Buckels, E.E., Trapnell, P.D., & Paulhus, D.L. (September, 2014). "Trolls just want to have fun." *Personality and Individual Differences*, 67: 97–102. Available from: http://bit.ly/1jNIiM0

Buckley, K.E., & Anderson, C.A. (2006). A theoretical model of the effects and consequences of playing video games. Play. Video Games Motiv. Responses Consequences, 363–378.

Burk, J. (1999). "Public Support for Peacekeeping in Lebanon and Somalia: Assessing the Casualties Hypothesis." *Political Science Quarterly*, 114 (1): 53–78.

Burke, K. (1969). *A Grammar of Motives.* Berkeley: University of California Press.

Busher, J. (2015). "Understanding the English Defence League: Living on the front line of a 'clash of civilisations'." http://blogs.lse.ac.uk/politicsandpolicy/understanding-the-english-defence-league-life-on-the-front-line-of-an-imagined-clash-of-civilisations

Bushman, B.J., & Anderson, C.A. (2009). "Comfortably Numb Desensitizing Effects of Violent Media on Helping Others." *Psychological Science*, 20: 273–277.

Bushman, B.J., & Geen, R.G. (1990). "Role of Cognitive-Emotional Mediators and Individual Differences in the Effects of Media Violence on Aggression." *Journal of Personality and Social Psychology*, 58: 156–163.

Butler, J. (2010). *Frames of War: When Is Life Grievable?* London: Verso.

Butt, R., & Tuck, H. (2014). *European Counter-Radicalisation and De-Radicalisation: A Comparative Evaluation of Approaches in the Netherlands, Sweden, Denmark and Germany.* London: Institute for Strategic Dialogue.

Buzzfeed. (January 10, 2017). These Reports Allege Trump Has Deep Ties To Russia. Available from: www.buzzfeed.com/kenbensinger/these-reports-allege-trump-has-deep-ties-to-russia?utm_term=.qlXG93m6W5#.hwjpL1aDj6

Buzzsumo. (2018). Search for Most Shared Pages of https://wikileaks.org/ on 3 March 2018. Available from: https://app.buzzsumo.com/research/most-shared?type=articles&result_type=total&num_days=365&general_article&infographic&video&how_to_article&list&what_post&why_post&q=https:%2F%2Fwikileaks.org%2F&page=1

Byers, D. (2017). "Facebook Estimates 126 Million People Were Served Content From Russia-linked Pages." *CNN*, October 31. Available from: http://money.cnn.com/2017/10/30/media/russia-facebook-126-million-users/index.html

Byman, D.L., & Williams, J.R. (2015). "ISIS vs. al Qaeda: Jihadism's Global Civil War." *Brookings*, February 24. Available from: www.brookings.edu/articles/isis-vs-al-qaeda-jihadisms-global-civil-war/

Cadwalladr, C. (2017). "The Great British Brexit Robbery: How Our Democracy Was Hijacked." *The Observer*, May 7. Available from: www.theguardian.com/technology/2017/may/07/the-great-british-brexit-robbery-hijacked-democracy

Cadwalladr, C. (2018a). "'I Made Steve Bannon's Psychological Warfare Tool': Meet the Data War Whistleblower." *The Guardian*, March 18. Available from: www.theguardian.com/news/2018/mar/17/data-war-whistleblower-christopher-wylie-faceooknix-bannon-trump

Cadwalladr, C. (2018b). "Cambridge Analytica's ruthless bid to sway the vote in Nigeria." *The Guardian*, March 21. Available from: www.theguardian.com/uk-news/2018/mar/21/cambridge-analyticas-ruthless-bid-to-sway-the-vote-in-nigeria

Carey, J. (1989). *Communication as Culture*. New York and London: Routledge.

Carruthers, S.L. (2000). *The Media at War: Communication and Conflict in the Twentieth Century*. New York: St. Martin's Press.

Casebeer, W.D., & Russell, J.A. (2005). "Storytelling and Terrorism: Towards a Comprehensive 'Counter-Narrative Strategy'." *Strategic Insights*, 4 (3). Available from: www.au.af.mil/au/awc/awcgate/nps/casebeer_mar05.pdf

Cassidy, J., & Manor, I. (2016). "Crafting Strategic MFA Communication Policies during Times of Political Crisis: A Note to MFA Policy Makers." *Global Affairs*, 2 (3): 331–343.

Castells, M. (2009). *Communication Power*. Oxford: Oxford University Press.

Chadwick, A. (2013). *The Hybrid Media System: Politics and Power (Oxford Studies in Digital Politics)*. Oxford: Oxford University Press.

Channel 4. Exposed: Undercover secrets of Trump's data firm. March 20, 2018. Available from: www.channel4.com/news/exposed-undercover-secrets-of-donald-trump-data-firm-cambridge-analytica

Cheng, J., Berstein, M., Danesu-Niculescu-Mizil, C., & Leskovec, J. (2017). "Anyone Can Become a Troll: Causes of Trolling Behaviour in Online Discussions." http://bit.ly/2jZY4ub

Chotikul, D. (1986). *The Soviet Theory of Reflexive Control in Historical and Psychocultural Perspective: Preliminary Study*. Monterey, CA: Naval Postgraduate School.

Chmielewski, D. (June 15, 2016). Here's the leaked opposition research document on Donald Trump that's circulating the web. Available from: www.recode.net/2016/6/15/11949066/leaked-dnc-opposition-research-donald-trump

Chmielewski, D. (2016). "White Supremacists Urge Trolling Clinton Supporters to Suicide." *USA Today*. Available from: https://usat.ly/2fGtBOW

Christensen, L.T., & Christensen, E. (2017). "The Nature of Strategic Communication: A Rejoinder to Nothhaft." *International Journal of Strategic Communication*, 11 (3): 180–183.

Clarke, V., & Braun V. (2014). "Thematic analysis." In *Encyclopedia of Critical Psychology* (pp. 1947–1952). Springer: Berlin, Heidelberg.

Cockfield, A.J. (2016). "Breaking Bad: What Does the First Major Tax Haven Leak Tell Us?" *Tax Notes International*, 83 (8): 691.

Coddington, M. (2012). "Defending a Paradigm by Patrolling a Boundary: Two Global Newspapers' Approach to WikiLeaks." *Journalism & Mass Communication Quarterly*, 89 (3): 377–396.

Coleman, G. (2013). "Anonymous and the politics of leaking." In B. Brevini, A. Hintz, & P. McCurdy (Eds.), *Beyond WikiLeaks* (pp. 209–228). London: Palgrave Macmillan.

Collins, A.M., & Loftus, E.F. (1975). "A Spreading-Activation Theory of Semantic Processing." *Psychological Review*, 82: 407.

Conway, M. (2012). "From al-Zarqawi to al-Awlaki: The Emergence and Development of an Online Radical Milieu." *CTX: Combating Terrorism Exchange*, 2 (4): 12–22.

Conway, M. (2016). "Determining the Role of the Internet in Violent Extremism and Terrorism: Six Suggestions for Progressing Research." *Studies in Conflict & Terrorism*, 40: 77–98.

Conway, M. (2017). "Determining the Role of the Internet in Violent Extremism and Terrorism: Six Suggestions for Progressing Research." *Studies in Conflict & Terrorism*, 40 (1): 77–98. doi:10.1080/1057610X.2016.1157408

Conway, M., & McInerney, L. (2008). "Jihadi video and auto-radicalisation: Evidence from an exploratory youtube study." In *Intelligence and Security Informatics* (pp. 108–118). Lecture Notes in Computer Science. Springer: Berlin, Heidelberg. Available from: https://link.springer.com/chapter/10.1007/978-3-540-89900-6_13

Conway, M., Khawaja, M., & Lakhani, S. (2017). "Disrupting Daesh: Measuring Takedown of Online Terrorist Material and Its Impacts." Vox-Pol. Available from: www.voxpol.eu/download/vox-pol_publication/DCUJ5528-Disrupting-DAESH-1706-WEB-v2.pdf

Cook, J., & Lewandowsky, S. (2012). *The Debunking Handbook (v2)*. St Lucia: University of Queensland.

Corman, S.R. (May 21, 2009). "What Power Needs to be Smart." Paper presented at the Digital Media and Security Workshop, University of Warwick.

Corman, S.R., Trethewey, A., & Goodall, B. (2007). *A 21st Century Model for Communication in the Global War of Ideas: From Simplistic Influence to Pragmatic Complexity*. Arizona State University: Consortium for Strategic Communication.

Corner, J. (2007). "Mediated Politics, Promotional Culture and the Idea of Propaganda." *Media, Culture & Society*, 29 (4): 669–677.

Cornish, P., Lindley-French, J., & Yorke, C. (2011). *Strategic Communications and National Strategy*. London: Chatham House.

Cosmides, L. (1989). "The Logic of Social Exchange: Has Natural Selection Shaped How Humans Reason? Studies with the Wason Selection Task." *Cognition*, 31 (3): 187–276.

Cowan, G., & Cull, N.J. (Eds.). (2008). *Public Diplomacy in a Changing World. The ANNALS of the American Academy of Political and Social Science* (p. 616). Thousand Oaks, CA: SAGE Publications.

Cramer, K.J. (2016). *The Politics of Resentment*. London: University of Chicago Press.

Crelinsten, R.D. (2002). "Analyzing Terrorism and Counter Terrorism: A Communication Model." *Terrorism and Political Violence*, 14 (2): 77–122.

Crone, M. (2014). "Religion and Violence: Governing Muslim Militancy through Aesthetic Assemblages." *Millennium*, 43 (1): 291–307.

Crouch, C. (2004). *Post-Democracy*. Cambridge: Polity.

Crowell, M. (2017). "What Went Wrong with France's Deradicalization Program?" *The Atlantic*, September 28. Available from: www.theatlantic.com/international/archive/2017/09/france-jihad-deradicalization-macron/540699/

Cryptome. (2013a). "Snowden Censored." https://cryptome.org/2013/06/snowden-censored.htm

Cryptome. (2013b). "Snowden Tally." https://cryptome.org/2013/11/snowden-tally.htm

Cull, N.J. (2009). "Public diplomacy before Gullion. The evolution of a phrase." In N. Snow & P. Taylor (Eds.), *Routledge Handbook of Public Diplomacy*. London: Routledge.

Curtis, C. (2017). "The demographics dividing Britain." *YouGov.uk*, April 25. Available from: https://yougov.co.uk/news/2017/04/25/demographics-dividing-britain/ (accessed April 13, 2017).

Daadler, I., & Goldgeier, J. (2006). "Global NATO." *Foreign Affairs*, 85 (5): 105–113.

d'Ancona, M. (2017). *Post-Truth: The New War on Truth and How to Fight Back*. London: Random House.

Darwish, K., Magdy, W., & Zanouda, T. (2017) Trump vs. Hillary: What Went Viral during the 2016 US Presidential Election. Available from: https://arxiv.org/pdf/1707.03375.pdf

Dauber, C.E. (2001). "The Impact Mogadishu on U.S. Military Intervention." *Armed Forces & Society*, 27 (2): 205–229.

Davies, W. (2016). "The Age of Post-truth Politics." *The New York Times*, August 24. Available from: www.nytimes.com/2016/08/24/opinion/campaign-stops/the-age-of-post-truth-politics.html (accessed August 25, 2016).

De Gouveia, P.F., & Plumridge, H. (2005). *European Infopolitik: Developing EU Public Diplomacy Strategy*. London: Foreign Policy Centre.

De Nevers, R. (2007). "NATO's International Security Role in the Terrorist Era." *International Security*, 31 (4): 34–66.

Del Vicario, M., Vivaldo, G., Bessi, A., Zollo, F., Scala, A., Caldarelli, G., & Quattrociocchi, W. (2016). "Echo Chambers: Emotional Contagion and Group Polarization on Facebook." *Scientific Reports*, 6. Available from: www.ncbi.nlm.nih.gov/pmc/articles/PMC5131349/

Denning, D. (1998). *Information Warfare and Security*. Boston, MA: Addison-Wesley

Department of Defense. (2009). *Strategic Communication Science and Technology Plan*. Washington, DC.

Dias, V.A. (2013). "The EU and Russia: Competing Discourses, Practices and Interests in the Shared Neighbourhood." *Perspectives on European Politics and Society*, 14 (2): 256–271.

Diez, T., & Manners, I. (2014). "Reflecting on normative power Europe." In T. Diez (Ed.), *A Different Kind of Power? The EU's Role in International Politics* (pp. 55–73). New York: Idebate Press.

Donatella, D.R. (2009). "Non-Western media and the EU perspectives from Al Jazeera." In S. Lucarelli & L. Fioramonti (Eds.), *External Perceptions of the European Union as a Global Actor*. London: Routledge.

Dreyfus, E. (2017). "Secret Facebook Groups are the Trump Era's Worst, Best Echo Chamber." *Wired*. Available from: http://bit.ly/2jGtkNt

Dryzek, J. (2000). *Deliberative Democracy and Beyond: Liberals, Critics, Contestations*. Oxford: Oxford University Press (on Demand).

Dubois, E., & Gaffney, D. (2014). "The Multiple Facets of Influence: Identifying Political Influentials and Opinion Leaders on Twitter." *American Behavioral Scientist*, 58 (10): 1260–1277. doi:10.1177/0002764214527088

Duke, S.W. (2002). "Preparing for European Diplomacy?" *Journal of Common Market Studies*, 40 (5): 849–870.

Duke, S. (2013). "The European External Action Service and Public Diplomacy." In *European Public Diplomacy* (pp. 113–136). Palgrave Macmillan Series in Global Public Diplomacy. New York: Palgrave Macmillan.

Edström, H. (2011). Utility for NATO – Utility of NATO? In H. Edström, J. Matlary, & M. Petersson (Eds.), *NATO: The Power of Partnerships*. London: Palgrave Macmillan.

Eichenberg, R.C., Stoll, R.J., & Lebo, M. (2006). "War President: The Approval Ratings of George W. Bush." *Journal of Conflict Resolution*, 50: 783–808.

Eldridge, S., II. (2017). *Online Journalism from the Periphery: Interloper Media and the Journalistic Field*. London: Routledge.

Electoral Geographies. (2016). "The Politics of Place and Polarization." Available from: http://electoralgeographies.web.unc.edu/how-political-segregation-has-changed-american-electoral-geography/

Elshimi, M. (2017). *De-Radicalisation in the UK Prevent Strategy: Security, Identity and Religion*. London: Routledge.

Entman, R.M. (2012). *Scandal and Silence: Media Responses to Presidential Misconduct*. Cambridge: Polity.

Eugene, C. (2015). "The Bottom-Up Formation and Maintenance of a Twitter Community: Analysis of the #FreeJahar Twitter Community." *Industrial Management & Data Systems*, 115 (4): 612–624. doi:10.1108/IMDS-11-2014-0332

Evans, N.G., & Commins, A. (2017). "Defining Dual-Use Research: When Scientific Advances Can Both Help and Hurt Humanity." *The Conversation*, February 3. Available from: https://theconversation.com/defining-dual-use-research-when-scientific-advances-can-both-help-and-hurt-humanity-70333 (accessed April 26, 2018).

Farwell, J.P. (2014). "The Media Strategy of ISIS." *Survival*, 56 (6): 49–55.

Farrar, K.M., Krcmar, M., & Nowak, K.L. (2006). "Contextual Features of Violent Video Games, Mental Models, and Aggression." *Journal of Communication*, 56: 387–405.

Feaver, P.D., & Gelpi, C. (2004). *Choosing Your Battles: American Civil-Military Relations and the Use of Force*. Princeton, NJ: Princeton University Press.

Ferguson, K. (2016). "Countering Violent Extremism through Media and Communication strategies." *Reflections*, 27: 28.

Ferguson, C.J., & Colwell, J. (2017). "Understanding Why Scholars Hold Different Views on the Influences of Video Games on Public Health." *Journal of Communication*. doi:10.1111/jcom.12293

Figenschou, T., & Ihlebæk, K. (September 19, 2017). "The Mainstream is Fake: Media Criticism and Mistrust in Radical Right-Wing Alternative Media." Paper presented at C-REX Internal Seminar. Centre for Research on Extremism, University of Oslo.

Flynn, K. (2006). "Covert Disclosures: Unauthorized Leaking, Public Officials and The Public Sphere." *Journalism Studies*, 7 (2): 256–273.

Flyvbjerg, B. (2001). *Making Social Science Matter*. Cambridge: Cambridge University Press.

Fodor, J. (1983). *The Modularity of The Mind: An Essay on Faculty Psychology*. Cambridge, MA: MIT Press.

France24. (March 14, 2017). "French 'De-Radicalisation' Pioneer in Court Over Embezzlement Charges." Available from: www.france24.com/en/20170313-france-jihadist-de-radicalisation-pioneer-sonia-imloul-embezzlement-case

Freedman, L. (2015). *Strategy: A History*. Oxford: Oxford University Press.

Frey, K.P., & Eagly, A.H. (1993). "Vividness Can Undermine the Persuasiveness of Messages." *Journal of Personality and Social Psychology*, 65: 32–44.

Friis, S.M. (2015). "'Beyond Anything We Have Ever Seen': Beheading Videos and the Visibility of Violence in the War Against ISIS." *International Affairs*, 91 (4): 725–746.

Friis, S.M. (2017). "'Behead, Burn, Crucify, Crush': Theorizing the Islamic State's Public Displays of Violence." *European Journal of International Relations*. doi:1354066117714416

Fuchs, S. (1988). "The Constitution of Emergent Interaction Orders: A Comment on Rawls." *Sociological Theory*, 6 (1): 122–124.

Fuchs, S. (2001). *Against Essentialism: A Theory of Culture and Society.* London: Harvard University Press.

Fuchs, S. (2009). "The Behaviour of Cultural Networks." *Soziale Systeme,* 15 (2): 345–366.

Fuchs, C. (2017). *Social Media: A Critical Introduction.* London: Sage.

Garrett, R.K., & Weeks, B.E. (2013). "The Promise and Peril of Real-Time Corrections to Political Misperceptions." *CSCW '13,* February 23–27. Available from: http://rkellygarrett.com/wp-content/uploads/2014/05/Garrett-and-Weeks-Promise-and-peril-of-real-time-corrections.pdf

Garrison, W.C. (1999). *Information Operations and Counter-Propaganda: Making a Weapon of Public Affairs.* Carlisle, PA: Army War College Carlisle Barracks.

Gartenstein-Ross, D., & Grossman, L. (2009). *Homegrown Terrorists in the US and UK: An Empirical Examination of the Radicalization Process.* Washington, DC: Foundation for the Defense of Democracy.

Gartner, S. (2008). "The Multiple Effects of Casualties on Public Support for War: An Experimental Approach." *American Political Science Review,* 102 (1): 95–106.

———. (2011). "On Behalf of a Grateful Nation: Conventionalized Images of Loss and Individual Opinion Change in War." *International Studies Quarterly,* 55. doi:10.1111/j.1468-2478.2011.00655.x

Gartner, S.S., & Segura, G.M. (1998). "War, Casualties, and Public Opinion." *Journal of Conflict Resolution,* 42: 278–300.

Gayle, D. (2016). "Prevent Strategy 'Could End Up Promoting Extremism.'" *The Guardian,* April 21. Available from: www.theguardian.com/politics/2016/apr/21/government-prevent-strategy-promoting-extremism-maina-kiai

Gearan, A. (2014). "NATO Chief Recommits to Defending Eastern European, Baltic Nations." *The Washington Post,* April 1. Available from: www.washingtonpost.com/world/europe/nato-sees-no-evidence-russia-pulling-back-troops-from-ukrainian-border/2014/04/01/eea9b6fe-b99f-11e3-96ae-f2c36d2b1245_story.html (accessed May 18, 2017).

Gelpi, C., Feaver, P., & Reifler, J. (2005/2006). "Success Matters: Casualty Sensitivity and the War in Iraq." *International Security,* 30 (3): 7–46.

Gelpi, C., Feaver, P.D., & Reifler, J. (2009). *Paying the Human Costs of War: American Public Opinion and Causalities in Military Conflicts.* Princeton, NJ: Princeton University Press.

Gerasimov, V. (2013). "The Value of Science is in the Foresight: New Challenges Demand Rethinking the Forms and Methods of Carrying out Combat Operations." *Voyenno-Promyshlennyy Kurier.*

Giddens, A. (1990a). *Modernity and Self-Identity: Self and Society in the Late Modern Age.* Cambridge: Polity Press and Oxford: Blackwell.

Giddens, A. (1990b). *The Consequences of Modernity.* Stanford, CA: Stanford University Press.

Gilboa, E. (2005). "Global Television News and Foreign Policy: Debating the CNN Effect." *International Studies Perspectives,* 3: 325–341.

Gilboa, E. (2008). "Searching for a Theory of Public Diplomacy." *The Annals of the American Academy of Political and Social Science,* 616 (1): 55–77.

Githens-Mazer J., & Lambert, R. (2010). "Why Conventional Wisdom on Radicalization Fails: The Persistence of a Failed Discourse." *International Affairs,* 86 (4): 889–901.

Gitlin, T. (1978). "Media Sociology: The Dominant Paradigm." *Theory and Society,* 6 (2): 205–253. Available from: www.jstor.org/stable/657009

Glaser. (2018). "The Cambridge Analytica Scandal Is What Facebook-Powered Election Cheating Looks Like." *Slate,* March 17 (accessed March 24, 2018).

Glazzard, A. (2017). "Losing the Plot: Narrative, Counter-Narrative and Violent Extremism." *The International Centre for Counter-Terrorism - The Hague*, 8 (8). Available from: https://icct.nl/wp-content/uploads/2017/05/ICCT-Glazzard-Losing-the-Plot-May-2017.pdf

Graham, J., Haidt, J., & Nosek, B.A. (2009). "Liberals and Conservatives Rely on Different Sets of Moral Foundations." *Journal of Personality and Social Psychology*, 96 (5): 1029–1046.

Gråtrud, H. (2016). "Islamic State Nasheeds as Messaging Tools." *Studies in Conflict & Terrorism*, 39 (12): 1050–1070. doi:10.1080/1057610X.2016.1159429

Grattan, M. (1998). "The Politics of Spin." *Australian Studies in Journalism*, 7: 32–45, P 41.

Grim, R., & Walsh, B. (2017). "Leaked Documents Expose Stunning Plan to Wage Financial War on Qatar - and Steal the World Cup." *The Intercept*. Available from: https://theintercept.com/2017/11/09/uae-qatar-oitaba-rowland-banque-havilland-world-cup/

Gripsrud, J. (1992). "The aesthetics and politics of melodrama." In P. Dahlgren & C. Sparks (Eds.), *Journalism and Popular Culture*. London: Sage.

Grizzard, M., Tamborini, R., Sherry, J.L., Weber, R., Prabhu, S., Hahn, L., & Idzik, P. (2015). "The Thrill Is Gone, But You Might Not Know: Habituation and Generalization of Biophysiological and Self-Reported Arousal Responses to Video Games." *Communication Monographs*, 82 (1): 64–87. doi:10.1080/03637751.2014.971418

Grizzard, M., Shaw, A.Z., Dolan, E.A., Anderson, K.B., Hahn, L., & Prabhu, S. (2016). "Does Repeated Exposure to Popular Media Strengthen Moral Intuitions? Exploratory Evidence Regarding Consistent and Conflicted Moral Content." *Media Psychology*. doi:10.1080/15213269.2016.1227266

Grizzard, M., Huang, J., Weiss, J.K., Novotny, E.R., Fitzgerald, K.S., Chu, H., Ngoh, Z.Y., Plante, A., & Ahn, C. (2017). "Graphic Violence as Moral Motivator: The Effects of Graphically Violent Content in News." *Mass Communication & Society*, 20 (6): 763–783.

Grusin, R. (2015). "Radical Mediation." *Critical Inquiry*, 42 (1): 124–148.

Guadagno, R.E., Rhoads, K.V., & Sagarin, B.J. (2011). "Figural Vividness and Persuasion: Capturing the 'Elusive' Vividness Effect." *Personality and Social Psychology Bulletin*, 37: 626–638.

Guilluy, C. (2014). *La France Périphérique*. Paris: Flammarion.

Habermas, J. (1962, transl. 1989). *The Structural Transformation of the Public Sphere: An Inquiry into a Category of Bourgeois Society*. Cambridge: Polity Press.

Haidt, J. (2012). *The Righteous Mind* (Kindle ed.). London: Penguin.

Hall, K. (2017). "Russian General ID's in Activity around Shootdown of Malaysian Passenger Jet." *McClatchy DC Bureau*, December 8. Available from: www.mcclatchydc.com/news/nation-world/world/article188720184.html

Hallahan, K. (2004). "Communication management." In R.L. Heath (Ed.), *Encyclopedia of Public Relations* (Vol. 1, pp. 161–164). Thousand Oaks, CA: Sage.

Hallahan, K., Holtzhausen, D., van Ruler, B., Verčič, D., & Sriramesh, K.. (2007). "Defining Strategic Communication." *International Journal of Strategic Communication*, 1 (1): 3–35.

Halverson, J., Corman S., & Goodall, H.L. (2011). *Master Narratives of Islamist Extremism*. Springer: Berlin, Heidelberg.

Hamilton, K., & Langhorne, R. (1995). *The Practice of Diplomacy: Its Evolution, Theory, and Administration*. London and New York: Routledge.

Hansen, L. (2011). "Theorizing the Image for Security Studies Visual securitization and the Muhammad Cartoon Crisis." *European Journal of International Relations*, 17 (1): 51–74.

Harding, L., & Roth, A. (2018). "Spy Poisoning: Why Putin may have Engineered Gruesome Calling Card." *The Guardian*, March 13. Available from: www.theguardian.

com/uk-news/2018/mar/13/spy-poisoning-why-putin-may-have-engineered-gruesome-calling-card (accessed March 19, 2018).

Hariman, R., & Lucaites, J.L. (2007). *No Caption Needed: Iconic Photographs, Public Culture, and Liberal Democracy*. Chicago, IL: University of Chicago Press.

Harris-Hogan, S., Barrelle, K., & Zammit, A. (2016). "What is Countering Violent Extremism? Exploring CVE Policy and Practice in Australia." *Behavioral Sciences of Terrorism and Political Aggression*, 8 (1): 6–24.

Haukkala, H. (2015). "From Cooperative to Contested Europe? The Conflict in Ukraine as a Culmination of a Long-Term Crisis in EU–Russia Relations." *Journal of Contemporary European Studies*, 23 (1): 25–40.

Hayden, C. (2013). "Logics of Narrative and Networks in US Public Diplomacy: Communication Power and US Strategic Engagement." *Journal of International Communication*, 19 (2): 196–218.

Hedayah. (2016). "Launch of the Counter Narrative Library." www.hedayahcenter.org/activites/80/activities/511/2016/665/launch-of-the-counter-narrative-library

Hedayah. (n.d.). "About Us." www.hedayahcenter.org/about-us/177/history

Hellman, M., & Wagnsson, C. (2017). "How Can European States Respond to Russian Information Warfare? An Analytical Framework." *European Security*, 26 (2): 153–170.

Henley, J., & Garside, J. (2017). "Murdered Panama Papers Journalist's Son Attacks Malta's 'Crooks.'" *The Guardian*. Available from: www.theguardian.com/world/2017/oct/17/murdered-panama-papers-journalist-son-malta-crooks-daphne-caruana-galizia

Hern, A. (2017). "How Social Media Filter Bubbles and Algorithms Influence the Election." *The Guardian*, March 22. Available from: www.theguardian.com/technology/2017/may/22/social-media-election-facebook-filter-bubbles

Hille, K., Foy, H., & Seddon, M. (2018). "Moscow Thanks UK for Helping Putin win Landslide Vote in Russia." *Financial Times*, March 18. Available from: www.ft.com/content/efab0a30-2ad4-11e8-a34a-7e7563b0b0f4 (accessed March 19, 2018).

Himelboim, I., Smith, M.A., Rainie, L., Shneiderman, B., & Espina, C. (2017). "Classifying Twitter Topic-Networks Using Social Network Analysis." *Social Media + Society*, 3 (1): 1–13. doi:10.1177/2056305117691545

Hobolt, S. (2016). "The Brexit Vote: A Divided Nation, a Divided Continent." *Journal of European Public Policy*, 23 (9): 1259–1277.

Hoffman, B. (2006). *Inside Terrorism*. New York: Columbia University Press.

Hoffman F.G. (2009). "Hybrid vs Compound War. The Janus Choice: Defining Today's Multifaceted Conflict." *Armed Forces Journal*, October 1. Available from: http://www.armedforcesjourn al.com/hybrid-vs-compound-war/ (accessed May 28, 2015).

Home Office. (2011). *CONTEST United Kingdom's Strategy to Counter Terrorism*. London: The Cabinet Office.

Homeland Security. (2017). "Countering Violent Extremism." www.dhs.gov/countering-violent-extremism

Hoskins, A., & O'loughlin, B. (2007). *Television and Terror: Conflicting Times and the Crisis of News Discourse*. Basingstoke: Palgrave.

Hoskins, A., & O'Loughlin, B. (2015). "Arrested War: The Third Phase of Mediatization." *Information, Communication & Society*, 18 (11): 1320–1338.

Hoskins, A., O'Loughlin, B., & Awan, A. (2011). *Radicalisation and the Media: Connectivity and Terrorism in the New Media Ecology*. London: Routledge.

Hutchison, E. (2016). *Affective Communities in World Politics*. Cambridge: Cambridge University Press.

Horton, D., & Wohl, R. (1956). "Mass Communication and Para-Social Interaction: Observation on Intimacy at a Distance." *Psychiatry*, 19: 215–229.

Howard, P., Kollanyi, B., Bradshaw, S., & Neudert, L.-M. (2017). Social Media, News and Political Information during the US Election. COMPROP Data Memo September 2017. comprop.oii.ox.ac.uk/wp-content/uploads/sites/89/2017/09/Polarizing-Content-and-Swing-States.pdf

Hulcoop, A., Scott-Railton, J., Tanchak, P., Brooks, M., & Deibert, R. (2017). "TAINTED LEAKS: Disinformation and Phishing with a Russian Nexus." *The Citizen Lab*, May 25. Available from: https://citizenlab.ca/2017/05/tainted-leaks-disinformation-phish/ (accessed May 14, 2017).

Ionov, M.D. (1995). "On Reflexive Control of the Enemy in Combat." *Military Thought - A Russian Journal of Military Theory and Strategy*, 1 (English ed.): 46–48.

InfoWatch. (2017). "Global Data Leakage Report, H1 2017." *InfoWatch Analytics Center*. https://infowatch.com/sites/default/files/report/infowatch_global_data_leak_report_h1__2017_ENG.pdf

ITV. (2016). "Assange on Peston on Sunday: 'More Clinton Leaks to Come.'" *Peston on Sunday*. www.itv.com/news/update/2016-06-12/assange-on-peston-on-sunday-more-clinton-leaks-to-come/

Iceland Monitor. (2017). "General Elections 2017 in Iceland." http://icelandmonitor.mbl.is/elections2017/

Institute for Strategic Dialogue. (n.d.) "Case Studies." www.counterextremism.org/download_file/106/134/413/

Intelligence and Security Committee of Parliament. (2017). "Annual Report 2016–2017." https://b1cba9b3-a-5e6631fd-s-sites.googlegroups.com/a/independent.gov.uk/isc/files/2016-2017_ISC_AR.pdf?attachauth=ANoY7col3ws8Yv3Te7fiDJ4lrtcl2H1Dy3KzjFwjOdZf6oJIUpu2lnxwqglo7F9M9ydMqJ7R-PNdQqqNcrzEjw3LCmnbyWaDPs6zwMwFkq6DpS-jDo6oU_o8oyR4HNEGXxR3R_yjaeLcYvqFcQB53GdgfLe5O_9HGb2ohLcR74IkMSGTOEUKLIt-UUqOyDG84Jt-VYZxMkg0ou6_Ue4FPpCIox81yTVKVi6wLG5WqfNXEbJTV0bJ-IU%3D&attredirects=0

Ioffe, J. (2017). "The Secret Correspondence between Donald Trump Jr. and WikiLeaks." The Atlantic, November 13. Available from: www.theatlantic.com/politics/archive/2017/11/the-secret-correspondence-between-donald-trump-jr-and-wikileaks/545738/

Ipsos Mori. (2016). "Perils of Perception." *Ipsos Mori*. Available from: www.ipsos.com/ipsos-mori/en-uk/perceptions-are-not-reality-what-world-gets-wrong

Jakobsen, P.V., & Ringsmose, J. (2015). "In Denmark, Afghanistan Is Worth Dying For: How Public Support for the War Was Maintained in the Face of Mounting Casualties and Elusive Success." *Cooperation and Conflict*, 50 (2): 211–227.

Jenks, J. (2006). *British Propaganda and News Media in the Cold War*. Edinburgh: Edinburgh University Press.

Jentleson, B.W. (1992). "The Pretty Prudent Public: Post-Vietnam American Opinion on the Use of Military Force." *International Studies Quarterly*, 36: 49–74.

Jentleson, B.W., & Britton, R.L. (1998). "Still Pretty Prudent: Post-Cold War American Public Opinion on the Use of Military Force." *Journal of Conflict Resolution*, 42 (4): 395–417.

Jeong, E.J., Bohil, C.J., & Biocca, F.A. (2011). "Brand Logo Placements in Violent Video Games." *Journal of Advertising*, 40: 59–72.

Johnson, L.K. (1986). "The CIA and the Media." *Intelligence and National Security*, 1 (2): 143–169.

Jörgens, H., Kolleck, N., & Saerbeck, B. (2016). "Exploring the Hidden Influence of International Treaty Secretariats: Using Social Network Analysis to Analyse the Twitter Debate on the 'Lima Work Programme on Gender'." *Journal of European Public Policy*, 23 (7): 979–998. doi:10.1080/13501763.2016.1162836

Kaczynski. (2014). "State Department's Terrorist Trolling Team Releases Graphic Angti-ISIS Video." *BuzzFeed*, September 4. Available from: www.buzzfeed.com/andrewkaczynski/state-departments-terrorist-trolling-team-releases-graphic-a#.qwXyNZ7OA

Kahneman, D. (2011). *Thinking, Fast and Slow.* New York: Farrar, Straus and Giroux.

Kampf, R., Manor, I., & Segev, E. (2015). "Digital Diplomacy 2.0? A Cross-National Comparison of Public Engagement in Facebook and Twitter." *The Hague Journal of Diplomacy*, 10 (4): 331–362.

Kandyla, A.A., & De Vreese, C. (2011). "News Media Representations of a Common EU Foreign and Security Policy. A Cross-National Content Analysis of CFSP Coverage in National Quality Newspapers." *Comparative European Politics*, 9 (1): 52–75.

Kang, C. (2016). "Fake News Onslaught Targets Pizzeria as Nest of Child-Trafficking." *The New York Times.* http://nyti.ms/2iB2s24

Karoliny, E. (2010). "Communicating the EU to the World: A European Communication Policy for the External Relations of the Union." *Studia Iuridica Auctoritate Universitatis Pecs Publicata*, 147: 35.

Katalenas, D. (2016). "Join the US Freedom Army." *LinkedIn.* Available from: http://bit.ly/2r99cov

Katz, E., & Lazarsfeld, P.F. (1955). *Personal Influence: The Part Played by People in the Flow of Mass Communications.* New York: The Free Press.

Keller, P. (2017). "Divided by geography? NATO's internal debate about the eastern and southern flanks." In K. Friis (Ed.), *NATO and Collective Defence in the 21st Century. An Assessment of the Warsaw Summit.* London: Routledge.

Kelley, C.A. (1989). "A Study of Selected Issues in Vividness Research: The Role of Attention and Elaboration Enhancing Cues." *Advances in Consumer Research*, 16: 574–580.

Keuleers, F. (2015). "Explaining External Perceptions: The EU and China in African Public Opinion." *Journal of Common Market Studies*, 53 (4): 803–821.

Kiely, E. (2017). "Gingrich Spreads Conspiracy Theory." FactCheck.org. Available from: www.factcheck.org/2017/05/gingrich-spreads-conspiracy-theory/

King, T. (2017). "Fixing Misinformation is a Misguided and Insufficient Strategy." *Medium.* Available from: https://medium.com/@tallgeekychap/fixing-misinformation-is-a-misguided-and-insufficient-strategy-7934c2fa2b38

Kirby, E.J. (2016). "The City Getting Rich from Fake News." *BBC*, December 5. Available from: www.bbc.com/news/magazine-38168281

Klarevas, L. (2002). "The 'Essential Domino' of Military Operations: American Public Opinion and the Use of Force." *International Studies Perspectives*, 3: 417–437.

Knight, B. (2016). "Teenage Girl Admits Making up Migrant Rape Claim that Outraged Germany." *The Guardian*, January 31. Available from: www.theguardian.com/world/2016/jan/31/teenage-girl-made-up-migrant-claim-that-caused-uproar-ingermany (accessed May 2, 2016).

Knightley, P. (2004). *The First Casualty: The War Correspondent as Hero and Myth-Maker From the Crimea to Iraq.* Baltimore, MD: Johns Hopkins Press.

Knowlton, B. (2014). "Digital War Takes Shape on Websites Over ISIS." *The New York Times*, September 26. Available from: www.nytimes.com/2014/09/27/world/middleeast/us-vividly-rebuts-isis-propaganda-on-arab-social-media.html

Kollanyi, B., Howard, P.N., & Woolley, S.C. (2016). "Bots and Automation over Twitter during the US Election." *Data Memo*. Available from: http://politicalbots.org/?p=787

Korn, J. (2016). "European CVE Strategies from a Practitioner's Perspective." *The Annals of the American Academy of Political and Social Science*, 668 (1): 180–197.

Kramer, X.H., Kaiser, T.B., Schmidt, S.E., Davidson, J.E., & Lefebvre V.A. (2003). "From Prediction to Reflexive Control." *Reflexive Processes and Control*, 2 (1): 86–102.

Krcmar, M., & Hight, A. (2007). "The Development of Aggressive Mental Models in Young Children." *Media Psychology*, 10: 250–269.

Kulesa, L., & Frear, T. (May, 2017). *NATO's Evolving Modern Deterrence Posture: Challenges and Risks*. London: ELN Issue Brief.

Kundnani, A. (2012). "Radicalisation: The Journey of a Concept." *Race & Class*, 54 (2): 3–25.

Kurtz, H. (1998). *Spin Cycle: Inside the Clinton Propaganda Machine*. London: Simon & Schuster.

Kuus, M. (2009). "Cosmopolitan Militarism? Spaces of NATO Expansion." *Environment and Planning A*, 41 (3): 545–562.

Kwong, M. (2017). "Trump Is Hyping a Uranium Scandal about Hillary Clinton. Here's Why Some Observers Call It 'Bogus'." *CBC*. Available from: www.cbc.ca/news/world/trump-bogus-clinton-uranium-one-deal-conspiracy-1.4383957

Laclau, E. (2004). "Glimpsing the future." In S. Critchley & O. Marchart (Eds.), *Laclau: A Critical Reader* (pp. 279–328). London: Routledge.

Laclau, E. (2007). *On Populist Reason* (Reprint ed.). London and New York: Verso.

Lacquement, R.A. (2004). "The Casualty-Aversion Myth." *Naval War College Review LVII*, 1: 38–57.

Lamothe, D., & Birnbaum, M. (2017). "Defense Secretary Mattis issues new ultimatum to NATO Allies on Defense Spending." *The Washington Post*, February 16.

Lang, M. (2017). "Number of Americans Exposed to Russian Propaganda Rises, as Tech Giants Testify." *San Francisco Chronicle*, November 1. Available from: www.sfchronicle.com/business/article/Facebook-Google-Twitter-say-150-million-12323900.php (accessed December 13, 2017).

Lapowsky, I., & Marshall, A. (2017). "Ford's US Expansion is a Victory for Trump's Trolling Tactics." *Wired*. Available from: http://bit.ly/2ixfWKZ

Laqueur, W. (2004). "The Terrorism to Come." *Policy Review*, 126: 49–64.

Larson, E. (1996). *Casualties and Consensus: The Historical Role of Casualties in Domestic Support for U.S. Military Operations*. Santa Monica, CA: RAND.

Lasswell, H.D. (1927). "The Theory of Political Propaganda." *American Political Science Review*, 21 (3): 627–631.

Laurence, J., & Vaïsse, J. (2006). *Integrating Islam: Political and Religious Challenges in Contemporary France*. Washington, DC: Brookings Institution Press.

Lazarsfeld, P., & Merton, R. (1948). "Mass communication, popular taste, and organized social action." In W. Schramm (Ed.), *Mass Communication* (pp. 492–503). Urbana: University of Illinois Press.

Leander, A. (2017). "Digital/Commercial (In)Visibility: The Politics of DAESH Recruitment Videos." *European Journal of Social Theory*, 20 (3): 348–372.

Le Bars, S. (2013). "74% des Français jugent l'islam intolérant : « Les musulmans doivent entendre cet avertissement »." *Le Monde*, January 24. Available from: http://religion.blog.lemonde.fr/2013/01/24/74-des-francais-jugent-lislam-intolerant-les-musulmans-doivent-entendre-cet-avertissement/

Lee, H., Abdar, M., & Yen, N.Y. (2018). "Event-Based Trend Factor Analysis Based on Hashtag Correlation and Temporal Information Mining." *Applied Soft Computing*. doi:10.1016/j.asoc.2018.02.044

Lefebvre, V.A., & Lefebvre, V.D. (1984). *Reflexive Control: The Soviet Concept of Influencing an Adversary's Decision Making Process*. Englewood: Science Applications.

Lefebvre, V.A., & Smolyan, G.L. (1968 [1971]). *Algebra of Conflict*. Translated from the original title "Algebra konflikta". Springfield, VA: National Technical Information Service.

Legendary American. (2016). "Introducing MostDamagingWikileaks.com!" *Reddit Post*. Available from: www.reddit.com/r/The_Donald/comments/59lpwh/introducing_mostdamagingwikileakscom/

Lemieux, A., & Nill, R. (2011). "The role and impact of music in promoting (and countering) violent extremism." In S. Canna (Ed.), *Countering Violent Extremism: Scientific Methods and Strategies* (p. 146). Wright-Patterson Air Force Base, OH: Air Force Research Laboratory.

Lesaca, J. (2015). "On Social Media, ISIS Uses Modern Cultural Images to Spread Anti-Modern Values." *Brookings Institution*, September 24. Available from: www.brookings.edu/blog/techtank/2015/09/24/on-social-media-isis-uses-modern-cultural-images-to-spread-anti-modern-values/

Leuprecht, C., Hataley, T., Moskalenko, S., & McCauley, C. (2010). "Containing the Narrative: Strategy and Tactics in Countering the Storyline of Global Jihad. *Journal of Policing, Intelligence and Counter Terrorism*, 5 (1): 42–57.

Lewis, P., & Hilder, P. (2018). "Leaked: Cambridge Analytica's Blueprint for Trump Victory." *The Guardian*, March 23. Available from: www.theguardian.com/uk-news/2018/mar/23/leaked-cambridge-analyticas-blueprint-for-trump-victory (accessed March 24, 2018).

Linebarger, P. (2015). *Psychological Warfare* (Kindle ed.)

Linz, D.G., Donnerstein, E., & Penrod, S. (1988). "Effects of Long-Term Exposure to Violent and Sexually Degrading Depictions of Women." *Journal of Personality and Social Psychology*, 55 (5): 758.

Lippman, W. (1922). *Public Opinion*. New York: Harcourt, Brace and Company.

Livingston, S. (1994). *The Terrorism Spectacle*. Boulder, CO: Westview Press.

———. (1997). *Clarifying the CNN Effect: An Examination of Media Effects According to Type of Military Intervention*. Cambridge, MA: Joan Shorenstein Center on the Press Politics and Public Policy John F. Kennedy School of Government Harvard University.

Livingston, S., & Eachus, T. (1995). "Humanitarian Crises and U.S. Foreign Policy: Somalia and the CNN Effect Reconsidered." *Political Communication*, 12: 413–429.

Lord, K.M. (2008). *Voices of America: U.S. Public Diplomacy for the 21st Century*. Washington, DC: Brookings Institution.

Lotan, G. (2016). "Fake News Is Not the Only Problem." *Points*. Available from: http://bit.ly/2qzAA1U

Lucarelli, S., & Fioramonti, L. (2009). "Conclusion self-representations and external perceptions – can the EU bridge the gap?" In S. Lucarelli & L. Fioramonti (Eds.), *External Perceptions of the European Union as a Global Actor* (pp. 218–225). London: Routledge.

Luhmann, N. (1995). *Social Systems*. Stanford, CA: Stanford University Press.

Luhmann, N. (1998). *Die Gesellschaft der Gesellschaft I*. Frankfurt/M.: Suhrkamp.

Luik, J. (2016). "Estonian Perspective." Presentation at NATO Information and Communicators Conference (NICC). Tallinn, September 12.

Lycarião, D., & dos Santos, M.A. (2017). "Bridging Semantic and Social Network Analyses: The Case of the Hashtag #precisamosfalarsobreaborto (we need to talk about abortion) on Twitter." *Information, Communication & Society*, 20 (3): 368–385. doi:10.1 080/1369118X.2016.1168469

Lynch, P. (June 2, 2015). Introduction to the course "Building Safer Communities: Options for Civil Society." Nairobi.

Lynch, M., Freelon, D., & Aday, S. (2015). "Online Self-Segregation in Wartime: A Longitudinal Network Analysis of Tweets About Syria, 2011–2013." *Annals of the American Academy of Political and Social Science*, 659 (1): 166–179.

MacFarquhar, N. (2016). "A Powerful Russian Weapon: The Spread of False Stories." *The New York Times*, August 28. Available from: www.nytimes.com/2016/08/29/ world/europe/russia-sweden-disinformation.html

Madrigal, A. (2017). "What Facebook Did to American Democracy." *The Atlantic*, October 12. Available from: www.theatlantic.com/technology/archive/2017/10/ what-facebook-did/542502/

Maheshwari, S. (2017). "10 Times Trump Spread Fake News." *The New York Times*. http://nyti.ms/2jBM9C4

Mai'a, K. (2013). "Conceptualizing European public diplomacy." In M. Cross & J. Melissen (Eds.), *European Public Diplomacy: Soft Power at Work* (pp. 1–11). New York: Palgrave Macmillan.

Maltby, S. (2012a). *Military Media Management: Negotiating the 'Front' Line in Mediatized War*. Abingdon: Routledge.

Maltby, S. (2012b). "The Mediatization of the Military." *Media, War & Conflict*, 5 (3): 255–268.

Maltby, S. (2015). "Imagining influence: Logic(al) tensions in war and defence." In S. Hjarvard, M. Mortensen, & M. Fugl Eskjær (Eds.), *The Dynamics of Mediatized Conflict* (pp. 165–184). New York: Peter Lang.

Mann, S. (2004). "Sousveillance: Inverse surveillance in multimedia imaging." In *Proceedings of the 12th annual ACM International Conference on Multimedia* (pp. 620–627). New York.

Manners, I., & Whitman, R. (2013). "Normative power and the future of EU diplomacy." In M. Cross & J. Melissen (Eds.), *European Public Diplomacy: Soft Power at Work* (pp. 183–203). New York: Palgrave Macmillan.

Mansoor, P., & Murray, W. (2012). *Hybrid Warfare: Fighting Complex Opponents from the Ancient World to the Present*. Cambridge: Cambridge University Press.

Marlin, R. (2011). "Propaganda and the Ethics of WikiLeaks." *Global Media Journal: Australian Edition*, 5 (1): 1–8.

Marantz, A. (2016). "Trolls for Trump: Meet Mike Cernovich, the Meme Mastermind of the Alt-Right." *The New Yorker*. Available from: http://bit.ly/2f9w9Fe

Maronkova, B. (2016). "NATO's Embrace of Digital Outreach." *CPD Blog*. Available from: https://uscpublicdiplomacy.org/blog/natos-embrace-digital-outreach (accessed February 13, 2017).

Marshall, J. (2016). "Trump & Putin. Yes, It's Really a Thing." *Talking Points Memo*. Available from: http://talkingpointsmemo.com/edblog/trump-putin-yes-it-s-really-a-thing

Mathew, G. (2017). "Behind the Scenes of Behavioral Advertising." Kissmetrics. Available from: http://bit.ly/XJ6DtZ

Mazzetti, M., & Gordon, M. (2015). "ISIS is Winning the Social Media War, U.S. Concludes." *New York Times*, June 12. Available from: www.nytimes.com/2015/06/13/ world/middleeast/isis-is-winning-message-war-us-concludes.html?_r=1

McCauley, C. (1998). "When screen violence is not attractive." In J.H. Goldstein (Ed.), *Why We Watch: The Attractions of Violent Entertainment* (pp. 144–162). Oxford: Oxford University Press.

McGreal, C. (2010). "Wikileaks Reveals Video Showing US Air Crew Shooting Down Iraqi Civilians." *The Guardian*. Available from: www.theguardian.com/world/2010/apr/05/wikileaks-us-army-iraq-attack

McGuire, W.J. (1986). "Personality and Attitude Change: An Information-Processing Theory." *Psychological Foundations of Attitudes*, 171: 196.

Meister, S. (2016). "The 'Lisa Case': Germany as a Target of Russian Disinformation." *NATO Review*. Available from: www.nato.int/docu/review/2016/also-in-2016/lisa-case-germany-target-russian-disinformation/EN/index.htm (accessed May 2, 2016).

Meleagrou-Hitchens, A. Alexander, A., & Kaderbhai, N. (2017). "The Impact of Digital Communications Technology on Radicalization and Recruitment." *International Affairs*, 93 (5): 1233–1249.

Melissen, J. (Ed.). (2005a). *The New Public Diplomacy. Soft Power in International Relations*. Basingstoke: Palgrave Macmillan.

Melissen, J. (2005b). "The new public diplomacy: Between theory and practice." In *New Public Diplomacy* (pp. 3–27). London: Palgrave Macmillan.

Mellon, J. & Prosser, C. (2017). "Twitter and Facebook Are Not Representative of the General Population: Political Attitudes and Demographics of British Social Media Users." *Research & Politics*, 4 (3). doi:10.1177/2053168017720008

Meyer, C. (1999). "Political Legitimacy and the Invisibility of Politics: Exploring the European Union's Communication Deficit." *Journal of Common Market Studies*, 37 (4): 617–639.

Michalski, A. (2005). "The EU as a soft power: The force of persuasion." In J. Melissen (Ed.), *The New Public Diplomacy* (pp. 124–144). Basingstoke: Palgrave Macmillan.

Miller, J. (2017). "Germany Votes for 50m Euro Social Media Fines." *BBC News*, June 30. Available from: www.bbc.com/news/technology-40444354

Miller, G., & Mekhennet, S. (2015). "Inside the Surreal World of the Islamic State's Propaganda Machine." *Washington Post*, November 20. Available from: www.washingtonpost.com/world/national-security/inside-the-islamic-states-propagandamachine/2015/11/20/051e997a-8ce6-11e5-acff-673ae92ddd2b_story.html?tid=sm_tw

Ministry of Defence. (2011). *Strategic Communication: The Defence Contribution. Shrivenham: The Development, Concepts and Doctrine Centre*. Available from: www.gov.uk/government/uploads/system/uploads/attachment_data/file/33710/20120126jdn112_Strategic_CommsU.pdf

Ministry of Defence. (2012). *Joint Doctrine Note 1/12 Strategic Communication: The Defense Contribution*. Ministry of Defence.

Ministry of Foreign Affairs. (2017). *Strategic Communication and Countering Violent Extremism*. The Hague.

Mirzoeff, N. (2011). *The Right to Look: A Counterhistory of Visuality*. Durham, NC: Duke University Press.

Miskimmon, A., O'Loughlin, B., & Roselle, L. (2013). *Strategic Narratives: Communication Power and the New World Order* (Vol. 3). New York: Routledge.

Miskimmon, A., O'Loughlin, B., & Roselle, L. (2017). *Forging the World: Strategic Narratives and International Relations*. Ann Arbor, MI: University of Michigan Press.

Missiroli, A., Andersson, J.J., Gaub, F., Popescu, N., & Wilkins, J.-J. (2016). *Strategic Communications East and South*. Paris: European Union Institute for Security Studies.

Mitts, T. (2017). "From Isolation to Radicalization: Anti-Muslim Hostility and Support for ISIS in the West." Unpublished paper, October 6. Available from: http://tamarmitts.com/wp-content/uploads/2016/06/Mitts_JMP.pdf (accessed December 20, 2017).

Moloney, K. (2006). *Rethinking Public Relations: PR Propaganda and Democracy*. London: Routledge.

Mook, R. (2016). "Clinton Camp: DNC Hack a Russian Plot to Help Trump." *CNN*. Available from: http://edition.cnn.com/videos/politics/2016/07/24/wikileaks-clinton-campaignmanager-robby-mook-intv-tapper-sotu.cnn

Moore, C. (2006). "Reading the Hermeneutics of Violence: The Literary Turn and Chechnya." *Global Society*, 20 (2): 179–198.

Moore, C., & Shepherd L.J. (2010). "Aesthetics and International Relations: Towards a Global Politics." *Global Society*, 24 (3): 299–309.

Moz. (2017). "External Links." http://bit.ly/1NEfEuo

MSNBC. (March 30, 2018). World Exclusive: Whistleblower Blasts Facebook 'Exploitation'. Available from: www.msnbc.com/the-beat-with-ari-melber/watch/world-exclusive-whistleblower-blasts-facebook-exploitation-1199152195803

Mueller, J. (1973). *War, Presidents, and Public Opinion*. New York: John Wiley & Sons.

Murphy, D. (2009). "Talking the Talk: Why Warfighters Don't Understand Information Operations." Issue Paper 4(9). Carlisle, PA: U.S. Army War College Center for Strategic Leadership.

Murphy, D. (2010). "In Search of the Art and Science of Strategic Communication." Issue Paper 4(9). Carlisle, PA: U.S. Army War College Center for Strategic Leadership.

Mustafaraj, E., & Metaxas, P. (2010). "From Obscurity to Prominence in Minutes: Political Speech and Real-Time Search." In *Proceedings of the WebSci10: Extending the Frontiers of Society On-Line*, April 26–27th, Raleigh, NC.

MyKettleIsNotBlack. (2016). *Reddit Post*, July 27. Available from: www.reddit.com/r/The_Donald/comments/4uua1j/dnc_data_director_seth_rich_was_likely/

Nabi, R.L. (2009). "Emotion and media effects." In R.L. Nabi & M.B. Oliver (Eds.), *The Sage Handbook of Media Processes and Effects* (pp. 205–221). Thousand Oaks, CA: Sage.

National Coordinator for Counterterrorism. (Ed.). (2010). *Countering Violent Extremist Narratives*. The Hague: National Coordinator for Counterterrorism.

Neumann, P.R. (2008). "Introduction." In P. Neumann, J. Stoil, & D. Esfandiary (Eds.), *Perspectives on Radicalisation and Political Violence: Papers from the First International Conference on Radicalisation and Political Violence*. London: ICSR

Neumann, P. (2010). *Prisons and Terrorism Radicalisation and De-Radicalisation in 15 Countries*. London: International Centre for the Study of Radicalisation. Available from: http://icsr.info/wp-content/uploads/2012/10/1277699166PrisonsandTerrorismRadicalisationandDeradicalisationin15Countries.pdf

Neumann, P. (2012). *Countering Online Radicalization in America*. Washington, DC: Bipartisan Policy Centre, Homeland Security Project. Available from: http://bipartisanpolicy.org/wp-content/uploads/sites/default/files/BPC%20_Online%20Radicalization%20Report.pdf

Newport, F., Singh, L., Soroka, S., Traugott, M., & Dugan, A. (2016). "'Email' Dominates What Americans Have Heard About Clinton." *Gallup News*. Available from: http://news.gallup.com/poll/195596/email-dominates-americans-heard-clinton.aspx

New York Times Co. v. United States (No. 1873). (1971). Available from: www.law.cornell.edu/supremecourt/text/403/713

Newsweek. (2017). "Donald Trump Calls White House Kushner Leaks 'Fake News'." Available from: www.newsweek.com/donald-trump-calls-white-house-kushner-links-fake-news-616919

Nickerson, R.S. (1998). "Confirmation Bias: A Ubiquitous Phenomenon in Many Guises." *Review of General Psychology*, 2 (2): 175–220.

Nimmo, B. (2017). "How A Russian Troll Fooled America." *Atlantic Council's Digital Forensic Research Lab*, November 14. Available from: https://medium.com/dfrlab/how-a-russian-troll-fooled-america-80452a4806d1 (accessed March 24, 2017).

Nimmo, B. (2018). "#ElectionWatch: Beyond Russian Impact." *DFR Lab*. Available from: https://medium.com/dfrlab/electionwatch-beyond-russian-impact-2f5777677cc0

Nisbett, R.E., & Ross, L. (1980). *Human Inference: Strategies and Shortcomings of Social Judgment*. Englewood Cliffs, NJ: Prentice-Hall.

Niţoiu, C. (2013). "The Narrative Construction of the European Union in External Relations." *Perspectives on European Politics and Society*, 14 (2): 240–255.

Nix, A. (2016). "Power of Big Data and Psychographics." *YouTube*, September 27. Available from: http://bit.ly/2gD8FbL

Noelle-Neumann, E. (1993). *The Spiral of Silence: Public Opinion – Our Social Skin* (2nd ed.). Chicago, IL: University of Chicago Press.

Noetzel, T., & Schreer, B. (2012). "More Flexible, Less Coherent: NATO after Lisbon." *Australian Journal of International Affairs*, 66 (1): 20–33.

Nulty, P., Theocharis, Y., Popa, S.A., Parnet, O., & Benoit, K. (2016). "Social Media and Political Communication in the 2014 Elections to the European Parliament." *Electoral Studies*, 44: 429–444.

Obama, B. (2013). "Speech on National Security." *The Washington Post*, May 23. Available from: www.washingtonpost.com/politics/president-obamas-may-23-speech-on-national-security-as-prepared-for-delivery/2013/05/23/02c35e30-c3b8-11e2-9fe2-6ee52d0eb7c1_story.html?noredirect=on&utm_term=.ece996e46ffc (accessed June 20, 2018).

Obama, B. (2015). "Remarks by the President at the Summit on Countering Violent Extremism." *whitehouse.gov*, February 19. Available from: https://obamawhitehouse.archives.gov/the-press-office/2015/02/19/remarks-president-summit-countering-violent-extremism-february-19-2015 (accessed November 6, 2017).

Offman, C. (2016). "Donald Trump Seems to be Campaigning to be Troll-in-Chief." *The Globe and Mail*. Available from: https://tgam.ca/2r15Jv1

Okenyi, P., & Owens, T. (2007). On the Anatomy of Human Hacking. *Information Security and Risk Management*. Available from: www.tandfonline.com/doi/full/10.1080/10658980701747237

O'Loughlin, B. (2011). "Images as Weapons of war: Representation, Mediation and Interpretation." *Review of International Studies*, 37 (1): 71–91.

O'Loughlin, B. (2018). "Deflating the Iconoclash: Shifting the Focus from Islamic State's Iconoclasm to Its Realpolitik." *Critical Studies in Media Communication*, 35 (1): 89–102.

Olsson, E. K., & Hammargård, K. (2016). "The Rhetoric of the President of the European Commission: Charismatic Leader or Neutral Mediator?" *Journal of European Public Policy*, 23 (4): 550–570.

Olsson, E.K., Deverell, E., Wagnsson, C., & Hellman, M. (2016). "EU Armed Forces and Social Media: Convergence or Divergence?" *Defence Studies*, 16 (2): 97–117.

Osborne, S., & Carroll, O. (2018). "Russia Tells May It Is 'Not to Blame' for Nerve Agent Poisoning of Former Spy Sergei Skripal." *The Independent*, March 13. Available from: www.independent.co.uk/news/uk/crime/sergei-skripal-russia-nerve-agent-novichok-demands-sample-lavrov-vladimir-putin-kremlin-a8253121.html (accessed March 19, 2018).

Packer, G. (2015). "The Other Paris." *The New Yorker*, August 24. Available from: www.newyorker.com/magazine/2015/08/31/the-other-france

Pamment, J. (2012). *New Public Diplomacy in the 21st Century*. London: Routledge.

Pamment, J. (2015). "Strategic Communication Campaigns at the Foreign and Commonwealth Office: Managing Mediatization during the Papal Visit, the Royal Wedding, and the Queen's Visit to Ireland." *International Journal of Strategic Communication*, 9 (2): 118–133.

Pamment, J., & Wilkins, K. (Eds.). (2018). *Communicating National Image through Development and Diplomacy: The Politics of Foreign Aid*. Cham, Switzerland: Palgrave Macmillan.

Pamment, J., Nothhaft, H., Agardh-Twetman, H., & Fjällhed, A. (2018). *Countering Information Influence Activities*. Stockholm: MSB.

Papacharissi, Z. (2015). *Affective Publics: Sentiment, Technology, and Politics*. Oxford: Oxford University Press.

Patrick, J.J. (February 28, 2018). Cambridge Analytica CEO Gives Evidence to Fake News Inquiry. Available from: www.byline.com/column/67/article/2069

Paul, C. (2009). *Whither Strategic Communication: A Survey of Current Proposals and Recommendations*. Santa Monica, CA: RAND.

Paul, C. (2011). *Strategic Communication: Origins, Concepts, and Current Debates*. Santa Barbara, CA: Praeger.

Penrod, J. (2001). "Refinement of the Concept of Uncertainty." *Journal of Advanced Nursing*, 34 (2): 238–245.

Peters, J.D. (2015). *The Marvelous Clouds: Towards a Philosophy of Elemental Media*. London: University of Chicago Press.

Pew Research Center. (2006). "The Great Divide: How Westerners and Muslims View Each Other." Washington, DC: Pew Global Attitude Project. Available from: www.pewglobal.org/files/pdf/253.pdf

Pew Research Center. (2017). "Digital News Fact Sheet." Available from: www.journalism.org/fact-sheet/digital-news/

Pfau, M., Haigh, M.M., Fifrick, A., Holl, D., Tedesco, A., & Nunnally, D. (2006). "The Effects of Print News Photographs of the Casualties of War." *Journalism & Mass Communication Quarterly*, 83: 150–168.

Pfau, M., Haigh, M.M., Shannon, T., Tones, T., Mercurio, D., & Williams, R. (2008). "The Influence of Television News Depictions of the Images of War on Viewers." *Journal of Broadcasting & Electronic Media*, 52: 303–322.

Pinker, S. (2013). "Science Is Not Your Enemy. An Impassioned Plea to Neglected Novelists, Embattled Professors and Tenure-Less Historians." *New Republic*, August 7.

Plouffe, D. (2010). *The Audacity to Win: How Obama Won and How We Can Beat the Party of Limbaugh, Beck, and Palin*. New York: Penguin Books.

Poole, E. (2002). *Reporting Islam: Media Representations of British Muslims*. London and New York: I.B. Tauris; In the United States of America and Canada distributed by Palgrave Macmillan.

Poole, E., & Richardson, J.E. (Eds.). (2006). *Muslims and the News Media*. London: Tauris.

Pouliot, V. (2010). *International Security in Practice. The Politics of NATO-Russia Diplomacy*. Cambridge: Cambridge University press.

Potter, W.J., & Smith, S. (2000). "The Context of Graphic Portrayals of Television Violence." *Journal of Broadcasting & Electronic Media*, 44: 301–323.

Potter, W.J., Pashupati, K., Pekurny, R.G., Hoffman, E., & Davis, K. (2002). "Perceptions of Television: A Schema." *Media Psychology*, 4: 27–50.

Powers, S.M. (2014). "Conceptualizing Radicalization in a Market for Loyalties." *Media, War & Conflict*, 7 (2): 233–249.

Pozen, D. (2013). "The Leaky Leviathan: Why the Government Condemns and Condones Unlawful Disclosures of Information." *Harvard Law Review*, 127 (2): 512–635.

Prokop, A. (2018). "All of Robert Mueller's Indictments and Plea Deals in the Russia Investigation So Far." *Vox*, February 23. Available from: www.vox.com/policy-and-politics/2018/2/20/17031772/mueller-indictments-grand-jury

Quinn, B. (2016). "French Police Make Woman Remove Clothing on Nice Beach Following Burkini Ban." *The Guardian*, August 23. Available from: www.theguardian.com/world/2016/aug/24/french-police-make-woman-remove-burkini-on-nice-beach

Rainie, L., Anderson, J., & Albright, J. (2017). "The Future of Free Speech, Trolls, Anonymity and Fake News Online." *Pew Research Center*. Available from: www.pewinternet.org/2017/03/29/the-future-of-free-speech-trolls-anonymity-and-fake-news-online/

Ramsay, G. (2010). "Conceptualising Online Terrorism." *Perspectives on Terrorism*, 2 (7), 3–10.

Ramsay, G. (2015). *Jihadi Culture on the World Wide Web* (Reprint ed.). Bloomsbury Academic.

Rancière, J. (2006). *The Politics of Aesthetics*. London and New York: Continuum.

Reddit. "His name was seth rich." 2016: Rasmussen, S.B. (2010). "The Messages and Practices of the European Union's Public Diplomacy." *The Hague Journal of Diplomacy*, 5 (3): 263–287. www.reddit.com/r/The_Donald/comments/4yk6q7/his_name_was_seth_rich/

Reding, A., Weed, K., & Ghez, J.J. (2010). *NATO's Strategic Communications Concept and Its Relevance for France*. Cambridge: RAND.

Richardson, L. (1988). "Secrecy and Status: The Social Construction of Forbidden Relationships." *American Sociological Review*, 53: 209–219.

Ricoeur, P. (1984). *Time and Narrative* (Vol. I.), translated by K. McLaughlin & D. Pellauer. Chicago, IL: University of Chicago Press.

Riddle, K. (2013). "Transportation into Vivid Media Violence: A Focus on Attention, Emotions, and Mental Rumination." *Communication Quarterly*, 61: 446–462.

———. (2014). "A Theory of Vivid Media Violence." *Communication Theory*, 24: 291–310.

Risen, J. (2018). "The biggest secret: My Life as a New York Times Reporter in the Shadow of the War on Terror." *The Intercept*. Available from: https://theintercept.com/2018/01/03/my-life-as-a-new-york-times-reporter-in-the-shadow-of-the-war-on-terror/

Risso, L. (2014). *Propaganda and Intelligence in the Cold War: The NATO Information Service*. Oxon and New York: Routledge.

Roberts, A. (2011). "The WikiLeaks Illusion." *The Wilson Quarterly (1976-)*, 35 (3): 16–21.

Robinson, P. (1999). "The CNN Effect: Can the News Media Drive Foreign Policy?" *Political Communication*, 25: 301–309.

Robinson, P. (2002). *The CNN Effect: The Myth of News, Foreign Policy, and Intervention*. Oxford: Routledge Press.

Robinson, J. (2012). "Wikileaks, disclosure, free speech and democracy: New media and the Fourth Estate." In *More of Less: Democracy and the New Media*. Sydney: Future Leaders.

Robinson, P., Goddard, P., Parry, K., Murray, C., & Taylor, P. (2010). *Pockets of Resistance*. Manchester: Manchester University Press.

Roselle, L., Miskimmon, A., & O'Loughlin, B. (2014). "Strategic Narrative: A New Means to Understand Soft Power." *Media, War & Conflict*, 7 (1): 70–84.

Roskos-Ewoldsen, B., Davies, J., & Roskos-Ewoldsen, D.R. (2004). "Implications of the Mental Models Approach for Cultivation Theory." *Communications*, 29: 345–363.

Ross, A.A. (2013a). *Mixed Emotions: Beyond Fear and Hatred in International Conflict*. Chicago, IL: University of Chicago Press.

Ross, A. (2013b). *Tweet*, July 11. Available from: https://twitter.com/AlecJRoss/status/355432597188386817 (accessed May 2, 2018).

Roth, G. (1997). *Das Gehirn und seine Wirklichkeit*. Frankfurt/M.: Suhrkamp.

Roth, G. (2003). *Fuehlen, Denken, Handeln*. Frankfurt/M.: Suhrkamp.

Roth, G., & Dicke, U. (2005). "Evolution of the Brain and Intelligence." *Trends in Cognitive Science*, 9 (5): 2050–2257.

Rudy, R., & Linz, D. (November, 2007). "Domains of Media Desensitization: A Model of the Relationships among Cognitive, Emotional, Physiological, and Behavioral

Response Systems." Paper presented at the meeting of the National Communication Association, Chicago, IL.

Russell, A., & Waisbord, S. (2017). "The Snowden Revelations and the Networked Fourth Estate." *Journal of Communication*, 11: 58–878.

Sagar, R. (2016). *Secrets and Leaks: The Dilemma of Tate Secrecy.* Princeton, NJ: Princeton University Press.

Sageman, M. (2004). *Understanding Terror Networks.* Philadelphia, PA: University of Pennsylvania Press.

Sageman, M. (2011). *Leaderless Jihad: Terror Networks in the Twenty-First Century.* Philadelphia, PA: University of Pennsylvania Press.

Samuel, A. (2016). "Psychographics Are Just as Important for Marketers as Demographics." *Harvard Business Review*, March 11. Available from: https://hbr.org/2016/03/psychograp hics-are-just-as-important-for-marketers-as-demographics (accessed March 24, 2016).

Samuel, H. (2017). "French Attempts to 'De-Radicalise' Homegrown Jihadists Pronounced a 'Total Fiasco'." *The Telegraph*, February 23. Available from: www.telegraph.co.uk/ news/2017/02/23/french-attempts-de-radicalise-homegrown-jihadists-pronounced/

Sandhu, S. (2017). "Heading for Mars While We Haven't Been on the Moon: A Reply to Nothhaft." *International Journal of Strategic Communication*, 11 (3): 184–188.

Sanger, D.E., & Haberman, M. (2016). "Donald Trump Sets Conditions for Defending NATO Allies against Attack." *New York Times*, July 20. Available from: www.nytimes. com/2016/07/21/us/politics/donald-trump-issues.html (accessed February 20, 2017).

Schacter, D.L. (2002). *The Seven Sins of Memory.* Boston, MA and New York: Houghton Mifflin.

Scheuer, M. (2008). *Imperial Hubris: Why the West Is Losing the War on Terror.* Washington DC; Poole: Potomac; Chris Lloyd [distributor].

Scheufele, D. (1999). "Framing as a Theory of Media Effects." *Journal of Communication*, 49 (4): 103–122.

Schmid, A.P. (2013). "Radicalisation, De-Radicalisation, Counter-Radicalisation: A Conceptual Discussion and Literature Review." *ICCT Research Paper*, 97: 22.

Schmid, A.P. (2014). "Al-Qaeda's 'Single Narrative' and Attempts to Develop Counter-Narratives: The State of Knowledge." *The Hague: ICCT*, 26(2): 208–225.

Schreckender, B. (2017). "World War Meme." *Politico.* Available from: http://politi. co/2lNQpvN

Schultz, T. (2017). "Why the 'Fake Rape' Story against German NATO Forces Fell Flat in Lithuania." *Deutsche Welle*, February 23. Available from: www.dw.com/en/whythe- fake-rape-story-against-german-nato-forces-fell-flat-in-lithuania/a-37694870.

Sedgwick, M. (2010). "The Concept of Radicalization as a Source of Confusion." *Terrorism and Political Violence*, 22 (4): 479–494.

Selim, G. (2016). "Approaches for Countering Violent Extremism at Home and Abroad." *The ANNALS of the American Academy of Political and Social Science*, 668 (1): 94–101.

Senate, C.O. (2018). *Putin's Asymmetric Assault on Democracy in Russia and Europe: Implications for U.S. National Security.* Washington, DC: US Government Publishing Office.

Sharp, P. (2009). *Diplomatic Theory of International Relations.* Cambridge: Cambridge University Press.

Shear, M.D., & Rosenberg, M. (2016). "Released Emails Suggest the D.N.C. Derided the Sanders Campaign." *The New York Times.* Available from: www.nytimes. com/2016/07/23/us/politics/dnc-emails-sanders-clinton.html

Sherer, M., & Rogers, R.W. (1984). "The Role of Vivid Information in Fear Appeals and Attitude Change." *Journal of Research in Personality*, 18: 321–334.

Sherwood, H. (2016). "Polish Magazine's 'Islamic Rape of Europe' Cover Sparks Outrage." World News. *The Guardian*, February 18. Available from: www.theguardian.com/world/2016/feb/18/polish-magazines-islamic-of-europe-cover-sparks-outrage

Shorrock, T. (2016). Cryptome's Searing Critique of Snowden Inc. TimShorrock.com.

Sidman, A.H., & Norpoth, H. (2012). "Fighting to Win: Wartime Morale in the American Public." *Electoral Studies*, 31: 330–341.

Silke, A., & Veldhuis, T. (2017). "Countering Violent Extremism in Prisons: A Review of Key Recent Research and Critical Research Gaps." *Perspectives on Terrorism*, 11 (5). Available from: www.terrorismanalysts.com/pt/index.php/pot/article/view/640/1258

Silver, N. (2015). "Donald Trump Is the World's Greatest Troll." *FiveThirtyEight*. Available from: http://53eig.ht/2r7BD5q

Silverman, B. "Managing Public Relations through the Strategic Press Leak." Available from: www.ereleases.com/pr-fuel/managing-public-relations-through-the-strategicpress-leak/

Simmel, G. (1906). "The Sociology of Secrecy and of Secret Societies." *American Journal of Sociology*, 11 (4): 441–498.

Smith, K.E. (2000). "The End of Civilian Rower EU: A Welcome Demise or Cause for Corncern? *The International spectator*, 35 (2): 11–28.

Snow, N., & Taylor, P.M. (Eds.). (2009). *Routledge Handbook of Public Diplomacy*. London and New York: Routledge.

Solomon, T. (2014). "The Affective Underpinnings of Soft Power." *European Journal of International Relations*, 20 (3): 720–741.

Solomon, N., & Lee, M.A. (1990). *Unreliable Sources*. New York: Lyle Stuart.

Solon, O. (2017). "How Syria's White Helmets Became Victims of an Online Propaganda Machine." *The Guardian*, December 18. Available from: www.theguardian.com/world/2017/dec/18/syria-white-helmets-conspiracy-theories

Sparrow, A. (2001). "Sept 11: 'A Good Day to Bury Bad News'." *The Telegraph*. Available from: www.telegraph.co.uk/news/uknews/1358985/Sept-11-a-good-day-to-bury-bad-news.html

Stephens, B. (2017). "The President versus 'Fake News,' Again." *New York Times*, June 29. Available from: www.nytimes.com/2017/06/29/opinion/trump-cnn-fake-news-russia.html

Stuart, D. (2004). "NATO and the Wider World: From Regional Collective Defence to Global Coalitions of the Willing." *Australian Journal of International Affairs*, 58 (1): 33–46.

Swigger, N. (2013). "The Online Citizen: Is Social Media Changing Citizens' Beliefs About Democratic Values?" *Political Behavior*, 35 (3): 589–603. doi:10.1007/s11109-012-9208-y

Tanz, J. (2017). "Journalism Fights for Survival in the Post-Truth Era." *Wired*. Available from: www.wired.com/2017/02/journalism-fights-survival-post-truth-era/

Tatham, S., & Le Page, R. (2014). *NATO Strategic Communication: More to Be Done?* Riga: National Defence Academy of Latvia.

Taylor, P. (1990). *Munitions of the Mind: A History of Propaganda from the Ancient World to the Present Day*. Manchester: Manchester University Press.

Taylor, P.M. (2009). "Public diplomacy and strategic communication." In N. Snow & P.M. Taylor (Eds.), *Routledge Handbook of Public Diplomacy* (pp. 12–17). London & New York: Routledge.

Taylor, C. (2018). "Structured vs. Unstructured Data." *Datamation*, March 28. Available from: www.datamation.com/big-data/structured-vs-unstructured-data.html (accessed April 12, 2018).

Taylor, M., & Kent, M.L. (2014). "Dialogic Engagement: Clarifying Foundational Concepts." *Journal of Public Relations Research*, 26 (5): 384–398.

Taylor, S.E., & Thompson, S.C. (1982). "Stalking the Elusive 'Vividness' Effect." *Psychological Review*, 89: 155–181.

The Guardian. (2016). "Germany must soon Close Borders to Refugees, Transport Minister Tells Merkel." *The Guardian*. Available from: www.theguardian.com/world/2016/jan/19/germany-must-soon-close-borders-to-refugees-transport-minister-tells-merkel (accessed May 3, 2016).

The Guardian. (2017). "Isis Faces Exodus of Foreign Fighters as Its 'Caliphate' Crumbles." *The Guardian*, April 26. Available from: www.theguardian.com/world/2017/apr/26/isis-exodus-foreign-fighters-caliphate-crumbles?CMP=share_btn_tw

The Guardian. (2018). "The Cambridge Analytica Files." *The Guardian*. Available from: www.theguardian.com/news/series/cambridge-analytica-files

The Telegraph. (2008). "Vandals Desecrate 500 French Muslim War Graves." *The Telegraph*, December 8. Available from: www.telegraph.co.uk/news/worldnews/europe/france/3684187/Vandals-desecrate-500-French-Muslim-war-graves.html

Thiessen, M.A. (2016). "The Democrats' Well-Deserved WikiLeaks Blowback." *The Washington Post*. Available from: www.washingtonpost.com/opinions/the-democrats-well-deserved-wikileaks-blowback/2016/07/27/ab15766c-5402-11e6-b7de-dfe509430c39_story.html?utm_term=.b1ae4007d104

Thomas, T. (2004). "Russia's Reflexive Control Theory and the Military." *The Journal of Slavic Military Studies*, 17 (2): 237–256. doi:10.1080/13518040490450529

Thomas, T. (2015). "Russia's Military Strategy and Ukraine: Indirect, Asymmetric—and Putin-Led." *The Journal of Slavic Military Studies*, 28 (3): 445–461. doi:10.1080/13518046.2015.1061819

Thompson, J.B. (2013). *Political Scandal: Power and Visibility in the Media Age*. Hoboken, NJ: John Wiley & Sons.

Tiffen, R. (1989). *News and Power*. Sydney: Allen & Unwin.

Todd, E. (2016). *Who Is Charlie? - Xenophobia and the New Middle Class*. Polity Press.

Tooby, J., & Cosmides, L. (1992). "The psychological foundations of culture." In J. Barkow, L. Cosmides, & J. Tooby (Eds.), *The Adapted Mind*. New York: Oxford University Press.

Tooby, J., & Cosmides, L. (2005). "Conceptual foundations of evolutionary psychology." In D. Buss (Ed.), *The Handbook of Evolutionary Psychology* (pp. 5–67). Hoboken, NJ: Wiley.

Traynor, I. (2014). "NATO Moves to Bolster Eastern European Defences against Russia." *The Guardian*, April 1. Available from: www.theguardian.com/world/2014/apr/01/nato-eastern-europe-defences-russia-putin-crimea (accessed May 5, 2017).

Trump, Donald. Twitter Post. (July 23, 2016a, 5:20 P.M.). Available from: https://twitter.com/realDonaldTrump/status/756962332228612096

Trump, Donald. Twitter Post. (October 12, 2016b, 9:46 A.M.). Available from: https://twitter.com/realDonaldTrump/status/786201435486781440

Turcotte, J., York, C., Irving, J., Scholl, R.M., & Pingree, R.J. (September, 2015). "News Recommendations from Social Media Opinion Leaders: Effects on Media Trust and Information Seeking." *Journal of Computer-Mediated Communication*, 20 (5): 520–535.

Twiplomacy. (May 31, 2016). "Twiplomacy Study 2016." Available from: http://twiplomacy.com/blog/twiplomacy-study-2016/ (accessed July 7, 2016).

Uchill, J. (2017). "Timeline: Campaign Knew Russia had Clinton Emails Months before Trump 'Joke'." *The Hill*. thehill.com/homenews/administration/357851-timeline-campaign-knew-russia-had-clinton-emails-months-before-trump

University of Edinburgh. (2017). "WikiLeaks Gave Trump Edge in Campaign Race, Twitter Study Finds." *School of Informatics*. Available from: www.ed.ac.uk/informatics/news-events/stories/2017/wikileaks-trump-edge-in-campaign-race-twitter

US Department of Defense. (2018). "The Expanding Spectrum of Espionage by Americans, 1947–2015." *Defense Personnel and Security Research Center*. Available from: https://publicintelligence.net/perserec-espionage-by-americans/

US National Intelligence Council. (2017). "Assessing Russian Activities and Intentions in Recent US Elections." *Intelligence Community Assessment*. Available from: www.dni.gov/files/documents/ICA_2017_01.pdf

Van Dijck, J. (2013). *The Culture of Connectivity: A Critical History of Social Media*. Oxford and New York: Oxford University Press.

Van Ginkel, B., & Entenmann, E. (Eds.). (2016). "The Foreign Fighters Phenomenon in the EU - Profiles, Threats & Policies." *The International Centre for Counter-Terrorism – The Hague*, 7 (2). Available from: https://icct.nl/publication/report-the-foreign-fighters-phenomenon-in-the-eu-profiles-threats-policies/

Veebel, V. (2016). "Estonia Confronts Propaganda." *Journal of European Security and Defense Issues*, 7: 14–19.

Vermeir, K., & Margócsy, D. (2012). "States of Secrecy: An Introduction." *The British Journal for the History of Science*, 45 (2): 53–164.

Vidino, L., & Hughes, S. (2015). "Isis in America: From Retweets to Raqqa." *Program on Extremism*, George Washington University.

Viner, K. (2016). "How Technology Disrupted the Truth." *The Guardian*, July 12. Available from: www.theguardian.com/media/2016/jul/12/how-technology-disrupted-the-truth

Virilio, P. (1994). *The Vision Machine*. Bloomington: Indiana University Press.

Vosoughi, S., Roy, D., & Aral, S. (2018). "The Spread of True and False News Online." *Science*, 359 (6380): 1146–1151.

Wagnsson, C. (2011a). "A Security Community in the Making? Sweden and NATO Post-Libya." *European Security*, 20 (4): 585–603.

Wagnsson, C. (2011b). "NATO's Role in the Strategic Concept Debate: Watchdog, Fire-Fighter, Neighbour or Seminar Leader?" *Co-operation and Conflict*, 46 (4): 482–501.

Walker, C., & Ludwig, J. (2017). "The Meaning of Sharp Power." *Foreign Affairs*, November. Available from: www.foreignaffairs.com/articles/china/2017-11-16/meaning-sharp-power?cid=int-fls&pgtype=hpg (accessed April 15, 2018).

Walker, P., & Roth, A. (2018). "UK, US, Germany and France Unite to Condemn Spy Attack." *The Guardian*, March 15. Available from: www.theguardian.com/uk-news/2018/mar/15/salisbury-poisoning-uk-us-germany-and-france-issue-joint-statement (accessed March 19, 2018).

Wanless, A., & Berk, M. (2017). "Participatory Propaganda: The Engagement of Audiences in the Spread of Persuasive Communications." In *Proceedings of the Social Media and Social Order, Culture Conflict 2.0 Conference*, December 1, Oslo.

Weiss, M. (2017). "Revealed: The Secret KGB Manual for Recruiting Spies." *The Daily Beast*, December 27. Available from: www.thedailybeast.com/the-kgb-papers-how-putin-learned-his-spycraft-part-1?ref=home

Welsh, J., & Fearn, D. (Eds.). (2008). *Engagement: Public Diplomacy in a Globalised World*. London: Foreign & Commonwealth Office (FCO).

White, H.C. (2008). *Identity and Control: How Social Formations Emerge*. Princeton, NJ: Princeton University Press.

Wikileaks. Twitter Post. (July 22, 2016a, 7:04 P.M.). Available from: https://twitter.com/wikileaks/status/756626079314575360

Wikileaks. Twitter Post. (July 24, 2016b, 6:05 P.M.). Available from: https://twitter.com/wikileaks/status/757335823754887168

Wikileaks. Twitter Post. (July 24, 2016c, 7:24 P.M.). Available from: https://twitter.com/wikileaks/status/757355749588738052

Wikileaks. Twitter Post. (August 9, 2016d, 11:48 A.M.). Available from: https://twitter.com/wikileaks/status/763041804652539904

Wikileaks. (March 6, 2016e). "Hillary Clinton Email Archive." Available from: https://wikileaks.org/clinton-emails/

Wikileaks. Twitter Post. (November 5, 2016f.). Available from: https://twitter.com/wikileaks/status/795073756599291904

Wikileaks. Twitter Post. (November 6, 2016g, 11:58 P.M.). Available from: https://twitter.com/wikileaks/status/795490673411686404

Williams, M.C. (2003). "Words, Images, Enemies: Securitization and International Politics." *International Studies Quarterly*, 47 (4): 511–531.

Wilson, E.O. (1998). *Consilience. The Unity of Knowledge*. New York: Vintage.

Wilson, E. (2012). *The Social Conquest of Earth* (Kindle ed.). New York: Liveright.

Winter, C. (2015). "The Virtual 'Caliphate': *Studies in Conflict and Terrorism*, 1067. Understanding Islamic State's Propaganda Strategy" (London: Quilliam Foundation, 2015), 32. Available from: www.quilliamfoundation.org/wp/wp-content/uploads/publications/free/thevirtualcaliphate-understanding-islamic-states-propaganda-strategy.pdf (accessed August 7, 2015).

Wodak, R., & Boukala, S. (2015). "European Identities and the Revival of Nationalism in the European Union: A Discourse Historical Approach." *Journal of Language and Politics*, 14 (1): 87–109.

Woodward, B. (2005). "How Mark Felt became Deep Throat." *The Washington Post*, 2: A01.

Woolley, S., & Guilbeault, D. (2017). *Computational Propaganda in the United States of America: Manufacturing Consensus Online*. Working Paper. Available from: http://comprop.oii.ox.ac.uk/

Wright, L. (2007). *The Looming Tower: Al-Qaeda and the Road to 9/11*. 1. Vintage Books ed. National Bestseller. New York: Vintage Books.

Youyou, W., Kosinski, M., & Stillwell, D. (2015). "Computer-Based Personality Judgments Are More Accurate Than Those Made by HUMANS." *Proceedings of the National Academy of Sciences*. doi:10.1073/pnas.1418680112

Zaharna, R.S. (2007). "The Soft Power Differential: Network Communication and Mass Communication in Public Diplomacy." *The Hague Journal of Diplomacy*, 2 (3): 213–228.

Zempi, I., & Awan, I. (2017). *Islamophobia: Lived Experiences of Online and Offline Victimisation*. Available from: http://dx.doi.org/10.1332/policypress/9781447331964.001.0001

Zendle, D. (2016). *Priming and Negative Priming in Violent Video Games*. Thesis submitted to University of York.

Zenor, J. (2015). "Damming the Leaks: Balancing National Security, Whistleblowing and the Public Interest." *Lincoln Memorial University Law Review*, 3: 61–90.

Zwiebel, M.J. (2006). "Why We Need to Reestablish the USIA." *Military Review*, November–December: 130–139, http://usacac.army.mil/CAC2/MilitaryReview/Archives/English/MilitaryReview_2008IAR0630_art019.pdf

Official documentation

Appathurai, J. (September 16, 2009). *Weekly Press Briefing.* Available from: www.nato.int/ cps/iw/natohq/opinions_57633.htm?selectedLocale=en

Council of the European Union. (May 19, 2014). *Revised EU Strategy for Combating Radicalisation and Recruitment.* Brussels: Council of the European Union.

di Paola, G. (2009). "The military aspects of the new Strategic Concept", address at the 56th Annual Conference of NATO, September 25.

European Commission. (2002). "On information and communication strategy for the European Union." COM (2002) 350 final. Available from: http://ec.europa.eu/ transparency/regdoc/rep/1/2002/EN/1-2002-350-EN-F11.Pdf

European Commission and High Representative of the European Union for Foreign Affairs and Security Policy. (2015). Joint Communication to the European Parliament, The Council, the Economic and Social Committee and the Committee of the Regions, Brussels, 18.11.2015 JOIN (2015) 50 final, "Review of the European Neighbourhood Policy [SWD (2015) 500 final].

European Parliament. (2016). "European Parliament resolution of 23 November 2016 on EU strategic communication to counteract propaganda against it by third parties", 2016/2030 (INI). Available from: www.europarl.europa.eu/sides/getDoc. do?pubRef=-//EP//TEXT+TA+P8-TA-2016-0441+0+DOC+XML+V0//EN

Mogherini, F. (2016a). *"Remarks by F. Mogherini on EU strategic communication to counteract anti-EU propaganda by third parties"*, Press release, European External Action Services. Available from: https://eeas.europa.eu/headquarters/headquarters-homepage/15765/ remarks-f-mogherini-eu-strategic-communication-counteract-anti-eu-propaganda-third-parties_ru

Mogherini, F. (July 13, 2016b). Speech by the High Representative/Vice-President. Chinese Academy of Social Sciences, Beijing. Available from: https://europa.eu/ globalstrategy/en/speech-high-representativevice-president-federica-mogherini-chinese-academy-social-sciences-0

NATO. (1949). The North Atlantic Treaty. Available from: www.nato.int/nato_static/ assets/pdf/stock_publications/20120822_nato_treaty_en_light_2009.pdf (accessed May 16, 2017).

NATO. (1999). Information Warfare and International Security Committee Report. Available from: www.nato-pa.int/archivedpub/comrep/1999/as285stc-e.asp (accessed May 20, 2017).

NATO. (September 14, 2009). "NATO Strategic Communications Policy." Brussels: Office of the General Secretary. Available from: https://info.publicintelligence.net/ NATO-STRATCOM-Policy.pdf

NATO. (May 31, 2010a). International Military Staff Memorandum, Hybrid threats description and context.

NATO. (2010b). Active Engagement, Modern Defence. Strategic Concept for the Defence and Security of the Members of the North Atlantic Treaty Organisation Adopted by the Heads of State and Government in Lisbon. Available from: www. nato.int/cps/sl/natohq/official_texts_68580.htm?selectedLocale=en (accessed May 15, 2017).

NATO. (August 18, 2010c). "Military Concept for NATO Strategic Communications." Brussels: Office of the General Secretary. Available from: https://info.publicintelli gence.net/NATO-STRATCOM-Concept.pdf

NATO. (2012). Deterrence and Defence Posture Review. May 20, 2012. Available from: www.nato.int/cps/en/natohq/official_texts_87597.htm (accessed February 13, 2018).

NATO. (2017a). Communications and Public Diplomacy. Available from: www.nato.int/cps/en/natohq/topics_69275.htm

NATO. (2017b). Principal Officials. Available from: www.nato.int/cps/po/natohq/who_is_who_51639.htm (accessed May 15, 2017).

NATO. (2017c). NATO Welcomes Opening of European Centre of Countering Hybrid Threats in Helsinki. Available from: www.nato.int/cps/en/natohq/news_143143.htm?selectedLocale=en (accessed May 15, 2017).

NATO. (2017d). Countering Terrorism. Available from: www.nato.int/cps/en/natolive/topics_77646.htm?selectedLocale=en (accessed May 15, 2017).

Rasmussen, A.F. (2009a). NATO and Russia: A New Beginning Speech by NATO Secretary General Anders Fogh Rasmussen at the Carnegie Endowment, Brussels. September 18, 2009.

Rasmussen, A.F. (2009b). Speech by NATO Secretary General Anders Fogh Rasmussen at the NATO Parliamentary Assembly meeting in Edinburgh. November 17, 2009.

Rasmussen, A.F. (2009c). "NATO as a Guarantor of Territorial Defence and a Provider of Global Security", Speech at the conference "NATO Talk around the Brandenburger Tor" in Berlin. November 26, 2009.

Rasmussen, A.F. (2011). "NATO and the Mediterranean: The Changes Ahead." Speech at the Spanish Senate.

Rasmussen A.F., Albright, K., & van der Veer J. (September 4, 2009). Point de presse. Launch of the work of the group on the new Strategic Concept.

Russian Government. (September 9, 2000). *Information Security Doctrine of the Russian Federation.*

Russian Government. (December 25, 2014). *The Military Doctrine of the Russian Federation.* 2014 No. Pr.-2976. Available in English translation: http://rusemb.org.uk/press/2029 (accessed May 15, 2017).

Russian Government. (2015). National Security Strategy of the Russian Federation.

The Council. (2015). "Council Conclusions on Cyber Diplomacy." Available from: http://data.consilium.europa.eu/doc/document/ST-6122-2015-INIT/en/pdf

United Nations. (2015). "Secretary-General's Remarks to Security Council Meeting on Threats to International Peace and Security Caused by Terrorist Acts (Foreign Terrorist Fighters)." *United Nations Secretary-General*, May 29. Available from: www.un.org/sg/en/content/sg/statement/2015-05-29/secretary-generals-remarks-security-council-meeting-threats

United States Congress. (2011). *Ten Years On: The Evolution of Strategic Communication and Information Operations Since 9/11.* Washington, DC: U.S. Government Printing Office.

US Department of State. (n.d.) "Global Engagement Centre." Available from: www.state.gov/r/gec/

White House. (2010). *National Framework for Strategic Communication.* Washington, DC. Available from: https://fas.org/man/eprint/pubdip.pdf

Youtube. (2015). "EU participates in the Silent March in Paris in honour of the victims of the Charlie Hebdo attack." Available from: www.youtube.com/watch?v=hZFmnz4ROEo (retrieved March 03, 2017).

INDEX

Abu Dhabi 10, 84; Hedayah 84–85
Agents of influence 7, 99, 103, 114–116, 120
Al Jazeera 67, 73, 143
Al Qaeda 8, 121, 124, 126, 140–141, 143, 158, 162, 174; media message 141, 153
Algorithms 15, 47, 49, 51, 59, 89, 90
Alienation 111, 113, 165–167
Apostasy 164
Artificial intelligence 16, 49, 116
Audiences 4–6, 9, 14, 19–20, 22, 26, 45, 49, 50, 53–55, 59, 63, 68, 74, 77–78, 81, 84, 89, 91–92, 108–109, 110, 112, 115, 121–124, 127, 129, 130, 136–137, 139, 141, 146–149, 151–153, 157, 158, 160, 162–163, 166, 171

Believers 148, 163–164
Bellingcat 117–118, 175
Big data 21, 47, 51, 91

Cambridge Analytica 21, 45, 58–59
China 74; Weibo 74
the "CNN Effect" 140, 146
Cognitive filter 5, 18, 19, 20, 21, 26; layers of 20
Cognitive mapping, *see* filter mapping
Cognitive science 5, 29–31
Conspiracy theories 2, 58, 103, 117
Counterterrorism 7, 9, 73, 82, 84–86, 108, 110, 112, 156, 157, 158, 160, 174

Dabiq 164
Daesh 2, 8, 100–101, 103, 109, 116, 122, 129–134, 136, 137, 138, *see also* ISIS
Deception 4, 14, 18, 27, 43, 46, 50, 52, 93
Denmark 7, 85, 126, 133; "Back on Track" 85
the Digital Age 1, 4, 6, 7, 8, 19, 44, 54, 57, 60–61, 64, 99, 101, 103–105, 107, 113, 115, 118, 119, 121, 126, 128, 138, 172, 177
Digital diplomacy 1–4, 9, 114, 175
Disbelievers 164
Discourse 2, 10, 49–50, 52–53, 65, 68, 114, 120, 127, 165, 173, 179
Disinformation 1, 2, 3, 4, 5, 7, 9, 10, 14, 15, 17, 22, 23, 25, 26, 28, 29, 45, 73, 77, 78, 103, 116, 118, 119, 172, 173, 174, 175, 176, 177, 179; campaign 2–6, 13, 18, 21–22, 25–27, 34, 45–46, 48–50, 52, 54–60, 64, 85, 90, 103–104, 108, 112, 130, 141, 148, 156–157, 164–165, 169–170, 174–175, 177
Digital 1–10, 13–15, 19, 21–27, 35, 42, 44–45, 47, 49, 51, 53–55, 57–65, 68, 74–75, 78, 85–88, 99, 101, 103–105, 107, 113–119, 121, 126, 128, 138, 140, 147, 153–154, 156–157, 160, 165, 169–170, 172, 174–177; operators 5, 29, 34, 38–40, 43, 119–120; strategy 5–8, 14–15, 24–26, 44–45, 48, 55, 57, 75, 77, 82–84, 88, 95, 100, 119, 141, 143, 154–155, 158, 177

European Union (EU) 3, 5–6, 25, 66–80, 94, 133, 167, 168–169

Foreign policy 1, 4, 14, 22, 23, 26, 48, 52, 72–73, 168, 177–178; extremism 3–4, 7–8, 82–85, 87–88, 91–92, 94–95, 97, 99–101, 103, 105–106, 110–113, 118–124, 127–128, 139, 156, 158, 160, 164, 170, 172; countering 1, 3, 7–8, 10, 47, 77, 81–84, 87–88, 91–92, 97, 100, 103, 106, 108–109, 114, 119, 141, 156, 170, 172, 174, 176–177, 179
Facebook 19, 21, 25, 27–28, 50–51, 59, 78, 89, 107, 138, 161
Fake news 1, 2, 7, 50, 55, 58–60, 81, 83, 89–90, 93, 99, 102, 119, 176
Filter mapping 5, 21, 26
France 13, 75, 80, 88, 94, 157, 164–168; Charlie Hebdo 164; Paris, 33, 164, 167

Germany 13, 22, 25, 80, 85, 133; the "Lisa case" 24–25; the "Violence Prevention Network" 85
Global networks 67
Grayzone 164

Hacking 42, 44–46, 55, 57, 60, 62, 116
Hezbollah 101
Human cognition 30–32, 39
Hybrid warfare 77, 99–105, 107, 109, 111, 113, 115–120, 198

Identity 9, 31–33, 39, 43, 51, 62, 69, 75, 79–80, 90, 104, 157, 161
Identity Narratives 161, 163
Information 1–10, 13–20, 22–29, 32–37, 39–52, 54–55, 57–58, 61, 63, 65–70; Bubbles 89–90, 94, 155
Information influence 5, 9–10, 28–29, 31, 33–35, 37, 39–43, 173–179, 201; techniques 2, 9, 29, 39–41, 104, 152, 174–176, 179
Information operations 17, 92, 119, 172–173, 175
Information war 13, 17, *see also* information warfare
Information warfare 2, 4–6, 14, 26, 66–68, 76–80
International organizations 66
IS (Islamic State) 77–78, 157–167, 169–171, *see also* ISIS (Islamic State in Iraq and Syria)
ISIS (Islamic State in Iraq and Syria) 8, 17, 81, 87–88, 126–127, 129, 140–146, 149–155, 168, 174

media messages 141, 153; the Global Coalition against 122, 129; journalistic collaboration 61; leaks 5–6, 41, 44–56, 58–61, 63–65; fake 1–2, 7, 22, 24, 41, 50, 54–55, 58–60, 81, 83, 89–90, 93, 99, 102, 118–119, 176; liberal democracy 49
manipulation 3, 14, 27, 46, 49, 54, 59, 63, 64, 94
media 1–3, 5–9, 14, 19–20, 22–26, 28–30, 35–37, 39–42, 45–55, 57–65, 67–78, 80, 82–83, 85, 87, 89, 91, 93, 95, 99, 101–108, 110, 113–117, 119–123, 125–130, 134, 137–143, 145–155, 157–158, 160–161, 163–167, 169, 172, 177–178; ecology 121, 126–127, 161; visual 87, 126–129, 138–139, 151
MH17, 22, 175
Muslims 22, 111, 123, 144, 154, 162–167, 170

narrative resonance 162, 165–166
narratives 6, 8–9, 43, 59, 68, 71, 75–76, 85, 90, 101–103, 105–106, 108–117, 119–129, 135, 138–140, 154, 156–165, 167–170, 178; contestation 9, 157, 170, 178; counter-, 3–4, 8–9, 44, 51, 55, 57, 62, 77, 82–83, 85, 95, 100, 106, 108–110, 112, 117, 121, 124–125, 157–159, 162, 167, 169–170, 176–178; democratisation of 7–8, 99–103, 107, 116–117, 119–120; extremist-, 4, 7–9, 43, 81, 84–85, 88, 91, 94, 99, 102–103, 105–112, 115–116, 118–121, 129, 131, 133–135, 137–138, 157–158, 160–161, 165, 169–171, 174
native 105, 108–110
NATO (North Atlantic Treaty Organization) 6, 25, 28, 46, 66, 68–72, 74–81, 86, 91; Strategic Communications Center of Excellence, 77; the Strategic Concept process 69, 76

Open source intelligence 175
Opinion formation 5, 28–30, 33–36, 38–39, 41–42, 176–177; model 5, 8–9, 18–19, 21, 24, 26, 28, 30, 34–36, 38, 40–41, 47, 57, 59, 68, 70, 74–75, 86–87, 110, 116, 118, 140, 142, 149–154, 157, 161, 170, 173; vulnerabilities 5, 9, 22, 28, 34–35, 38–40, 42, 47, 103, 109, 173

the Panama Papers 6, 44, 60, 63–64
Persuasion 5, 9, 41, 50, 53, 91–92, 94, 124–125, 157–158, 169–170; environment 2, 4–5, 23–26, 33, 44, 49–51, 54, 61, 65–66, 77, 81–82, 87, 89, 94, 112, 123, 159–161, 165–166
Political communication 6, 33, 66–69, 71, 73–74, 79–80
Power 6–8, 16, 18, 21, 29–30, 44–49, 51–52, 63, 66–68, 71–72, 74, 80, 86, 94, 99, 114, 119, 140–141, 153–155, 168–169, 175; structure 19, 44, 67, 73, 77, 80, 93, 127, 150
Propaganda 1–7, 10, 13–16, 18, 22, 43–45, 47–55, 57, 59–61, 63–64, 68, 77–78, 81, 83–84, 88; campaigns 4–5, 18, 22, 25–26, 34, 49, 52, 54, 85, 103–104, 108, 112, 156–157, 164–165, 169–170, 174–175, 177; digital 1–10, 13–15, 19, 21–24, 26–27, 35, 42, 44–45, 47, 49, 51, 53–55, 57–65, 68, 74, 85, 87–88, 99, 101, 103–105, 107, 113–119, 121, 126, 128, 138, 140, 147, 153–154, 156–157, 160, 165, 169–170, 172, 174–177; recruitment-, 2–3, 7–8, 105, 121–122, 127, 131, 141, 154, 167; strategy 4–8, 14–15, 24–26, 26, 44–45, 48, 55, 57, 73, 75, 77, 82–84, 88, 95, 100, 119, 141, 143, 154–155, 158, 177
Public diplomacy 4, 6–7, 9, 30, 40, 67–70, 72–83, 86, 92, 158–159, 169, 174–176
Public opinion 5–6, 36, 39–42, 44–45, 49, 145–146, 160–161

Racism 113, 164, 166
Radicalization 28, 82, 85, 88, 123–124, 126
Reflexive control 5, 13–19, 24; 4E funnel, 5, 23–26; strategies 3, 6–7, 19, 23, 51, 55, 60, 63, 80, 108, 121, 124, 127, 158–159, 163; theory 5, 14–18, 21–23, 26, 29, 31, 53, 89, 124–125, 141, 148, 160
Russia 174; disinformation 1–5, 7, 9–10, 14–15, 17, 22–23, 25–26, 28–29, 45, 73, 77–78, 103, 116, 118–119, 172–177, 179; propaganda 1–7, 10, 13–16, 18, 22, 43–45, 47–55, 57, 59–61, 63–64, 68, 77–78, 81, 83, 87–92, 101, 109, 116, 122, 124–125, 127–129, 138, 158–159, 166–167, 169, 175–178; documents 52, 56, 61–62, 65, 81, 164

Social media 1–2, 6, 8–9, 14, 19–20, 25, 28, 30, 38, 40–42, 54, 63, 67–72, 74–78, 80, 87, 89, 93, 95, 102, 104–108, 110, 113–116, 120–124, 129–130, 134, 137–138, 140, 158, 163–164, 167, 169, 178
Social networks 53, 60, 90, 123
Strategic communication 3–7, 11, 29–30, 73, 77, 81–87, 89, 91–92, 94–95, 105, 116, 118–119, 159, 172; implementation 6, 82–84, 86
Strategic narratives 8, 140, 154, 160–161, 170, 178
Surveillance 6, 44, 46–47, 49, 51, 53, 61–63, 77, 173
Sweden 80, 85; EXIT Fryshuset 85; the "Tolerance" program 85
System Narrative 161–162, 168, 170

Terrorism 7, 9, 28, 77, 82, 84–86, 100, 102, 107, 112, 114, 116, 120, 124–125, 140, 157, 159–160, 167–168; attacks 25, 40, 68, 77, 88, 101, 103, 105, 107, 111–112, 116, 140, 153, 164, 166–167, 179
Theory of Vivid Media Violence 148
Trolling 2, 54, 59, 90
Truth 8, 10, 32, 78, 89–90, 92–93, 95, 99–103, 109, 115, 120, 179; the battle for 101
Twitter 8, 19, 21–22, 28, 51, 54, 56, 58, 60, 65, 72, 75, 78, 105, 107, 122, 129–130, 133, 138, 158, 169–171

Ukraine 17, 25, 75, 77, 91, 159, 174–175; crisis 4, 17, 48, 75, 79, 114, 168–169
United Kingdom 84; Brexit 13, 28, 34, 89, 94, 168; military doctrine 81, 108, 124; prevent strategy 88; Salisbury nerve agent attack 13; the Research, Information and Communication Unit, 84
United States 60, 65; Center for Strategic Counter Communication 141; The Global Engagement Centre 84

Whistle-blowing 44–47, 54, 63–65
Wikileaks 51–52, 55–60, 65

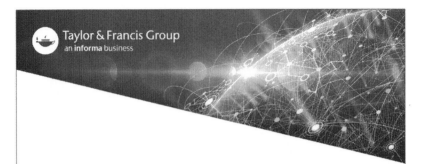